ANTHROPOLOGICAL PAPERS

MUSEUM OF ANTHROPOLOGY, UNIVERSITY OF MICHIGAN
NO. 29

13-18

THE PREHISTORIC ANIMAL ECOLOGY AND ETHNOZOOLOGY OF THE UPPER GREAT LAKES REGION

by
CHARLES EDWARD CLELAND

ANN ARBOR
THE UNIVERSITY OF MICHIGAN, 1966

PREFACE

Much of the data which serves as the basis of this volume was collected as a part of a research program designed to investigate the relationship between the post glacial ecologies and prehistoric cultures of the Upper Great Lakes area. This program was undertaken by the Museum of Anthropology of the University of Michigan between 1960 and 1964 with the support of the National Science Foundation. The faunal reports, which are included here as appendices, were compiled during the course of this project and were intended to be included in the archaeological site reports of other participants in the program. It soon became apparent that these collected faunal reports not only provided sufficient information for an independent study but that such a study had the potential of contributing to our understanding of environmental change in the Great Lakes region and the ways in which man dealt with the resources of his natural surroundings through the adaptation of his culture. This study was completed in 1966 and submitted to the University of Michigan as a doctoral dissertation.

During the preparation of the drafts of this study my doctoral committee offered many suggestions, most of these were useful and all were appreciated. Thanks is, therefore, gratefully extended to the members of this committee which included Dr. William H. Burt, Dr. James E. Fitting, Dr. Arthur J. Jelinek and Volney H. Jones under the able chairmanship of Dr. James B. Griffin.

Many others have also contributed to this document in a variety of ways. Joan Kearney identified many of the animal bones from the Schultz Site and helped in compiling much of the quantitative data presented in these pages. Her skill and dedication to these often laborious tasks in commendable. Patricia Hughes devoted herself to the difficult job of proof-reading and criticising the original manuscript, and her help and good judgment is greatly appreciated. Linda Britton deserves credit for the final editing of the present volume.

I am also indebted to Lyle Stone, Peter Murray and George Stuber for their artistic contributions. G. Richard Peske, Dr.

Warren Wittry and Dr. Paul Parmalee were all kind enough to permit free use of their unpublished data.

Finally, I wish to acknowledge the help, support and wise advice given to me over a number of years by my wife, Mary, my father, Charles E. Cleland, and by my teachers, James B. Griffin, Charles R. McGimsey III and Robert Alrutz. To these friends I owe my greatest debt.

Charles E. Cleland

CONTENTS

TABLES

FIGURES

I

INTRODUCTION

The plants and animals which inhabit the land areas of the world are not, as we all know, randomly distributed over the face of the globe. Most organisms tend to occur in association with certain other plants and animals which have become adapted to similar conditions of climate, soil and physiography. More important, these species become adapted to each other and by virtue of these interlocking relationships form delicately balanced natural communities. Although man is not as rigidly bound to his environment as the fauna and flora around him, he does adapt to the natural community in which he lives. Neither the natural environment nor human culture can be understood without knowledge of the effect of each upon the other. Herein lies the basic premise of this study. To understand culture we must investigate it in an environmental matrix viewing both external stimuli and the adaptive responses which they invoke. This idea was concisely stated by A. L. Kroeber (1939:1) in the introduction to his classic work Cultural and Natural Areas of Native North America:

the present work in no sense represents a relapse toward the old environmentalism which believed it could find the causes of culture in environment. While it is true that cultures are rooted in nature, and can therefore never be completely understood except with reference to that piece of nature in which they occur, they are no more produced by that nature than a plant is produced or caused by the soil in which it is rooted. The immediate causes of cultural phenomena are other cultural phenomena. At any rate, no anthropologist can assume anything else as his specific working basis. But this does not prevent the recognition of relations between nature and culture nor the importance of these relations to the full understanding of culture.

If environment, which in the broadest sense includes not only natural but cultural phenomena as well, is the basis for cultural adaptation, then we must explore the nature of adaptation as a phenomenon of interaction between the environment and a cultural system. White (1949:366) has envisioned a culture as an interaction between three subsystems or horizontal strata. The technological layer is on the bottom articulating closely with the natural environment, the sociological stratum overlies this and is, in turn, overlain by the ideological stratum. As we proceed from technology to ideology, the effect of the environment becomes progressively weakened, yet each subsystem conditions the other. It is the technology, however, which is the strongest determining factor for the cultural system as a whole. As appealing as this analogy may be to archaeologists, Harding (Sahlins and Service 1960:48) points out that White is discussing culture as a closed system while adaptive phenomena are functions of open systems:

Adaptation to nature will shape a culture's technology and derivatively its social and ideological components. Yet adaptation to other cultures may shape society and ideology which in turn act upon technology and determine its further course. The total result of the adaptive process is the production of an organized cultural whole, an integrated technology, society, and ideology, which copes with the dual selective influences of nature on the one hand and the impact of outside cultures on the other. Such are, in general outline, the mechanics of cultural adaptation.

The study of cultural adaptation is, thus, a wholistic one, a study of integrated systems. It is also a study of dynamic systems, a study which must place culture in a temporal-spatial context. Mason (1896), Wissler (1917), and other pioneer anthropologists who first undertook the correlation of cultural and natural phenomena did not adopt this view. These investigators were concerned with the spatial distribution of cultural traits or trait complexes. It remained for Kroeber (1939) to develop fully the culture area concept by relating cultural systems to natural areas in a spatial context. Kroeber's study was an important contribution because it dealt with cultural adaptations rather than the distribution of cultural traits. Jenks' (1900) earlier study of the Wisconsin wild rice area, and Steward's (1938) study of the cultures of the Great Basin utilized this approach within limited geographic areas. Driver and Massey's (1957) recent compendium on North American Indians reverts to the trait-listing approach to culture areas. This study of the Upper Great Lakes region is designed to add a temporal dimension to the relationship between the cultural and natural areas.

Since the advent of radiocarbon dating, archaeologists have been able to establish firm control over the temporal as well as the spatial dimensions of the data which their excavations produce. Prehistoric cultures can now be examined as dynamic, adaptive systems, systems which have limits in both time and space.

The archaeologist cannot excavate the non-material parts of a culture, however. These he must infer from the relationship which exists between material objects he recovers and the context in which they are found. Consequently, those areas of culture which would be placed in the ideological subsystem are extremely difficult to reconstruct since they are least seldom manifested in material objects. Attitudes about deer, copper ore, or the afterlife may or may not be indicated by deer bone, copper tools, or burial goods, And though social and political systems are very often directly and vitally related to game populations and hunting practices, it is often misleading to infer these systems from the shape of projectile points or the habits of the game animals represented in an archaeological site.

Fortunately, the relationship between man and his environment is most directly expressed by elements of the technological subsystem, and this subsystem may be accurately reconstructed from the recovered material culture. It is through this subsystem of culture that man articulates directly with his environment. It is with technological elements that he provides warmth, food, and shelter for himself and assures his survival in his natural environment. The recovery of arrow points and quantities of burned deer bone from archaeological sites assures us that people of this culture hunted deer with a bow and arrow, that they were competent enough in the use of this weapon to kill deer, and finally, that the deer meat was consumed as food.

It is also important that archaeological data permit statements about the geographic and temporal distribution of such a technological and economic pattern. If, for example, we have a series of prehistoric cultural complexes of known time span, and a wide distribution in space, it may be possible to record the time of the introduction of hunting deer with bows and arrows, and to trace the spread and evolution of this hunting technique. Mac White (1956) has discussed in some detail the levels of archaeological interpretation for predocumentary periods in view of latitudes of inference from material remains.

This study is focused on the prehistoric ecology and ethnozoology of the Upper Great Lakes area. It is designed to view the prehistoric cultures of this area as dynamic adaptive systems in terms of both space and time. Prefaced in the belief that culture, past or present, can be fully understood only in terms of the natural environment in which it occurs, this study will explore the relationship between prehistoric culture and prehistoric ecology. Even though this relationship may be expressed completely in technological terms, an adaptive or ecological approach requires exploration of its non-material phases. For this reason, speculation on the non-material aspects of the prehistoric cultures under consideration will be freely offered.

The basic data for this study is a series of reports on faunal remains from a number of Upper Great Lakes sites. Each report is a statement of the prehistoric animal ecology of the site area at the time the site was occupied and of the relationship between the culture(s) of the site and its natural environment(s). These site reports are included as appendices. From these and other published sources, a body of data is available which permits conclusions about the changing ecology of the Upper Great Lakes area through time. This information is presented in the section on paleoecology.

If prehistoric cultures were adapted to a particular ecological situations, then changes in the environment would logically produce cultural changes. Cultural changes, on the other hand, would also have an effect on the environmental relationship and, in some cases, might even change the natural environment. Consideration of these factors is presented in the section called Ethnozoology of the Upper Great Lakes.

The Modern Biotic Communities
of the Upper Great Lakes

Geographically, the Upper Great Lakes area may be defined as that region which comprises the watersheds of Lake Superior, Lake Michigan, and Lake Huron. The drainage basins of these lakes cover 220,480 square miles including both peninsulas of Michigan, eastern and northern Wisconsin, the eastern tip of Minnesota, and those areas of Ontario which border Lake Superior and Lake Huron (Figure 1). Within this relatively small area, there are such drastic changes from south to north that it is impossible to discuss the climate, physiography, ecology, or the prehistoric cultures of this region as a static whole. The Upper Great Lakes region is in every sense of the word an area of transition.

The modern natural communities of the Upper Great Lakes can be broadly classified into four large, relatively homogenous assemblages which have been called biotic provinces. Dice (1943) observed that communities of plants and animals must differ from region to region in correspondence with the regional distribution of climate and of the other features of the physical habitat. Each major ecologic division of a continent that covers a continuous geographic area may be called a biotic province. These four biotic provinces are the Carolinian, Illinoian, Canadian, and Hudsonian.

Strictly speaking, the Canadian biotic province covers nearly all of the drainage system of the Upper Great Lakes. It is bordered on the south by the Carolinian province, on the west and southwest by the Illinoian province, and on the north by the Hudsonian province. Although these latter communities have their major distribution outside of the Upper Great Lakes watershed, it is essential that they be considered in this study since the fauna and flora of the Canadian biotic province are, in fact, composed of elements which have their widest distribution in either the Carolinian or Hudsonian provinces. Thus, the Canadian province is, itself, a transitional community. There is, of course, another equally important reason why these two large marginal provinces must be discussed. If we are to consider the distribution of former climates and their effects on plant-animal associations, then changes toward either cooler or warmer climatic conditions would logically result in either the southward or northward mobility of all three of these biotic communities. Certainly, there were times after the retreat of glacial ice when most of the drainage basin of the Upper Great Lakes fell almost entirely within either the Hudsonian or Carolinian biotic provinces.

Grouping the natural communities of the Upper Great Lakes into only four biotic communities appears to border on the absurd, yet, like all classificatory systems, these groupings are an expedient method of eliminating unruly variables. The biotic provinces are, themselves, composed of many discrete, smaller natural communities, each occurring where local conditions of soil and climate afford the proper medium for the growth and propagation of that community. While these smaller local communities were undoubtedly important to the prehistoric people of the Upper Great Lakes, our techniques for delimiting their extent and distribution are as minimal as is our knowledge of their role in prehistoric cultures. Since the available paleoecological data lend themselves to the discussion of large biotic communities,

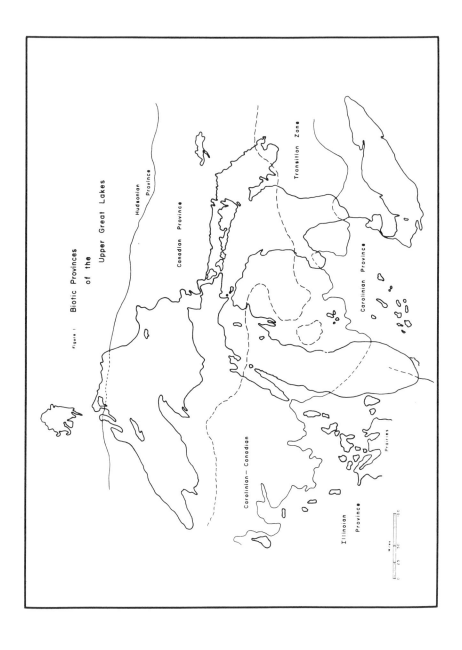

Figure 1   Biotic Provinces of the Upper Great Lakes

and since the culture area comcept seems to indicate that communities of this order of magnitude did exert certain influences on prehistoric cultures, the biotic province will be used in this study as the most meaningful unit of ecological reference. However, when the data lends itself to the investigation of smaller natural communities within these provinces, every effort will be made to evaluate their relevance to prehistoric culture. It is, after all, from these small communities that the fauna and flora of archaeological sites is primarily drawn.

Before discussing the biotic provinces themselves, mention must be made of the natural communities which frequently characterize the transition from one to another. These communities called ecotones, edges, or transition zones, are composed of floral and faunal elements typically associated with the larger communities which form them. Edge communities vary in width from a few miles to hundreds of miles, depending upon climatic and physiographic factors. In some areas the transition from one biotic province to another does not involve a discrete edge community but takes place gradually over a long distance. On the other hand, edges may be sharp and well-defined, such as the one which has developed between the Carolinian and Canadian provinces through central Wisconsin and Michigan. Edges exhibit a number of features which render them extremely favorable for man and beast, a phenomenon known as the "edge effect." Odum (1953:207) defines this effect by observing that "often, both the number of species and the population density of some of the species are greater in the ecotone than in the communities flanking it." Finally, like the large biotic communities which form them, the edge communities' geographic position shifts with climatic change and may not considered to be stable in the temporal dimension.

The Carolinian Biotic Province

Figure 1 shows the location of the Carolinian province in the Upper Great Lakes area. The topography of this province in southern Ontario, Michigan, and Wisconsin is level to gently rolling, although glacial moraines are common in some places. Soils vary in texture from sand to clay with occasional bog soils in low swampy situations. The soils of this region are grayish-brown and brown podzolic soils, formed under temperate forest conditions. Very dark brown prairie soils or Wiesenboden soils, which are formed under temperate grasslands, also appear sporadically in southwestern Michigan and south central Wisconsin (Kellogg 1941:277). The average growing season varies between 140 and 180 frost free days; the mean annual temperature varies from 46 to 50 degrees Fahrenheit; and the annual precipitation varies from 28 to 36 inches per year. Snowfall seldom exceeds 50 inches annually, and during the winter months the ground frequently lacks snow cover.

The presettlement forests of the Carolinian biotic province are commonly classified as the oak-hickory type. On dry sites, forest associations were dominated by black, red, and white oak, and by hickories, sugar maple, beech, walnut, butternut, elm, and tulip. On sites which were not well drained, forests were composed of elm, silver maple, ash, swamp white oak, basswood, shagbark hickory, sycamore, cottonwood, red oak, and bur oak. In swampy situtations this assemblage also included cedar and tamarack. On the northern fringe of the Carolinian province elm, red maple, ash, yellow birch, white birch, aspen, and white pine became predominant (Veatch 1959).

The vertebrates which occur within the biotic provinces of the northeastern United States are discussed in Appendix G (p. 224) in addition, the prehistoric archaeological distributions of some of these species are shown in Appendix I (p. 247). However, a few species which are typical of the Carolinian biotic province in the Great Lakes region will be mentioned here. The oppossum, raccoon, striped skunk, gray fox, bobcat, gray squirrel, southern flying squirrel, pine vole, cottontail rabbit, whitetail deer, turkey, red-shouldered hawk, barred owl, vulture, bobwhite, red-headed woodpecker, passenger pigeon, woodthrush, and cardinal are all, or probably were typical of areas with climax deciduous forest. This list can be lengthened considerably with the inclusion of a large number of reptiles and amphibians which are similarly restricted. In addition to these endemic species, the Carolinian forest is inhabited by a great number of species whose total ranges include other biotic provinces. These are black bear, longtailed weasel, mink, otter, badger, coyote, wolf, cougar, woodchuck, eastern chipmunk, fox squirrel, beaver, muskrat, elk, and bison.

At the period of earliest European contact, the Carolinian biotic province of the Upper Great Lakes was occupied by agricultural peoples who raised corn, beans, squash, and presumably other less important crops, in natural or artificial clearings within the forest. These people also hunted, primarily for deer, fished, trapped, and gathered wild plants when these were abundant. Tribes of this area include the Huron and Neutral in southern Ontario; the Potawatomi, Sauk-Fox, Miami, and perhaps Erie, in southern Michigan; and finally, the Siouan speaking tribes of southern Wisconsin.

The Canadian Biotic Province

Referring to Figure 1 again, we see that the southern margin of the Canadian biotic province extends across the Bruce Peninsula of lower Ontario into southern Michigan where it transects the state between Saginaw Bay and Little Traverse Bay. In Wisconsin the southern limits extend roughly from the northern tip of Green Bay to the western tip of Lake Superior. On the north this province bounds the Hudsonian province on a line which touches the northern tip of Lake Superior and passes 50 miles north of Lake Nipissing.

Most of this region has the uneven topography of a heavily glaciated country, gravelly hills (moraines) and ridges, sandy outwash plains, swamps, and rock outcrops. Most of the soils of this region are products of cool, moist forests, and are light colored, acid, rather infertile, and low in organic matter. They vary greatly because of the diverse nature of the parent materials that the glaciers moved and mixed. Stones, sands, and gravels are common. In addition to the organic soils which occupy millions of acres, there are also smooth uplands, rocky ridges, outwash plains, and former lake beds covered with deep silty or clayey soils (Muckenhirm and Berger 1957:547).

The climate of the Canadian province is cool, the average annual temperatures varying from 38 to 40 degrees Fahrenheit. The average annual per year growing season has between 80 and 140 frost-free growing days. Winter snowfall varies from 4 to 10 feet per year, and the ground may be covered with snow from 100 to 140 days of the year.

Potzger (1946:213-250) has considered the forests of the Canadian biotic province to be an artifact of the modifying effects of the large water masses which they surround; he has accordingly called this floral association the Lake Forest. As Dice (1938:514;1943:15) points out, the climatic climax of most of the forests of this province is a hardwood forest, but subclimaxes of several sorts play a predominant role in the composition of the total floral community. The dominant species of the climax Lake Forest is sugar maple while yellow birch, beech, elm, aspen, basswood, hemlock, and white pine are also members of the association. An important subclimax including black spruce, tamarack, cedar, fir, white pine, white birch, and alder occurs on extensive wet and swampy ground. Another subclimax which occurs on poor sandy soil includes Norway, jack, and white pine, and hemlock.

Few, if any, mammals are restricted to the Canadian biotic province. While those Carolinian mammals which do not extend northward into the Canadian province have already been discussed, other mammals which have a northern distribution do not, or formerly did not, cross the Canadian-Carolinian ecotone to the south. Some of these include the northern water shrew, arctic shrew, fisher, marten, wolverine, lynx, northern flying squirrel, northern bog lemming, boreal red-backed vole, porcupine, snowshoe hare, moose, and woodland caribou. Most of the birds of the Canadian biotic province are only summer visitors, but some of the indigenous birds include the spruce grouse, gray jay, raven, and the common loon.

Since the shores of the three Upper Great Lakes are generally bounded by the Canadian province, and since inland lakes and streams are so numerous within it, the fish of these lakes should be properly described as resources of the Canadian province. Rostlund (1952:73) gives us a thorough description of these waters.

This province is formed by the overlapping of the Mississippian and Canadian faunas [as used here these terms refer to the fish of the waters of the Mississippi River drainage and the waters of Canada], and therefore northern and southern fishes intermingle in the region. Whitefishes, lake herrings, lake trout, and pike-perch constitute the bulk of the resource, which consequently is high in quality, for these species are all prime food fishes. Other important fishes are brook trout, common pike, muskellunge, sauger, yellow perch, and lake sturgeon; burbot and mooneye occur; there are suckers and members of the minnow family but not in so large numbers of species as the Mississippian province. . . a number of Mississippian forms range northward into the Great Lakes province: catfishes, bowfin, gar pikes, white bass, black basses, crappies, sunfish and sheepshead.

Discussing the Upper Great Lakes as a fishing area, Rostlund says that,

In the smaller waters tributary to the main lakes or in narrow passages, such as the Straits of Mackinac and at Sault Ste. Marie, the fishes are seasonally highly available, but in the province as a whole the availability of the fish resource is low because of the prevalence of very large and deep water bodies. It is a region of lake fishery rather than river fishery, and aboriginal fishing in the main lakes may even be called an inland shore fishery. The best fishing season is clearly in summer, but winter fishing can be practiced under the ice.

At the time of first European contact, the Canadian province was inhabited by Algonquian speaking peoples. To the north and east of Lake Huron were many Algonquin bands (Tooker 1964:19) and the Ottawa. Most of northern Michigan and Canada north of Lake Superior was occupied by the Chippewa, while the Menomini inhabited the Canadian province in northern Wisconsin. These people were hunter-gatherers and fishermen who hunted in small family groups during the winter and lived in lake shore villages during the summer fishing season.

The Hudsonian Biotic Province

The Hudsonian biotic province is essentially transcontinental since it stretches from Newfoundland to Alaska, comprising the boreal forest zone which, in the east, lies between the Canadian province and the arctic tundra. Practically all of this region has been glaciated and, as consequence, the land is relatively flat with many lakes and bogs filling low areas. Soils are thin and are lacking entirely in many places, bare granite or other similar crystalline rock is common.

The climate of the Hudsonian province is characterized by long, severely cold winters, and by short, relatively warm summers. Snowfall is extremely heavy in winter and killing frosts may occur in any month of the year.

The most characteristic tree of this province is the black spruce which occurs in huge unbroken tracts. White spruce, paper birch, tamarack, balsam, poplar, fir, jack pine, willows, and alder also occur where situations are favorable to these species. Thick mats of sphagnum moss occur on the floor of the black spruce forests and in wetter places other bog plants, such as Labrador tea, and blueberries are also common.

Larger mammals of the eastern Hudsonian province include the fisher, marten, short-tailed weasel, wolverine, red fox, lynx, black bear, red squirrel, beaver, muskrat, porcupine, snowshoe hare, moose, and both barren ground and woodland caribou. (Moose were the principal game in this area, but this species was replaced by the caribou to the north and west.)

Indians of the Hudsonian province at the time of historic contact included the Naskapi, Montagnais, Cree, Ojibwa, and numerous Athabaskan speaking bands in western Canada. All of these people were hunters.

The Illinoian Biotic Province

The Illinoian province borders the Canadian province on both the west and the southwest where it extends through central

Minnesota, southern Wisconsin, and into central Illinois and northwestern Indiana. Studies of prairie remnants in Wisconsin by Whitford (1958) and in Michigan by Veatch (1928), as well as a study of the discontinuous distribution of prairie vertebrates by Smith (1957:205-218), indicate that the Illinoian biotic province once extended farther north and east into the Upper Great Lakes area.

The topography of this province is flat to very gently rolling, though steep bluffs border river valleys. Soils have developed under grasslands and are dark in color and high in organic material.

Average annual precipitation in this province is from 23 to 40 inches per year although those regions which border the Great Lakes receive between 30 and 35 inches per year. The frost-free growing period is between 140 and 180 days per year (Kincer 1941).

The vegetation of the Illinoian province is typically tall grass prairie, but scattered patches of oak-hickory forest are not uncommon, depending upon local conditions of soil and moisture. On flood plains deciduous species include elm, sycamore, bur oak, eastern cottonwood, hackberry, red bud, and buckeye. Maples, basswood, and beech are common in the eastern part of the province (Shelford 1913). Oak-hickory forests become increasingly frequent on the eastern edge of the Illinoian prairie area forming a parklike savannah. This area, which forms a wedge-shaped zone extending eastward into central Indiana and western Ohio, has been called the prairie peninsula. Sauer (1950), Stewart (1956), and many others have argued that oak-hickory forests are the climax vegetation of these fringe areas but that prairie intrusions have resulted from repeated firing of the expansive grasslands to the west.

Mammals which are usually associated with the grasslands of the Illinoian province include the badger, spotted skunk, coyote, Franklin ground squirrel, thirteen-lined ground squirrel, fox squirrel, plains pocket gopher, prairie vole, jack rabbit, elk, and bison. A few other vertebrates typical of the prairies include the prairie chicken, Swainson's hawk, sandhill crane, and ornate box turtle.

In the aboriginal period, the Illinoian biotic province was occupied by village farmers such as the Miami, Illinois, Kickapoo, Iowa, and Santee Dakota.

II

PALEOECOLOGY

In order to relate a culture to its natural environment it is necessary to refer to the specific resources available in its particular setting and to the relevant physical features such as terrain, precipitation, and temperature. Cultural responses are made to the natural environment in reference to these resources and conditions.

Paleoecological reconstruction is not a simple matter. No technique has evolved which will provide data on the relationship between physical and biotic elements, or between the biotic elements of a community at a particular point in time or space. These relationships must be presumed on the basis of modern associations and held as a constant in paleoecological reconstruction. When this assumption is made, and it may not always be valid, several techniques can be employed to determine the constituent parts of a natural community. The relationship between these parts, the prehistoric ecology, can then be reconstructed using associations implied from modern species. Paleoclimatology, geochronology, paleontology, paleobotany, and palynology may all be used to help reconstruct a particular prehistoric community.

Archaeologists are, of course, interested in man's role in the natural environment but this is seldom a major factor in paleoecological reconstruction. Although paleoecologists may use plant and animal remains from archaeological sites, these remains are not interpreted as artifacts of a cultural process, but rather as elements of a former natural environment. These remains are, of course, the result of cultural selection.

Since change in the interaction between physical and biotic factors in any particular area is an interdependent relationship and one which gradually changes through time, the study of such an interaction is most clearly demonstrated when either time or space is held as a constant. Consequently, this study is oriented to a particular point in space, the Upper Great Lakes region, and it will consider changes in the physical and biotic factors of the natural environment through time within this area.

The designation of temporal periods within the 14,000 year history of the post-Pleistocene Upper Great Lakes is difficult. Rather than being definitive, changes are often gradual making it necessary to delimit several periods which most accurately portray them. The criteria for the selection of these temporal categories are based upon: (1) stable periods of greatest ecological contrast, and (2) periods which most closely correspond to the recognized periods of cultural stability in which we are ultimately interested. It is a major premise of this study that the first factor stands in a causal relationship to the second.

The Boreal Woodland Period: 12,000 B.C. - 9,000 B.C.

At about 12,00 B.C., the retreat of the Cary substage of the Wisconsin glaciation opened up the southern part of the Great Lakes region to plant and animal colonization. During this early period, ice still covered northern Wisconsin, the Upper Peninsula of Michigan, the northern part of the Lower Peninsula of Michigan, and most of Ontario. After a short retreat of the ice, called the Cary-Port Huron interval (which dated a little before 11,000 B.C.), the ice again advanced until it occupied most of the land which was formerly covered by Cary ice. This advance is known as the Port Huron substage and its maximum southward extension is thought to be somewhat later than 11,000 B.C. By 10,500 B.C., the glacial ice had again retreated to a position just north of the Straits of Mackinac. This relatively short retreat marks a mild climatic phase called the Two Creeks interval which has been dated at ca. 9,850 B.C. (Broecker and Farrand 1963:795-802). Shortly before 10,000 B.C., the ice of the Valders substage advanced across the Straits of Mackinac and covered the Upper Peninsula of Michigan, northeastern Wisconsin, much of the Lake Michigan basin, and the western tip of the Lower Peninsula of Michigan (Hough 1963:97).

The biota of the Upper Great Lakes region during this three thousand year period reflects the cold climate produced by glacial activity. Terasmae (1961:666) estimates that the mean annual temperature for southeastern Canada during the period from 11,000 B.C. to 9,000 B.C. was between 8 and 15 degrees below present average temperatures. Climatic moderation which led to the gradual retreat of the continental glaciers shortly before 9,000 B.C. also produced a dramatic change in the biota, so that this date should mark the beginning of a new paleoecological period.

Palynological studies of the fossil pollen in the peat bogs of Michigan, Wisconsin, and Ontario, unanimously indicate that the earliest stable floral community in these regions was dominated by spruce (Potzger 1946:211-250; Winter 1962:526-528; Oltz and Kapp 1963:339-346; Anderson 1954:140-155; Benninghoff and Hibbard 1961: 155-159; Stoutamire and Benninghoff 1964:47-59; Semken, Miller and Stevens 1964:823-835). Other consistent but less frequent members of this plant community included fir, pine, larch, and birch. Spruce pollen usually comprised between 80 and 90 percent of the arboreal pollen. Deciduous pollen usually appeared in trace amounts. Non-arboreal pollen, which was abundant on early sites, became relatively scarce by 9,000 B.C. Pollen of this type represents grasses, sedges and such hydrophytic species as cattail, willow, alder, sphagnum, other mosses, and ground pine.

Mammal remains are also quite common in the bogs of this region. However, many of these species are now extinct or at least are no longer members of the modern faunal assemblage. Some of these species include the woodland musk-ox *(Symbos cavifrons)*, Jefferson mammoth *(Mammuthus jeffersoni)*, American mastodon *(Mammut americanus)*, the giant moose *(Cervalces)*, giant beaver *(Castoroides)*, barren ground caribou, peccary, and woodland caribou. In addition, the remains of many modern species such as elk, deer, moose, beaver, bear, and wolf are also encountered in bog deposits. Handley (1953: 252) has also reported the occurrence of a number of sea mammals from Arkona and Whittlesey Beach gravels. These beaches should date at about 11,000 B.C. This fauna includes the walrus *(Odobenus)*, fin whale *(Balaenoptera)*, sperm whale *(Physeter)*, and bowhead whale *(Balaena)*. If these sea mammals are correctly associated with Arkona and Whittlesey beaches, then they must have entered the Great Lakes by way of the Hudson River Valley during late recessional stages of the Cary glaciation.

We know very little about the habitats of most of these mammal species, yet, what little we do know indicates that many of these mammals had different habitat preferences. Skeels (1962:118) tells us that mammoths were grazers and "confined themselves to open grasslands and seldom entered deeply forested areas." Hibbard (1951) reports that mastodons were a forest animal, browsing on forest vegetation along bogs and streams. We can infer from the modern habitats of the barren ground caribou that this species preferred open or semi-open situations and that moose, giant moose, and beaver probably preferred forested regions. Although we know little of the habitat of the woodland musk-ox it probably preferred closed conifer forests. In addition, we know that bog formations contain animals which have been radiocarbon dated (Table 1) from 11,250 B.C. to 3,600 B.C., a span of about 8,000 years. In spite of this temporal span and the differences in habitat preference, writers have referred to bog species as one faunal assemblage simply because they are found in bogs. This is analogous to lumping all excavated archaeological material because it was found in the soil.

In fact, the pollen from these same bogs shows a number of successional stages leading to the development of the present climax vegetation of this area. Jelgersma (1962:528) notes that pollen profiles of the Great Lakes region do not show a wide tundra zone or pre-boreal phase as they do in Europe. Yet, Jelgersma's Zone I at the Madelia Marsh in southcentral Minnesota does contain large amounts of non-arboreal pollen, including pollen from such arctic-alpine plants as *Elaeagnus commutata, Shepherdia canadensis, Juniperus, Thalictrum, Saxifraga sp.,* and *Saxifraga oppositifolia.* These species indicate a short period of open tundra-like conditions preceding the spruce maximum. Jelgersma characterizes this tundra as small and narrow.

Stoutamire and Benninghoff (1964) examined the pollen from the skull of a mastodon excavated from a bog near Pontiac, Michigan. The skull of this beast, which has been dated at 9,950±350 B.C., contained sediments which gave a pollen count of 82 percent spruce, and, in addition, showed a high incidence of non-arboreal pollen. Stoutamire and Benninghoff (ibid:59) reconstruct the landscape at the time of the deposit as "mantled by stands of spruce, some closed, some parklike, with intervening stands of larch, meadows, marshes and lakes." They also note that the appearance of greater frequencies of pine pollen associated with a mastodon from Gratiot County, Michigan, some 90 miles northwest of the Pontiac site, dates the end of the pre-Pine period (Oltz and Kapp 1963). The Gratiot mastodon was dated at 8,750±400 B.C. (M-1254) and is thus 1,200 years younger than the Pontiac mastodon.

A date of 9,000 B.C. seems to be more accurate for the close of this pre-Pine period in more southern areas of Michigan. Semken, Miller, and Stevens (1964) examined the pollen from two woodland musk-ox skulls. The White Pigeon musk-ox is undated but yielded a pollen count of 57 percent spruce pollen and an arboreal pollen count of 78 percent. The Scotts musk-ox which has been dated at 9,150 B.C. yielded a pollen count of 55 percent pine pollen and 80 percent arboreal pollen. Presumably, the White Pigeon specimen is therefore earlier. These samples demonstrate that the woodland musk-ox *Symbos* occupied both the pine and earlier spruce-fir forests of southwestern Michigan. Fossil pollen associated with the vertebrae of woodland musk-ox from Kalamazoo County does not show a high percentage of non-arboreal pollen, even though it has been dated at 11,050 B.C. (M-639, Benninghoff and Hibbard 1961). This musk-ox also presumably lived in an extensive conifer forest, though Benninghoff and Hibbard (ibid:158) admit the possibility of local openings in the forest which occurred on gravelly and sandy flood plains.

The inconsistency of this sample with the one discussed by Stoutamire and Benninghoff, which dates 1,000 years later, may be explained by the difficulty of interpreting the pollen record. Not only was the vegetation, as a whole, undergoing rapid evolution, but each bog was itself influenced by various degrees of open water, the depth of the water, and the type of local habitat which surrounded it. A small sink hole bog surrounded by moraines would be expected to show a different pollen profile than an extensive lowland swamp even though the overall floral succession was much the same. Although we have some knowledge of the effect of climate on the vegetation of several widely separated localities, we do not know much about its effect on the vegetation of the whole Upper Great Lakes area. In all probability, the difference in vegetation on a given north-south line was probably as significant at 12,000 B.C. as it is today.

Guilday, Martin and McCrady (1964), in their classic study of the fauna of the New Paris Number 4 sinkhole in Bedford County, Pennsylvania, hypothesized open boreal woodland as the vegetation type in that area before 9,350 B.C. Fauna from the 8.5 meter level includes *Microtus xanthognathus, M. pennsylvanicus, M. chrotorrhinus, Synaptomys borealis, Sorex palustris,* and *Bufo americanus cf. copei.* These species can not be supported by either closed canopy forest or treeless tundra, but rather require subarctic open boreal woodlands. The succeeding faunal assemblage is typical of a closed boreal forest zone.

Considering the evidence from pollen profiles and the habitat preferences of the animals recovered from the bogs of the Great Lakes area, the following floral sequence is offered for the central part of the Great Lakes region between 12,000 B.C. and 9,000 B.C.:

1) 12,00 B.C. -11,500 B.C., a brief period in which recently deglaciated areas were covered with sedges, grasses, and tundra-like vegetation.

2) 11,500 B.C.-10,000 B.C., rapid colonization of low swampy areas with white spruce, black spruce, willow, alder, birch, and larch. The upland areas were still dominated by non-arboreal species but included occasional stands of conifers. Conifer colonization of the uplands was speeded by the moderate climate of the Two Creek interval

3) 10,000 B.C.-9,000 B.C., a period of rapid colonization of well-drained uplands by black spruce, fir, jack pine, white pine, and a few deciduous species such as maple. This phase was probably accomplished by the Valders maximum. The resulting forest had its closest analogy in the present boreal forest of the Canadian subarctic.

This sequence, of course, did not proceed at the same rate over the entire area. For example, phase 2 vegetation would have been well established in the south while more northern areas still would have had phase 1 vegetation. Similarly, by 9,000 B.C., the forest in the north was probably phase 3 type while that farther south was taking on characteristic elements of the next period.

The first colonization by animal species probably began soon after the retreat of glacial ice, and was characterized by the influx of open country grazing species such as mammoth, and barren ground carbou. These species occupied the higher, more open parkland areas, avoiding the closed spruce-fir forests which existed in moist situations. This fact may, in part, account for the relative scarcity of the remains of these species in bog deposits. The early placement and paucity of woodland musk-ox remains is not explained by this theory. Another, and equally plausible theory, is that the period of favorable habitat for these species was early and of short duration. Referring to Table 1 (p. 19) we see that radiocarbon dates tend to verify this assertion, since most of the mammoth and musk-ox remains have been assigned rather early dates, while mastodons, as a group, seem to date from later periods.

By 10,000 B.C., conifer forests were making inroads into better drained uplands so that most of the southern Upper Great Lakes area was covered with open boreal forests. The development of these conifer forests provided a habitat increasingly unfavorable to the pioneer grazing species, but favorable to browsers and other species which preferred forest habitat. By at least 9,000 B.C., mastodon, moose, and woodland caribou had probably largely replaced the mammoth, woodland musk-ox, and barren ground caribou in the southern Upper Great Lakes region. The date of 6,310±300 B.C. (M-1400) for a Jefferson mammoth

TABLE 1

RADIOCARBON DATES OF ANIMAL REMAINS OF THE UPPER GREAT LAKES

Species	Date	Location	Reference	Number
Woodland musk-ox (Coville)	11,250±300 B.C.	Kalamazoo County, Michigan	Crane and Griffin (1959:173)	M-639
Jefferson mammoth	10,250±350 B.C.	Jackson County, Michigan	Crane and Griffin (1958:2)	M-507
American mastodon (Perry)	10,050±200 B.C.	Tupperville, Ontario	McCallum and Wittenberg (1965:233)	S-172
American mastodon	9,950±350 B.C.	Oakland County, Michigan	Stoutamire and Benninghoff (1964:51)	Texas bionuclear lab 8013260000
Jefferson mammoth (Flint)	9,750±400 B.C.	Flint, Michigan	Crane and Griffin (1964:2)	M-1042
Woodland musk-ox (Scotts)	9,150±400 B.C.	Kalamazoo County, Michigan	Semken et al. (1964:825)	M-1042
American mastodon (Smith)	8,750±400 B.C.	Gratiot County, Michigan	Crane and Griffin (1965:123)	M-1254
American mastodon	8,704±188 B.C.	Novelty, Ohio	Ogden and Hay (1965:168)	OWU-126
American mastodon*	7,618±200 B.C.	Lenawee County, Michigan	Crane (1956:644)	M-282
American mastodon	7,370±400 B.C.	Elkhart, Indiana	Crane and Griffin (1961:106)	M-694
Jefferson mammoth (Prillwitz)	6,310±300 B.C.	Berrien County, Michigan	Crane and Griffin (1965:123)	M-1400
American mastodon*	5,870±225 B.C. 5,120±120 B.C.	Lenawee County, Michigan	Crane and Griffin (1958:2)	M-280 M-281
American mastodon (Ferguson)	4,300±250 B.C.	Tupperville, Ontario	McCallum and Dyck (1960:73)	S-16
American mastodon	4,150±100 B.C.	Washtenaw County, Michigan	Crane (1956:664)	M-67
American mastodon (Russell)	4,000±150 B.C.	Lapeer County, Michigan	Crane and Griffin (1959:173)	M-347
Woodland caribou	3,920±100 B.C.	Flint, Michigan	Crane (1956:664)	M-294
Gray fox	3,600±70 B.C.	Scarborough, Ontario	McCallum and Wittenberg (1962:74)	S-115A
Prairie vole	A.D. 1220±65	Leelanaw County, Michigan	Crane (1956:664)	M-208

*Same individual.

from Berrien County, Michigan, is, therefore, inconsistent with both this theory and with the much earlier dates obtained for other mammoth.

The Boreal Forest Period: 9,000 B.C. - 7,000 B.C.

A slow warming of the climate, shortly prior to 9,000 B.C., resulted in the northward retreat of Valders ice from the area north and east of Lake Michigan. Terasmae (1961) has estimated the temperature at this time at approximately 6 degrees Fahrenheit below present norms. By perhaps as early as 9,000 B.C. the ice had retreated north of Lake Nipissing so that a drainage channel was established between Lake Huron and the St. Lawrence Embayment in the St. Lawrence Valley. As a result, the water level in the Lake Michigan and Huron basins dropped to the Chippewa and Stanley low water stages. As a consequence, vast areas of former lake bottom were opened for the establishment of terrestrial communities.

It has been mentioned, that the gradual afforestation of recently unglaciated areas had been proceeding during the Boreal Woodland period, and that this process was nearly completed by 9,000 B.C. Just as the Broeal Woodland period was characterized by a subclimax vegetation, so was the Boreal Forest period. This brief and temporary stage in forest succesion had a deciduous forest element, unlike the climax boreal forest of the Canadian subarctic, to which it is often compared. Great Lakes pollen profiles show small amounts of oak, maple, and elm pollen plus lesser amounts of pollen from other deciduous species.

It is probable that a few mammals found in deciduous forest situations also inhabited the Great Lakes area at this time. In addition to mastodon, which have been dated to the Boreal Forest period, we would expect that these forests were inhabited by the black bear, marten, fisher, wolverine, lynx, snowshoe hare, beaver, muskrat, porcupine, woodland caribou, and moose.

The Pine Forest Period: 7,000 B.C. - 3,500 B.C.

Within the framework of dramatic climatic and ecological change in the paleoecological sequence of the Upper Great Lakes, the Pine Forest period represents a time of gradual change covering a span of some 4,000 years. The isostatic rebound of the land north of Lake Huron closed the Northbay outlet of the upper lakes and the water level began a long gradual rise to the Nipissing level at about 2,000 B.C. Forest composition underwent a slow evolution from spruce-pine to pine and finally to oak-pine.

All the while, deciduous forest animal species were gradually replacing boreal species in the north and pine forest species in the south. The climate became gradually warmer until it exceeded 5 degrees Fahrenheit above the present norms toward the end of this period (Terasmae 1961:666). This moderating trend has been called the Xerothermic period by paleoclimatologists.

Potzger's (1946) pollen profiles from Douglas Lake, Birge Bog, and Gilbert Bog in northern Michigan, and Forest Lake Bog, Allequash Lake, and Forest Lake in northern Wisconsin, all show a tremendous increase in pine pollen following the spruce maximum in those areas. Unlike the pollen profiles from the southern part of this region, which show an oak maximum following the Pine period, profiles in the north record pine pollen as 80 percent of the total sample and this frequency had been maintained since about 6,000 B.C. At Kirchner Marsh, in southcentral Minnesota, Winter (1962:527) reports a strong integration of non-arboreal pollen, particularly grasses, from about 5,000 B.C. to 3,500 B.C. This suggests prairie conditions in southcentral Minnesota and may also imply prairie expansion into southern Wisconsin and southern Michigan at the same period.

Potzger's pollen studies of Shipshewana Lake in northern Indiana, Third Sister Lake in southern Michigan, and Austin Bog in central Michigan show a south to north gradient in the intensity with which hardwood forest replaced pine at the close of the Pine period. Those on the northern end of the continuum show less deciduous pollen and fewer deciduous species. Profiles from Sodon Lake analyzed by Cain and Slater (1948:492-500), and more recently dated (M-162, M-163; Crane 1956), indicate that pine was the dominant forest species in southeastern Michigan at 5,000 B.C., and that it was replaced by oak at a slightly more recent date.

On the basis of Potzger's pollen profile, transects, and the dates which can now be inferred for them on the basis of a few more recently dated profiles, it appears that the modern Carolinian and Canadian biotic provinces were established in their present positions shortly after 5,000 B.C. (Figure 1, p.6). By the end of the Boreal Forest period, pine and spruce forest covered the northern part of the Upper Great Lakes area while pines and deciduous species comprised the forests farther south. In the north, pines gradually replaced spruce, except for stands in swampy areas; and, in the south, pines were replaced by oak-

dominated forests, except on very poor sandy soils where they
still remained as relic populations.

The frequency of pine pollen in the pollen profiles of this
period is so high that the forest compostion is generally pic-
tured as almost a pure stand of pine. This is probably a fal-
lacious assumption, both because pine is known to produce pollen in much greater quantities than other species, and because
pine pollen is transported great distances by wind. Ronald
Kapp (personal communication) has, in fact, questioned the whole
"Pine period" concept. He believes that forests of this period
probably had a substantial deciduous element. This Pine period
is designated as an ecological period in this study because the
appearance of an abundance of pine pollen in pollen profiles
marks the appearance of a new forest type—whatever its composition. Similarly, the replacement of pine pollen by that of deciduous species marks the close of this period. Used in this
way, "Pine period" does not imply that the forests were composed entirely of pine but that pine was an important element of
these forests.

Table 1 (p. 19) shows that mastodon may have been extant in
southern Michigan as late as 4,000 B.C. Woodland caribou remains, from a bog near Flint in east central Michigan, show
that this area was probably within the Lake Forest at about
4,000 B.C. The gray fox bones reported from a southwestern
Ontario bog at 3,400 B.C. are good evidence for a contemporary
deciduous forest in this area. The gray fox does not normally
range into conifer woodlands. The fauna of southern Wisconsin,
Michigan, and Ontario during the latter part of the Pine period
was probably similar in most respects to the contact period
Carolinian fauna of that area. The occurrence of an essentially
Carolinian fauna in the early Archaic levels of Raddatz Rockshelter, Sauk County, Wisconsin (Appendix A, p. 98) substantiates
this assertion. In the northern Pine Forest areas, the fauna
was probably of the Canadian type, and was also probably relatively impoverished since Pine Forest offers little cover or
food for herbivorous species.

During the opening stages of the Pine period, elements of the
Canadian biotic assemblage extend farther south than they do at
present, as demonstrated by the red fox, red squirrel and marten
in the lower levels of Raddatz Rockshelter. Yet, by the close
of this period, many typical Carolinian species probably had
reached farther north than they do today. This instability of the
ecotone between the two provinces is, of course, the result of
increasingly warmer temperatures through the Xerothermic

period. If this period brought dry weather as well as warmer weather, then we would expect the introduction of typical Illinoian prairie province species into southern Wisconsin and Michigan.

The Oak and Pine Period: 3,500 B.C. - Present

It has been suggested previously that the essential features of the Carolinian and Canadian biotic communities were established within their modern limits across the Upper Great Lakes area as early as 5,000 B.C. This is not to say that their ecotone has remained static since it is, in fact, still shifting. Oak-hickory forest became dominant to the south of the Carolinian-Canadian ecotone, and pine dominated the forests to the north. The final establishment of oak forest to the south has been used as a temporal marker for the beginning of this period. The term Oak and Pine is here used to refer to the two distinct floral associations of the Upper Great Lakes.

Changes in the fauna, flora, and climate of the Upper Great Lakes have taken place at a gradual pace since the retreat of glacial ice. Such changes were accomplished by gradual shifts in the composition of plant and animal assemblages by simple replacement of some species by others which were already present in low frequencies.

The appearance of oak-dominated forests in the southern part of the upper lakes area took place by a similar process, but seems to have been quite rapid. The rapidity of this evolution of forest types was, no doubt, the result of the Xerothermic period which reached its maximum shortly before 2,000 B.C. Although even the earliest pollen profiles show evidence of deciduous species in Great Lakes forests, it was probably not until 3,500 B.C. that the oak-hickory forest formation had completely replaced pine forests in the southern Great Lakes region. The establishment of forest of the beech-maple variety was proceeding at the same time in the north. Yarnell (1964:27) concluded, from his paleobotanical study of the Feeheley site, which has been dated at 2,000 B.C., that plant remains from this site seem to agree closely with the oak-hemlock-broadleaf forest which Zumberge and Potzger (1956:286) hypothesized as the forest type at South Haven in southwestern Michigan at the same period. The Feeheley site is located in Saginaw County, Michigan, and is very close to the modern Carolinian-Canadian ecotone, indicating that this ecotone was at least as far north 4,000 years ago as it is today (Appendix B p. 109).

A survey of the faunal remains from Archaic archaeological sites located on or near the present Carolinian-Canadian ecotone, gives support to the theory that a Carolinian floral and faunal assemblage was present in that area by at least 2,500 B.C. It has been suggested, however, that this forest type was surely established at a much earlier time. Levels 5 to 12 at the Raddatz Rockshelter in Sauk County, Wisconsin, the Schmidt site in Saginaw County, Michigan, and the Lamoka Lake site in Schuyler County, New York, all date from the early part of the Oak and Pine Forest period, i.e., around 2,500 B.C. - 2,000 B.C., and all are in the present Carolinian-Canadian ecotone. At the Raddatz Rockshelter, we find that both the Middle Archaic as well as the Late Archaic levels are dominated by deciduous forest and deciduous forest-edge species. Species such as the deer, elk, raccoon, gray squirrel, passenger pigeon, turkey, and box turtle are characteristic of these floral formations and do not normally occur in the Lake Forest of the Canadian biotic province. The disappearance of such typical Canadian forest species as the red squirrel, red fox, and marten from the Middle Archaic levels of the Raddatz Rockshelter is additional evidence for the establishment of a deciduous forest formation in southern Wisconsin, perhaps as early as 5,000 B.C. to 4,000 B.C.

Both deer and raccoon have been reported at the Schmidt site (Appendix B, p. 109). Although these species are not particularly sensitive ecological indicators, they are species which prefer deciduous forest associations and indicate that this type of vegetation was established in Saginaw County, Michigan, by 2,000 B.C.

Guilday (Ritchie 1965:54-59) has identified the remains of raccoon, gray fox, gray and fox squirrels, cottontail rabbit, deer, elk, turkey, and box turtles from the Lamoka Lake site in central New York. Northern Canadian biotic province counterparts of these species such as red fox, red squirrels, snow-shoe hare, woodland caribou, and moose, do not appear. Guilday points out that the box turtle and fox squirrel are record occurrences, since the eastern limits of the present range of these species is in extreme western New York. He believes their appearance at the Lamoka Lake site is a result of the warmer conditions of the Xerothermic.

Thus, we see that the fauna from archaeological sites along the present southern Carolinian-Canadian transition zone from Wisconsin to New York reflect warmer and probably dryer environmental conditions at the height of the Xerothermic period. Unfortunately, we do not have sites of this age in more northern

areas which would permit an evaluation of the northern limits
of the environmental changes produced by this climatic phenomenon.

Climatic Fluctuation of the Oak and Pine Forest Period

The climatic and ecological changes which have taken place
in the biotic provinces of the Great Lakes area since the beginning of the Oak and Pine period have been relatively slight
compared with the previous changes of the region. Griffin
(1960a:21-33, 1960b:809-868, 1961a:710-717, 1961b:147-155)
has presented some data suggesting a relationship between these
climatic and paleoecological fluctuations and the development
and demise of various cultural manifestations in North America.

This section is devoted to an examination Griffin's theories
of climatic change as they pertain to the changing biota of the
Upper Great Lakes. Griffin's theory is based upon the supposition that the expansions and recessions of the geographic distribution of a particular culture will be, in part, determined by
fluctuations in the geographic distribution of the natural environment to which that culture is adapted. An unfavorable climatic
phase could, therefore, cause a reduction in the distribution of
a culture or, in some severe cases, a decline in the culture
as a whole Conversely, favorable climatic conditions could produce the opposite effect. This theory has been most successfully
defended by pointing to simultaneous expansions or retractions of
far-flung but contemporary cultural developments around the
world. In some cases, changes in sea levels, the distribution
of plant and animal species, rainfall curves, soil types, and references in early historic sources have been used to document
the direction and intensity of ecological and climatic change.
In most cases, however, Griffin has not been able to specify
how or why these fluctuations affected changes within the cultures
he is discussing.

In his paper, "Post-Glacial Ecology and Culture Change in the
Great Lakes Area of North America, "Griffin (1961a) proposes
several paleoclimatological periods for this area during the Oak
and Pine period. These are as follows:

1) 2,300 B.C. - 1,800 B.C. —warm, period of Middle Archaic
florescence in the Great Lakes area.

2) 1,800 B.C. - 1,300 B.C.—cool climatic conditions.

3) 1,300 B.C. - 800 B.C.—warm, period of Late Archaic
development in the Upper Great Lakes.

4) 800 B.C. - 300 B.C. —cool climate.

5) 300 B.C. - A.D. 300 —warm, period of Middle Woodland

expansion into the Upper Great Lakes and florescence farther south.

6) A.D. 300 - A.D. 800 —cool, period of Middle Woodland decline.

7) A.D. 800 - A.D. 1200 —warm, period of Middle Mississippian expansion into southern Upper Great Lakes.

8) A.D. 1200 - A.D. 1700 —cool, period of decline to Upper Mississippi cultures in southern Upper Great Lakes.

These periods will be used in this study as a point of departure for the documentation of ecological change in the Upper Great Lakes during the Oak and Pine period.

Xerothermic Maximum: 2,300 B.C. - 1,800 B.C.

On the basis of Middle Archaic developments such as Old Copper, and Laurentian in the Great Lakes region, Griffin believes that this period was rather warm and therefore favorable for the northward movement of Archaic peoples. Although lack of faunal or floral evidence from related archaeological sites makes this rather hard to prove, there is no reason to believe that the warm climatic trend of the Xerothermic period did not continue for some time after its maximum at about 2,500 B.C. Kapp and Kneller (1962:135-145) analyzed paleobotanical material from an old Saline River terrace at Milan, Michigan, and concluded that this assemblage, dated at 2,130$\pm$100 B.C. (M-1149, Crane and Griffin 1962:183), represented climatic conditions which may have been warmer than the present climate of southeastern Michigan.

Cool Episode: 1,800 B.C. - 1,300 B.C.

As in the preceding period, there is little archaeological evidence that may be used to determine the climate of this period. Griffin believes it to be a relatively cool episode. Pollen profiles such as those at the Hartford Bog in southwestern Michigan (Zumberge and Potzger 1956:282), Kokomo Bog and Shipshewana Lake Bog in central and northern Indiana, Douglas Lake in northern Michigan, and Henzel Bog in central Minnesota (Potzger 1946) show a brief resurgence in the frequency of pine pollen following the Xerothermic maximum. Zumberge and Potzger regard this as evidence for climatic deterioration.

Late Archaic Episode: 1,300 B.C. - 800 B.C.

This was a period of rather intense cultural activity in the Upper Great Lakes and one which saw the highest development

of Archaic burial cermonialism. Griffin believes that this time was
characterized by a warm climatic phase. Unfortunately, there is
again little evidence to argue this hypothesis one way or another,
since most of the archaeological sites of this period are burial localities with few plant or animal remains. A cremated burial from
the Hodges site in Saginaw County, Michigan, contained a burned
portion of the distal end of a raccoon tibia (Binford 1963a:138). The
Hodges site occupation was on an Algoma river terrace and probably
dates at about 1,200 B.C. The remains of raccoon from this site
may be an indication of a warm climatic phase at this time. Writing
on the range changes of mammals in the Great Lakes area, de Vos
(1964:225) says that,

> The raccoon *(Procyon lotor)* not only has extended its range in a north-
> erly direction during recent decades, but it has also increased greatly
> in abundance in the Great Lakes region. Around [A.D.] 1900 the species
> was relatively rare in the southern sectors of Minnesota, Wisconsin,
> Michigan, and Ontario. Since then, the raccoon has gradually increased
> in numbers and extended its range northward.

Finally, raccoon bones have been reported from the Schmidt site,
also located in Saginaw County, Michigan (Appendix B, p. 109).
This site is believed to have been occupied during the 2,300 B.C.
to 1,800 B.C. warm period.

Cool Episode: 800 B.C. - 300 B.C.

Griffin (1961a:714) recognized this period as an unfavorable
one in the Upper Great Lakes area. He suggests that the onset of cool weather may have initiated a shift in burial cere-
monialism and perhaps the migration of people from the Great
Lakes area, southward into Ohio and Illinois. Here the burial
ceremonial complex underwent a remarkable florescence during
the next warm phase.

There is evidence which suggests that this is not the case.
Wright (1964:17-23) reports the occurrence of squash seeds,
Cucurbita at a transitional Late Archaic-Early Woodland camp
site near Saginaw, Michigan. This occupation has been dated at
530±120 B. C. (M-1432, Crane and Griffin 1965). This is by far
the most northern occurrence of squash prior to the Late Woodland period and may indicate a warm climatic phase on the
northern edge of the Carolinian biotic province at this time.

The Early Woodland component at the Schultz site near
Saginaw, Michigan, has also been radiocarbon dated at 500 B.C.
This site records a cultural sequence from Early Woodland
through Middle and Late Woodland occupations. Large quantities
of faunal material provide an excellent sequence for determining

changes in the prehistoric ecology as these changes are reflected
in the occurrences of various animal species. The only indication
of cooler climatic conditions at the Schultz site at this time, is
the occurrence of fisher and marten remains in the Early Woodland horizons. Although these species do not appear in later
horizons, their absence may be the result of other factors aside
from a warming of the climate. The fact remains, however,
that these typically northern species were present and provide
supporting evidence for the theory of a cool climate episode.

Hopewell Episode: 300 B.C. - A.D. 300

Griffin (1960a:28) has said that, "The Hopewell cultural height
of 200 B.C. to A.D. 200 corresponds neatly to a warm period
which had a rise of sea level of 5' to 6' above the present level
of the sea as recorded in the 'Abrolhos Terrace' of Australia
and the Perdue Chenier ridge of Louisiana and to the relatively
warm period of recurrence horizon II of northern Europe."
Griffin also has hypothesized that, "The gradual decline and
demise of the Hopewell culture in the Ohio and northern Mississippi Valley appears to correlate well with the cold period from
around A.D. 200 to A.D. 700." According to Griffin's theory,
this climatic deterioration reduced the reliability of agriculture
and, therefore, contributed to the decline in Hopewellian culture.

Baerreis and Bryson (1965) do not agree that the Hopewellian
period was one of relative warmth. They classify the period
from 600 B.C. - 500 B.C. to A.D. 300 - A.D. 400 as "more
severe" and identify it with the Sub-Atlantic period of Europe.
They emphasized, however, that the term "more severe" does
not have universal application and cite references to show that
the waters off California were cooler than at present, that Ari-
zona and New Mexico were warmer, and that both the Mediter-
ranean and central Canada were wetter. In Europe, glacial
accumulation during this period, due to more moisture rather
than lower temperatures, resulted in the Roman Emergence.

In view of the lack of agreement on climatic data, there are
several other kinds of arguments which can be invoked both for
and against Griffin's hypothesis. Griffin anticipated one of the
potential weaknesses in his theory by predicting that it would
be criticized on the grounds that it has not been demonstrated
that Hopewellian culture was reliant upon maize agriculture.
Not only is this still true, but most of the corn which has been
reported from Middle Woodland sites is from sites which date
during the latter part of this period, the period of supposed
climatic-deterioration.

On the basis of his study of the adaptation of the early Late Woodland peoples of the Illinois River Valley, Struever (1964) has argued that the Hopewellian communities in Illinois were dependent upon the exploitation of natural plant resources and hunting. Unfortunately, this economic pattern has not yet been adequately documented. Information from the Schultz site, in Saginaw County, Michigan, tends to substantiate Struever's claim, but this site is located on the northern periphery of Middle Woodland and may, therefore, have a different economy than the more "classic" Hopewellian centers of either Ohio or Illinois.

Another argument which tends to cast doubt upon Griffin's theory is that the distribution of Hopewellian culture, at least that within the Havana tradition, did not extend as far northward as even the present southern boundary of the Carolinian-Canadian ecotone. Hopewellian cultures of the southern variety penetrated neither the Lake Forest nor the Carolinian-Canadian edge. In fact, the most northerly distribution of this culture came late within the Middle Woodland period as exemplified by the North Bay complex in Wisconsin and the Goodall focus material from Newaygo County, Michigan. If the climate was warmer and Middle Woodland people were agriculturists, surely they would have established sites farther to the north. However, if these people were agricultural, but if the weather was cooler than it is at present, then they would have had the distribution which we now recognize.

Two other factors can be evoked to explain the southern distribution of Middle Woodland cultures, first the cultivation of a variety of corn which was not cold resistant and, second, the existence of a strong cultural preference for broad alluvial valleys. Unfortunately, we cannot evaluate the cold resistance of Hopewellian corn so that this first factor is open only to conjecture. And, in addition, the Middle Woodland sites in Michigan are not always found in large alluvial valleys. The hypothesis favored here is that Hopewellian peoples were not dependent upon food production until almost the second century after Christ, and that the climate, at least in the Upper Great Lakes, was not deteriorating but becoming increasingly warm during the late Middle Woodland period.

It will be suggested in a later section of this study, which deals with Middle Woodland adaptations, that there were three different adaptations during this period, and that each of these had a specific relationship to one of the three large natural communities of the upper lakes. It will also be suggested that by about A.D. 200, Middle Woodland peoples in the Carolinian

and even southern Carolinian-Canadian edge zones had become
dependent on corn agriculture. Evidence for this is seen in the
faunal remains at the Spoonville site (A.D. 215±110, M-1427;
A.D. 110±110, M-1428), at the late Middle Woodland horizon at
the Schultz site and to a lesser extent in the North Bay complex
in Door County, Wisconsin (A.D. 160; Mason 1966). Earlier
Middle Woodland manifestations, such as the Havana-like horizons
at the Schultz site, show more reliance on hunting and fishing
while Late Woodland occupations in these same localities, such
as Heins Creek in Door County (A.D. 732±150) and the later occupations at the Schultz site, provide some evidence for the
increased importance of agriculture by about A.D. 500.

In short, the above data is inconsistent with Griffin's theory
of decreasing agricultural potential during the late Middle Woodland period. It appears, instead, that the people of the southern
Upper Great Lakes were becoming more strongly agricultural
up to and beyond Griffin's A.D. 300 cut off date for the Hopewellian warm phase. If, as Griffin implies, Hopewellian peoples
were agriculturists who expanded northward during the Hopewellian
warm phase and were later thwarted in their effort to produce
corn in the face of cooler weather, we would expect to find both
a southward retraction and a decrease in the density of Middle
Woodland sites within this period. If, as it has been suggested,
the reverse situation is true, then we must follow the suggestion
of Baerreis and Bryson that the climate of the late Hopewell
period was becoming warmer and therefore more favorable to
the production of food.

Scandic Episode: A.D. 300 - A.D. 800

In the preceding section the "warm phase" which supposedly
nurtured the Middle Woodland developments of the Upper Mississippi Valley and Great Lakes area was discussed in regard
to a succeeding cool climatic phase which Griffin placed between
A.D. 200 and A.D. 700 - 800. Griffin (1960a:28) tells us that,

The gradual decline and demise of the Hopewell culture in Ohio and
northern Mississippi Valley appears to correlate well with the cold
period from around A.D. 200 to A.D. 700. This is the period attributed
to the "Whitewater Draught" in the Southwest which is expressed in tree
rings and evidences of erosion (Antevs, 1955: p. 330). It is also indicated by the RY11 recurrence horizon succeeded by cool moist conditions in southern Sweden around A.D. 400 (Goodwin, 1956) and the
climatic shift to a cooler period in Alaska dated about A.D. 500.

Baerreis and Bryson (1965:215) again disagree. In discussing
their Scandia Climatic Episode (A.D. 300 - 400 to A.D. 800 -
900) they note that,

Apparently the Sub-Atlantic ended about A.D. 300-400, though the end seems less definite than the beginning. The following episode was characterized by amelioration of the climate in Scandia [Greenland, Iceland and Scandinavia], glacial retreat, the post-Roman transgressions, and accelerated erosion in the Southwestern mountains.

Only two of the sites analyzed in this study have occupations which date from this period, the late Middle Woodland horizon at the Schultz site, and the Heins Creek site which is, in fact, very late within this period. Even though there is growing evidence for the persistence of Middle Woodland cultures until the sixth century after Christ, the apparent rarity of sites within the Scandic period gives credence to Griffin's position that this was a period of climatic and cultural regression. Yet, despite this fact, both the Heins Creek and late Middle and early Late Woodland occupations at Schultz show economies which are more dependent upon food production than those of earlier peoples in these locales. If this was period of climatic amelioration, as Baerreis and Bryson contend, we would expect to find early Late Woodland sites on more northerly latitudes than those of the late Middle Woodland period. There is little evidence to suggest that this was the case in Michigan and in southern Wisconsin the Effigy Mound culture was, in fact, restricted to about the same latitude as its Middle Woodland predecessors.

One faunal record from Ontario may indicate that the Scandic period was indeed cool. The occurrence of the moose bones at the Krieger site in Kent County constitutes the most southern record for the distribution of this species, (Appendix I p. 270). The Krieger site is classified as Owasco and probably dates between A.D. 500 and A.D. 1000. Since the climate seems to have undergone a warming trend at about A.D. 800, the occurrence of the moose probably dates from the Scandic Episode.

Neo-Atlantic Episode: A.D. 800 - A.D. 1200

There is general agreement among paleoclimatologists that the period spanning several centuries on either side of A.D. 1000 was one of warmth in eastern North America and northern Europe. Griffin (1960b) pointed out the importance of this climatic phase for the northward movement of strongly agricultural Middle Mississippian peoples into the upper Mississippi valley and Upper Great Lakes area. Baerreis and Bryson (1965) who refer to this period as the Neo-Atlantic, recognize the rather dramatic effect of this episode on the prehistoric cultures of this region, yet, it is not clear how this period

differed substantially from their preceding Scandic episode.
These authors extend the Neo-Atlantic period to A.D. 1300 when
there was a rather abrupt change in atmospheric circulation
bringing on cooler and wetter conditions.

The effect of the Neo-Atlantic period on the development of
the Upper Mississippian cultures of southern Wisconsin is
discussed in some detail in the section of this study dealing with
various adaptations of Oneota cultures. Although there is a
great deal of controversy on the temporal positioning of several
of the early sites of this sequence, their economies are basically
of two kinds: strongly agricultural, or primariiy agricultural
with some other important food resource. The sites which
seem to be the earliest stylistically are those with an intensely
agricultural economy. Developed Oneota sites, on the other
hand, have mixed economies and these are stylistically later in
the developmental sequence. All of the intesely agricultural
sites, i.e., Aztalan, Carcajou Point, and to a lesser extent
Lasley's Point, dating prior to A.D. 1300, have mixed agricultural or diffuse economies. Other late Upper Mississipian sites
in southern Wisconsin and northern Illinois seem to be strongly
agricultural.

It has been pointed out that there is no inherent relationship
between Oneota ceramic styles and diffuse economies. The fact
that this is the case for late Oneota sites in central Wisconsin
may be due to climatic deterioration after A.D. 1300. However,
this adaptation may also have developed in response to different
micro-environments of the Carolinian-Canadian edge which all
share environmental limitations for corn agriculture. If the
latter explanation is to be accepted, as it will be argued in this
study, it implies that Oneota cultures were not unlike their
counterparts in the Late Woodland cultures of the Carolinian-
Canadian edge of Michigan and Ontario. These societies drew
upon both northern and southern subsistence techniques and received cultural stimuli from both areas. This kind of adaptation
was a very flexible one and provided for maximum return in
food while preserving economic mobility. While climate has
some effect upon this kind of a society, its adaptation is one
which allows it to shift with climatic change. It is, therefore,
argued that while the onset of cooler climate at A.D. 1300 may
have been partially responsible for bringing about the diffuse
adaptations of the Oneota cultures of central Wisconsin, it appears as though these adaptations arose during the period of
relatively cool climate after A.D. 1300 in response to local environmental conditions within the Carolinian-Canadian edge.

During the Neo-Atlantic period there was a resurgence of cultural activity in southern Michigan. Agricultural people were pushing much farther to the north than at any earlier period. Yarnell (1964:14) reports that corn was grown near its northernmost aboriginal limit by A.D. 1000. Yarnell (ibid:123) also reports corn from the Juntunen site which presently lies well within the Canadian biotic province. This occurrence is in the context of occupations which date between A.D. 1070 and A.D. 1320.

Among the most interesting of these northern agricultural sites in Michigan are the ciruclar enclosures which are generally located on the extreme southern edge of the Canadian biotic province in centeral Michigan. Corn agriculture is not presently possible in these areas, yet corn has been reported from one of these sites, the Mikado earthwork in Alcona County, Michigan. This site has been dated at A.D. 1450 (M-777). The Linseman-Walters earthwork in Ogemaw County dates at A.D. 1350 (M-779) and a mound associated with the Atena enclosures of Missaukee County, Michigan, has been dated at A.D. 1270 (M-790). It seems reasonable to assume that these sites were occupied by agricultural people during the height of the Neo-Atlantic warm episode, which probably fell near the end of the period of A.D. 800 to A.D. 1300. The enclosures appear to be the remnants of fortifications which were perhaps necessitated during the succeeding cool climatic episode, by the fact that these people were in all probablility then competing with local hunters and gatherers of the Canadian province. It is known that this transition zone was an area of intertribal conflict at the historic period (see pages 75 and 76 for further discussion). Although the external cultural relationships of these enclosures is not well known at this time, it appears as though the return to cool moist conditions sometime after A.D. 1300 forced the abandonment of these northern agricultural outposts.

Pruitt (1954:253-256) reported the occurrence of bones of a prairie vole *(Microtus ochrogaster)* from a humus soil in Leelanau County, Michigan. This species currently occurs two hundred miles to the south in only the most southwestern counties of Michigan. The soil horizon from which the prairie vole was recovered has been dated at A.D. 1220±250 (M-208). Other faunal evidence for the Neo-Atlantic warm phase is the appearance of the turkey and deer in the Juntunen site at about A.D. 1000 to A.D. 1100. These Carolinian species do not appear in earlier or later deposits (Appendix E, p. 157).

The appearance of the opossum in the midden debris of the Fairport Harbor site near Cleveland, Ohio, constitutes the most northeasterly prehistoric record of this typically southeastern species (Guilday 1958:40). The opossum does not appear in either earlier or later prehistoric sites northeast of this point (Appendix I, Map 2 p. 253). In a recent discussion of the Whittlesey focus, Fitting (1964b:168) suggests an early placement of the Fairport Harbor site within this focus. In all probability this site dates from the Neo-Atlantic period and the occurrence of the opossum reflects warmer climatic conditions at that time.

Another record of the northern movement of a Carolinian species is the appearance of the remains of the cottontail rabbit in the midden deposit of the Iroquoian horizon of the Inverhuron site (Kenyon 1959:33). This occurrence is of particular interest in view of the blending of Canadian and Carolinian fauna in this occupation. The fisher, red fox, red squirrel, and porcupine belong to the former province while the woodchuck, cottontail rabbit, deer, and elk occur most typically in the latter. Kenyon (ibid:31) dates the Iroquois material at Inverhuron between A.D. 1100 and A.D. 1350. Again the mixed nature of the fauna and particularly this most northern occurrence of the cottontail rabbit is probably due to the climatic amelioration of the Neo-Atlantic period.

Protohistoric and Historic Climatic Episodes: A.D. 1200 - A.D. 1700

Some discussion has already been expended on the theory that the period following the Neo-Atlantic was cool and moist and that this fluctuation led to the demise of certain peripheral agricultural societies in Michigan, and perhaps influenced the developing Oneota economies of Wisconsin. It was, in fact, the effects of this climatic deterioration which first led Griffin (1960b) to explore the relationship between climate and culture in his classic essay "A Hypothesis for the Prehistory of the Winnebago." Since that time Baerreis and Bryson (1965) have distinguished several finer subdivisions within this period. These are as follows:

1) A.D. 1300 - A.D. 1450 — Pacific Climatic Episode; cool, dry conditions in the Midwest resulting in expansion of the prairie peninsula.

2) A.D. 1450 - A.D. 1550 — slight warming trend with a climate similar to the Neo-Atlantic.

3) A.D. 1550 - A.D. 1880 — Neo-Boreal Episode; a period of cool climate often referred to as the Little Ice Age in the Great Lakes area.

In the western Upper Great Lakes area, the climatic deterioration of this period seems to have had the effect of reducing the number and density of agricultural sites on the northern peripheries of corn agriculture. We have already seen its effects upon Oneota sites in Wisconsin and the earthwork enclosure sites of central Michigan. In addition, such sites as Juntunen in the Straits of Mackinac area, which had been occupied since shortly after A.D. 800, were apparently abandoned by about A.D. 1350 to A.D. 1400. The Skegemog Point site located on the western margin of the Carolinian-Canadian edge in the Grand Traverse Bay area of Michigan, which was recently excavated by Michigan State University, also appears to have been abandoned shortly before this time.

Griffin (1961b:711) has pointed out that the deleterious effects of this climatic shift were not felt in lower Ontario and New York, these locations being the scene of the development and florescence of Iroquoian culture between A.D. 1400 and A.D. 1600. Griffin has attributed this apparent exception to the modifying effect of the water mass of the Great Lakes. A more plausible, and probably more acceptable explanation would be the brief return to a favorable climate which Baerreis and Bryson place between A.D. 1450 and A.D. 1550.

There are, in fact, numerous examples of Carolinian fauna which attained their most northern aboriginal distribution in Ontario sites of this general period (Appendix I, p. 247). These records include turkey from the Sidey-Mackay site in Simcoe County, fox squirrel from the Lawson site in Middlesex County, and the Uren site in Oxford County, gray squirrel from the Roebuck Village site in Grenville County, and gray fox from both the Lawson and Roebuck sites. To be sure, some of these sites may date prior to the warm phase of A.D. 1450 - A.D. 1550 so that the presence of these species, though indicative of warmer conditions, cannot be considered as definitive as we would like to believe. Still, they do point to favorable climatic conditions during the Iroquois genesis.

There is no indication that the climate produced any adverse effect on the agricultural societies of the Carolinian province of south central Michigan. The highly selective hunting pattern exhibited on sites of the Younge Tradition in southeastern Michigan seem to have been as fully agricultural as sites such as Moccasin Bluff in Berrien County and the Silver Lake and Dumaw Creek sites in Oceana County in the western part of the state.

The Neo-Boreal Climatic Episode beginning in A.D. 1550 must certainly have had its effect upon the most northern agricultural societies, but as yet we have no solid evidence to demonstrate

the fact.   Fitting (personal communication) believes that the
sparse Late Woodland occupation of the Schultz site in Saginaw
County, Michigan, may be a reflection of a rather drastic change
in economic and settlement patterns in the Saginaw Valley at this
time.   While Fitting may be correct, the fauna of the Late Woodland occupation of the site indicates neither a cooler climate nor
a significant shift in subsistence activities.

One other bit of evidence may indicate a cooler climate during the late prehistoric period.   The remains of a woodland
caribou, the most southerly record of the distribution of this
species, has been recorded from the Lawson site in Middlesex
County, Ontario.   Since the Lawson site is late in the developmental Iroquois sequence, this specimen could quite possibly date
from the post-A.D. 1550 period.   Baerreis and Bryson (1965)
have suggested the intriguing possibility that the Neo-Boreal episode, through its adverse effect upon corn agriculture, may have
been very influential in producing a shift to the fur trading
economy of the early historic period in the Upper Great Lakes.

There has been a recent warming of the climate since the
1880's (Baerreis and Bryson 1965).   This change occurred too
late to register any effect upon Indian cultures since they had
all but disappeared by this time.   It did, however, affect the
distribution of many animals and presumably plant species.   The
exact effects are, of course, difficult to evaluate since they have
been complicated by the heavy influx of European population,
bringing about forest clearance, hunting with firearms, intensive
trapping, and other practices which grossly change the natural
environment.

De Vos (1964:210-231) has traced the range restrictions and
expansions of mammals in the Great Lakes region during the
nineteenth and twentieth centuries.   Unfortunately, many of his
original range estimates appear to be inaccurate, at least when
compared with the distribution of some species well represented
in late archaeological sites.   De Vos records range restrictions
for the woodland caribou, Canadian lynx, gray wolf, black bear,
marten, fisher, and snowshoe hare.   Species which have extended
their ranges northward include the moose, deer, opossum, cottontail rabbit, bobcat, raccoon, coyote, gray fox, gray squirrel, and
fox squirrel.   The thirteen-lined ground squirrel, Franklin ground
squirrel and jackrabbit have extended their ranges eastward
while a westward spread has been displayed by the smoky shrew
and the yellow-nosed vole.   Some species such as the elk, bison,
wolverine, and cougar have been exterminated entirely from this
region, except in areas where they have been recently reintro-
duced.

III

ETHNOZOOLOGY

Ethnozoology may be defined as the study of the relationship
between animal species and man within the bounds of a particular culture. Although ethnozoology encompasses such diverse
fields of study as the anatomical knowledge and taxonomic systems
of a culture, most of this kind of information cannot be reconstructed from the sort of data which the archaeologist has at
his disposal. We will never know precisely how people who occupied a particular archaeological site classified the animals,
whose bones the archaeologist recovers. The fact that certain
animals were utilized more intensely than others can yield information which leads to a fuller understanding of that culture. In
primitive cultural situations where people are dependent upon
hunting, gathering, simple agriculture or a combination of these
economic pursuits for food, clothing and shelter, the successful
exploitation of animal species is vital for survival.

If we intend to devote ourselves to a more complete knowledge
of cultures whether modern or prehistoric, it is necessary to
consider them in relation to their natural environments. As
Kroeber (1939:1) observed, . . ."cultures are rooted in nature
and can therefore never be understood except with reference to
that piece of nature in which they occur. . ." Animal remains
from archaeological sites represent not only a "piece of nature"
but the relationship between culture and the natural environment.

Within the limits of an environmental setting and a given
technological level, the people of a society are faced with a range
of choices in the selection of animal species. If moose, caribou,
field mice, sturgeon, and lake trout are available, an adapted
culture will prescribe which species will be hunted, in what season they are to be hunted, which techniques of hunting will be
used and who will employ these techniques. These processes
are not only technological but social, political, and philosophical
as well. The vital man-environmental relationship is bound up
in the process of cultural adaptation.

How or why a culture reaches a certain adaptive level is, perhaps, beyond the scope of this study. We can assume that the mechanics of adaptive processes are based upon a balance between energy expenditure and productivity. Given a number of possible food sources, it seems probable that a culture will come to utilize those plant and animal species which are most accessible, most abundant or easiest to capture with the technological methods available. Once such an adaptive pattern is acquired, change is made at the expense of tradition and is often slow and gradual. Adaptive revolutions are occasioned only by external pressure which causes disorder in either the natural or cultural environment.

It is not the nature of plant and animal species to flourish in continuous reaches of either time or space. Plants bear seed with season, rabbits are more numerous some years than others, deer do not frequent pine forests, and fish spawn where conditions suit them. Thus, people who must depend upon particular plants and animals are subject to those variables which condition the areal and spatial distribution of these species. Culture provides man with many ingenious methods to assure his survival in the face of nature's caprices. A man may hunt moose with a bow in the pine forest during the winter and join scores of other people to spear sturgeon in the spring. Such activities are geared to the animal resources he is able to exploit and are important as a major determinant of the characteristics of his cultural pattern.

If through the application of paleoecological techniques, we are able to acquire a knowledge of the natural environment in which a culture is rooted, the same primary data can yield important ethnozoological information. Instead of observing animal bones from archaeological sites as a segment of a larger surrounding natural community, we must find significance in the fact that these bones also represent a series of culturally determined choices. The people who killed the animals chose them within a technological, socio-political, and ideological framework in which some species were selected with great frequency, while others were selected infrequently, or not at all. If we know which animals were selected and how frequently, the season in which they were selcted, the method by which they were taken, and something of settlement patterns and demography, we are able to add a great deal of information to our knowledge of prehistoric cultures. Such information can be gained from archaeological sites when conditions are favorable for the preservation of organic material.

Just as the paleoecological record shows shifts in the distribution and composition of biotic provinces through time, so are there indications for change in the way cultures adapt to these environments. Archaeologists recognize the most obvious patterns in designating periods of cultural integrity. Thus, the Paleo-Indians were hunters of big game, Archaic peoples were hunters and gatherers, while Woodland people's practiced agriculture, etc. The application of recent sophisticated archaeological, ethnozoological, and ethnobotanical techniques makes possible the delineation of much narrower adaptive patterns. It is possible, for instance, to trace the seasonal movements and activities of Archaic hunters within one river valley, as recently illustrated by Winter's superb work with the Riverton culture in the Wabash River valley (1963:33-41). While micro-environmental studies of this nature are extremely important, it is not often that archaeological data permits this type of evaluation. More frequently, we must work with the adaptation which takes place within more inclusive environmental zones, for instance, river valleys, parklands or one of the dominant forest types. Although cultures which occur in these large communities exploit the resources of many micro-environments, the fact that boundaries of the larger communities are often coterminous with the boundaries of areas of cultural integrity indicates that the cultures within that community share a basic adaptive pattern. Kaplan (Sahlins and Service 1960:75) in formulating the "law of cultural dominance" tells us that "that cultural system which more effectively exploits the energy resources of a given environment will tend to spread in that environment at the expense of less effective systems." If this idea is correct, and there is little reason to doubt its validity, then the establishment of an efficient or a more efficient adaptive pattern within a particular environmental zone will result in the eventual spread of that pattern throughout that environmental zone.

One of the primary objectives of this study is to apply ethnozoological technique to the archaeological record of the Upper Great Lakes area in an effort to relate known cultural complexes to specific natural communities and to define and describe the types of adaptations which developed in these natural communities.

The Identification and Analysis of Faunal Remains

A thorough study of animal remains from archaeological sites must include two phases, the actual identification of the remains and an analysis of the significance of these remains.

The identification of animal bone from archaeological sites has been a standard part of a good site report for many years. However, this information was usually presented in a section of the report which discussed the environment of the site, or occasionally in a section devoted to animal foods. Typically, remains were submitted to a zoologist who provided the archaeologist with a list of the species represented on the site. Such lists usually included a count of the bones of each species, but seldom included provenience information. As a consequence, no record was provided of the number of individual animals represented, nor changes in fauna through time. The zoologist, whose valuable time was expended in the tedium of identification, was interested in former distribution of animal species. On the other hand, the archaeologist may have been interested in subsistence patterns and in the season that the site was occupied. However, his inability to interpret the information supplied to him by the zoologist usually mitigated against the appearance of the desired information.

In the last 15 or 20 years, archaeologists have come to realize the value of faunal and botanical analysis in interpreting and reconstructing prehistoric cultures. As a result, they have developed several methods of obtaining the proper kind of information. These include educating experts in other fields to the problem of the archaeologist, training archaeologists who are able to provide information in one or more of these specialized fields, and finally, learning to do it themselves. The first two alternatives have been most successful.

New methods which provide the kind of data necessary for archaeological interpretation include: (1) identification of remains by provenience unit, (2) identification of specific bones representing each species including notes indicating whether these bones came from the right or left side of the animal, (3) identification of minimum numbers of individual animals of each species, (4) calculation of the amount of meat provided by each species, (5) classification of unidentifiable bone into classes of animal, i.e., mammal, bird, and fish, and (6) noting special features of the faunal assemblage such as ages of animals, seasonal conditions such as the presence or absence of deer antler on deer skull, recording marks made in butchering and other secondary features such as charring.

If such information is recorded, then a number of meaningful kinds of analytic processes can be undertaken. (1) Changes in faunal assemblages through time can be recorded and used to trace changes in both the natural environment and cultural adaptation. (2) The amount of food provided by various species can be calculated and an accurate judgment may be made about the role of each species in the subsistence activities. (3) The presence or absence of seasonal species such as migratory fowl, notations on seasonal morphological changes and growth rates can be used to determine the season of occupancy. (4) Postmortem manipulations of animal remains can provide information about hunting techniques, and methods used in butchering, cooking, and preservation.

When the proper data is not gathered during the identification process, then the detailed analysis necessary to gain anthropological information is impossible. The interpretations of archaeological faunal material presented in this study are based upon the above mentioned identification practices. As a result, they are not always comparable with the few other faunal studies which have been done on archaeological sites of the Upper Great Lakes area. For instance, a meaningful comparison of the frequency of mammal bone on two sites is not possible when we know the numbers of identified and unidentified mammal bones from one site and only the number of identified mammal bones from the other. Even a comparison of identified mammal bone would be biased by the differential ability of the two specialists who identified the bone and other factors such as preservation and the degree of fragmentation.

Similarly, we cannot compare the amount of meat of various species represented on two sites if the minimum number of individuals of each species is not reported at both of the sites. The amount of meat represented can be calculated only if we know the minimum number of individuals of each species which were represented.

Difficulties such as these have resulted in the rejection of most other faunal studies which have been done on Upper Great Lake sites. Many of these do, however, provide information on the prehistoric distribution of animal species which is sometimes useful in plotting environmental change. The archaeological occurrences of many animal species in the eastern United States have been plotted and are presented in Appendix I p. 247). The authenticity of reports of the appearance of species outside of their present or known former ranges have not been checked by personal examination.

Appendices G and H are designed to serve the archaeologist who wishes to interpret a list of identified species which have been supplied to him by colleagues in the various fields of zoology. Appendix G (p. 224) is a list of the ranges of many species in regard to the biotic provinces of eastern North America. If a zonal concept of environmental change is applied, then the identification of a large number of Hudsonian species from a Paleo-Indian site in southern Ohio would indicate a boreal forest environment and imply the availability of other boreal species. Appendix H (p. 245) may be even more useful. Here are presented the habitat preferences of animals which are typical of the common habitat types of the eastern United States. Many of these species are not strictly limited to these habitats, but prefer them and are found in greatest abundance where these habitats are present.

Here again, the identification of an assemblage of prairie species in an area that is now wooded indicates the existence of prairie vegetation during a former period. Often the identification of habitats which differ from those of the present also indicate different climatic conditions such as higher or lower temperatures or more or less precipitation. Readers who use this information should be wary of several pitfalls. Judgments about former habitats should be made on the basis of an assemblage of animal species, not on lone individuals. Identifications which are incorrect can also lead to faulty conclusions so that all questionable records should be verified. Finally, many extant species have larger or smaller ranges today than they did in the prehistoric period, a result of their ability or inability to adapt to increasing human populations and to changes in the distribution of habitat types as a result of modern land use practices.

Focal and Diffuse Economies

Unfortunately, so little rigorous work has been done with the prehistoric subsistence patterns of the eastern United States that no descriptive system has yet been produced which promotes systematic thought on the subject. The terms which have been applied to the economies of these societies have been largely borrowed from social anthropology which also suffers from an inadequate terminology. Such designations as "hunters and gatherers" or "food producers" may be accurate descriptions of what people do, but they are not adequate for broad comparisons or for discussing the implications of the economy as it relates sectors of culture.

It is often difficult, or even impossible, to speak of the economies of primitive cultures *per se*. The reason is, of course, that economic activities are so integrally linked with the technological, socio-political, and ideological subsystems of these societies that the functioning of primitive economy must be understood in these contexts. For this reason, a classificatory system which describes economies must be inclusive enough to provide for the implications of economic activity on other cultural subsystems.

In order to facilitate this way of thinking about economy and economic activities, a system of classification is proposed, phrased in terms of economic adaptations. It has been useful to think of economies as belonging to one of two polar types. These are designated as focal and diffuse economies, or in terms of the whole cultural complex, focal and diffuse adaptations. These classifications are based upon the kinds of resources which a culture exploits, and, they take cognizance of the fact that such activities have important implications for the structuring of the cultural system itself.

The practice of a focal subsistence economy is directed toward the procurement of one or a few similar kinds of foods. Those societies which practice focal economies are specialized ones, depending upon specific methods and techniques for the exploitation of an abundant resource. However, the population density, types of economic residential stability, and sophistication of social and political systems achieved by peoples with focal adaptations may vary greatly, depending upon the level of productivity which can be attained through the exploitation of the primary resource. Specialized hunters, fishermen, as well as agriculturalists have focal economies. Whereas level of productivity of the economies of people who are exploiting game or fish populations is primarily determined by the natural availability of the resource, the level of productivity of people who produce food is determined primarily by cultural factors.

The advantage of a focal economy is the cultural stability which it produces. Given the level of availability of a resource which is necessary to support a focal economy, and the degree of cultural specialization needed to exploit it, the rate of change in the technological, socio-political, and ideological systems of the culture will be slow. The fact that focal adaptations can develop only in the presence of a very reliable resource means that the economy is seldom threatened. To be sure, there could be occasional crop failures or game shortages which would prove to be quite disastrous, but, normally, these would be only temporary setbacks. If such failures become too frequent then the primary resource is no longer reliable and new subsistence resources must be found, and new systems developed to exploit them.

There are, however, disadvantages which may result from the rigid nature of focal adaptations. Any major change which takes place within the society is made at the expense of well established traditions and, therefore, comes about only under drastic conditions. A society with a focal economy based upon hunting, for example, would have to undergo a major readaptation to begin growing crop plants or even to develop an economy based upon some other resources whose level of availability is naturally determined.

The second type of economic pattern, the diffuse economy, is based, not upon the reliability of one resource, but on an ability to exploit a variety of resources. Societies with diffuse adaptations are not specialized ones in the strict sense of the word, since they depend upon many specialized skills and techniques to exploit a number of different kinds of resources. No one of these resources is abundant enough, or reliable enough, to support the population level which is achieved by the systematic exploitation of them all. The failure of one resource would result in a shift of emphasis to one or more alternate resources. Unlike focal economies where "all the eggs are placed in one basket," the failure of one of the resources exploited by people with a diffuse economy would be detrimental, but not disastrous.

This is the great advantage of the diffuse adaptation, the relative flexibility and adaptability of those societies which practice it. The lack of economic specialization has significant implications for evolutionary change — it provides the milieu from which these societies can take advantage of new resources or methods of exploiting old ones by simply shifting the emphasis of subsistence activities. Diffuse adaptations are, to borrow a biological term, pre-adapted socieites.

This type of economic pattern has several innate disadvantages. It requires a great deal of mobility, and a large technological inventory. In addition, a diffuse economy does not profit for any length of time from food surpluses. And finally, it is bounded by the natural availability of food resources.

It should be noted that the focal-diffuse system of classification places these adaptations at opposite ends of a continuum. While we seldom encounter modern or prehistoric cultures which are purely focal or purely diffuse, there is seldom confusion over the question of whether a given society is practicing one kind of economy or the other. Thus, an agricultural group may occasionally hunt deer, or a society with a diffuse economy may

spend a whole summer fishing while ignoring other available resources; yet, these economic activities do not accurately reflect
the total adaptation of the culture. By definition, no culture can
occupy the middle of the focal-diffuse continuum. This is not
to say that a society cannot pass from one type of adaptation to
the other, only that to do so requires a quantum jump resulting
in a new adaptation. Since diffuse adaptations pre-adapt a culture for several kinds of subsistence activities upon which a
focal economy could be based, a readaptation of a diffuse economy to a focal economy based upon one of its alternate resources requires only a subtle cultural reorientation. The reverse is not true. A rapid and drastic readaptation is required
for a focal adaptation to either switch to a new primary resource
or to develop an adaptation of the diffuse type.

Paleo-Indian Cultures: 10,000 B.C. - 8,000 B.C.

Very little is known of the earliest cultures of the Upper
Great Lakes region. Fluted point surface finds (Byers 1942;
Fitting 1963; Mason 1958; Roosa 1963, 1965) and excavated sites
(Fitting 1964a; MacNeish 1952) indicate wide stylistic similarities
with Paleo-Indian material from other areas of the United States.
Details of Paleo-Indian subsistence and settlement patterns in the
eastern United States are extremely sketchy. It may be safely
assumed, however, that these cultural patterns as well as the
functional and stylistic traditions of tool manufacture represent
an adaptive pattern which was able to function for at least two
thousand years in a number of diverse environmental situations.
Fitting (1965b) has suggested that the minor stylistic differences
in fluted point types may be related to areas of cultural integrity
within some of these environmental zones.

The fact that Paleo-Indian peoples lived on small, rather
temporary and widely scattered sites, the fact that they made
tools for hunting and skin working, and because these tools have
been found with the remains of extinct Pleistocene mammals on
the Great Plains, we assume that Paleo-Indians were indeed
hunters. As a matter of fact, we have no evidence of the kind
of food these people consumed on a day to day basis. For, while
Paleo-Indians of the western United States occasionally killed an
elephant or giant bison, they may have sustained themselves on
much smaller game. In short, we have only circumstantial
evidence that Paleo-Indians were hunters, let alone that they
were hunters of extinct Pleistocene species as is so often assumed.

Although many hundreds or perhaps thousands of mammoth and mastodon remains have been unearthed in the eastern United States, only a single mastodon has been shown to have met its demise by human agent. In Warren Wittry's (1965:14-25) study of the Rappuhn mastodon in Lapeer County, Michigan, he states (ibid:19): "The association of man with the Rappuhn mastodon is proven beyond a doubt, . . ." Stone tools were not recovered with the Rappuhn mastodon, but there was strong, if not conclusive, evidence that this animal was butchered by man. Geochronological evidence places the death of this animal at least as early as 9,000 B.C.

The discovery of bones of a barren ground caribou, *Rangifer arcticus*, in a fire pit with Paleo-Indian tools at the Holcombe site in Macomb County, Michigan, is the only clear association of Paleo-Indian tools with an animal species in the eastern Unites States (Cleland 1965:350-351). The modern habitat of this gregarious species is the tundra and boreal woodland of the Canadian subarctic. The barren ground caribou spends the summer on the tundra and with the approach of winter, migrates in huge herds to the protection of the boreal woodlands. Unless its habitat has changed since the retreat of glacial ice from the Great Lakes region, which seems unlikely, we can hypothesize this type of environment in southern Michigan at the time it was occupied by Paleo-Indians. This does not imply, however, that the tundra of Michigan was of the same composition or extent as the modern arctic tundra.

The Holcombe find also indicates that Paleo-Indians were hunting medium-sized game. While the Rappuhn mastodon butchering site certainly indicates that early hunters of the Upper Great Lakes were not adverse to eating mastodon meat, it proves neither that Paleo-Indians were specialized elephant hunters nor that they were responsible for the extinction of large Pleistocene game. In fact, the Rappuhn mastodon and the Holcombe caribou tell us very little about Paleo-Indian subsistence activities. Indirect evidence in the form of inferred tool functions, i.e., spears, and hide-working tools, as well as the small scattered social units, indicated by the sparse and disperse nature of Paleo-Indian sites, certainly points to a hunting adaptation. The rather wide stylistic similarities of Paleo-Indian artifacts in general, as well as the rather low incidence of variation in tool type, indicates a focal or specialized technology and economy. The only game which will support such an economy must be those species which are very large, very common, or both. While the extinct Pleistocene species were large, they were presumably difficult to kill and probably not extremely common. Other likely species such as deer, are not gregarious during most of the year, and in addition, were probably difficult to kill with a spear. On the other hand, animals like the extinct *Bison antiquus* and *Bison occidentalis* of the plains and plains peripheries, and the barren ground caribou of the Great Lakes area were probably both numerous and vulnerable to spearmen since they were usually concentrated in large herds. Yet, even if we grant that these species were the main game of some Paleo-Indian groups, it would still be difficult to point to possible game species which could have been utilized on a regular basis by Paleo-Indians who occupied areas devoid of gregarious herbivores, the southern United States for example. Perhaps the necessity to turn to other subsistence resources was one of the factors which led to early experimentation with projectile styles in that area.

The strength of tradition is one of the characteristics of a focal adaptation, and Paleo-Indian culture was certainly tradition bound. In fact, Paleo-Indian hunters occupied a vast area of the New World with a technological and social system that exhibits so little areal variation that the area it covered can be equalled only by Lower Paleolithic cultures of the Old World. Such cultural stagnation may by explained by low population density, lack of indigenous cultural influences and, most important, a very specific adaptive pattern.

The nature of the transition from those cultures which we call Paleo-Indian to those we recognize as Archaic could not have been gradual in areas where biotic change was rapid. Where environments were comparatively static at the end of the Pleistocene e.g. the Great Plains, we would expect a great deal more cultural continuity than in areas such as the eastern United States and especially the Great Lakes region. Here, rapid environmental change must have forced a drastic change in the economic systems of Paleo-Indian groups, bringing about readaptations in all other sections of Paleo-Indian culture. Logically then, we would expect these areas to be the arena of rapid modifications of the Paleo-Indian tradition, modifications which must have taken place soon after the Great Lakes area was open for occupation.

Perhaps we can seek ethnographic parallels between the Paleo-Indians of the Upper Great Lakes and the Athabaskan hunters of the western Canadian subarctic. These latter people are not free wandering hunters [Fitting (1965b) has quite correctly made the same observations about the Paleo-Indians of south-eastern Michigan] but hold territories along the seasonal migration routes of caribou. Caribou are killed in large numbers during the migration period when members of the band cooperate to direct the flow of animals to positions where they are vulnerable to spearmen. Whereas we can be fairly safe in assuming that Paleo-Indians had a band level of socio-political integration, such as that defined and described by Service (1962), we must be cautious in making further generalizations without more precise knowledge of Paleo-Indian culture.

Early Archaic Cultures: 8,000 B.C. - 6,000 B.C.

Even less is known of the adaptation of the Early Archaic cultures of the Upper Great Lakes area than that of the Paleo-Indians. Some of the work with Early Archaic cultures by Greenman (1943:260-265), Greenman and Stanley (1940:194-199), Lee (1954:101-111, 1955:63-71), Mason (1963:199-211), Mason and Irwin (1961:43-58), Peske (1963:557-566), and Quimby (1959: 424-426, 1963:558-559) indicates the occupation of this area by Early Archaic people who manufactured large stemmed and lanceolate projectile points of argillite and quartzite. Lanceolate points of this type have a wide distribution throughout the United States following the fluted point tradition in time.

Although lanceolate points have been recovered in association with a great number of game species on the plains and plain peripheries (Agogino and Frankforter 1960:414-415; Schultz and Frankforter 1948:43-62), these faunal assemblages are not typical of the forested Great Lakes region. Within this area we have but one report of fauna associated with Early Archaic material. Shay (1963:24-27) reports the remains of *Bison occidentalis* deer, muskrat, wolf, black bear, turtle, bird, and fish bone with Meserve points at the Itasca kill sites in Clearwater County of northcentral Minnesota. This cultural assemblage seems to date at about 7,000 B.C. or slightly earlier.

Mason and Irwin (1961:55) argue that,

Because Eden, Scottsbluff, Plainview, Angostura and such point assemblages exhibit a markedly similar stone-working tradition with the fluted-point complexes and likewise shared a similar mode of life, we suggest that they should all be classified paleo-Indian. . . .

Numerous discoveries, they add,

have related this highly specialized stone-working tradition with the specific life-way of big-game hunting. . . .

Elsewhere, they state,

It seems the most reasonable course to infer that all these groups [Paleo-Indian and Eden-Scottsbluff assemblages] sharing a fundamentally similar economy and technology also shared a similar social system, one appropriate to the predominance of the male role in food getting.

Mason and Irwin disagree with the classification of Eden-Scottsbluff in a "Plains Archaic" category. They point out that the subistence and settlement patterns as well as the technology of these early plains groups are unrelated to the term Archaic as it is used in the East to imply a tendency toward relatively large semi-permanent habitation areas with corresponding implications for increased population density and regional adaptation. Such is not the case on the plains at this period, and the application of the term Archaic to both assemblages clouds their distinctiveness. Caldwell (1958:13) suggests that,

The unsholdered points, fluted or not, would seem better adapted to prairies or savannah than to forests. Where the pattern of hunting is one of using animal surrounds, where wounded beasts are milling and charging, the most effective weapon should be a spear used as a bayonet, to be thrust and withdrawn again and again.

It seems reasonable to accept Mason and Irwin's arguments that Eden-Scottsbluff point makers were hunters and Caldwell's suggestion that these points were at least functionally related to Paleo-Indian weaponry.

It seems unreasonable to believe, as Caldwell implies, that lanceolate point makers wandered about the woods of the eastern United States in a unadapted condition for several thousand years before they stumbled upon the idea of barbed points as a new method of killing game in the forests. Similarly unacceptable is Mason and Irwin's argument that Eden-Scottsbluff point makers closely resembled Paleo-Indian on a culture-type classification. At least in the Great Lakes region, the admittedly scanty evidence indicates an adjustment to forested conditions. Food remains such as beaver, black bear, muskrat, turtle, and fish do not indicate a "prairie or savannah-type adaptation" nor are these remains one of the "numerous discoveries which have related this [Paleo-Indian—Eden-Scottsbluff] highly specialized stone working tradition with the specific life-way of big-game hunting."

While the Early Archaic peoples of the Great Lakes were most certainly hunters, they were just as certainly hunters of the forest and must have been adapted to forest life. This being the case, we can predict the acquisition of new techniques and devices applicable to life in forested areas. The Itasca faunal

assemblage indicates that Early Archaic hunters were utilizing
forest game species. Traps, snares, harpoons, canoes, and
snowshoes may well have been used by Early Archaic people.
If the Paleo-Indians of the Upper Great Lakes were exploiting
large herding animals, then the disappearance of these species,
with the warming climate and resultant encroachment of pine
forest, must have brought about a change in hunting techniques
more suitable to the capture of the non-gregarious animals and
smaller game species of these forests.

At the time Early Archaic cultures occupied the Upper Great
Lakes region, its forests were probably composed of spruce,
fir, and pine, suitable habitat for moose and woodland caribou.
If these species were the major sources of food in this area,
then ethnographic parallels can be sought with the Algonquian
moose hunters of the Canadian boreal forest. Here, people
such as the Cree, Naskapi, and Montagnais live in small, scattered bands hunting moose, woodland caribou, beaver, and occasionally fishing during the warm season. Larger animals are
stalked and taken with spears during the winter and during
the summer, driven into water where they are speared. Speck
and Eiseley (1942) felt that population pressure in this forest
area which supported segregated nonmigratory game, resulted
in hereditary family-owned hunting tracts. Leacock (1954) has
since been able to demonstrate that the individual land owning
pattern of this area was an historic adaptation, a function of
the fur trade. Aboriginally, these people held large vaguely
defined communal territories where the population did not exceed 0.9 persons per square mile of territory (Kroeber 1939:
Table 18). It is interesting to point out that these people are
similar enough to Athabaskan barren ground caribou hunters
so that they are often classified within a single culture area.

Without evidence of many cultural traits, but based upon
a fair knowledge of Early Archaic technology and the kind of
natural environment these people had to deal with, it is not unreasonable to suppose a band level culture, similar to the
Algonkian cultures of the North American subarctic forests.

Middle Archaic Cultures: 6,000 B.C. - 3,000 B.C.

Sometime between the period of the initial adaptation to life
in forested areas and the appearance of specialized Late Archaic
cultures in the Upper Great Lakes' area, Archaic peoples of this
region developed a variety of new tools for utilizing both plant
and animal products of the forest. These include large notched

projectile points, knives, scrapers and drills of flint, ground
stone tools such as the grooved ax, adz and gouge, bannerstones,
and probably milling stones. In addition, these people probably
made a variety of bone tools including awls, antler points, and
needles.

The only excavated Middle Archaic site in the Great Lakes
region which preserved enough faunal material to permit a reconstruction of subsistence activities at that time is the Raddatz Rockshelter in south central Wisconsin (Wittry 1959a). A
re-analysis of the fauna of this site, which is included as part
of this study (Appendix A, p. 98), indicates the important role
of deer in Middle Archaic subsistence patterning. Deer provided
over 80 percent of the meat represented in all levels of the site
while deer and elk made up over 90 percent of the total meat.
It has been noted, however, that many other smaller animals were
represented and represented consistently. This indicates that
smaller species were important as a secondary or "stop gap"
resource. The small species are also indicative of a diffuse
economy. At least, they are usually not represented in quantity
on Woodland sites with focal economies where deer are often
hunted practically to the exclusion of other species. Since it
has been suggested that the Raddatz site was occupied much
more frequently during the winter than the summer, we must
remember that only part of the yearly subsistence cycle is represented. Wittry records the presence of a grinding stone
which was probably used to prepare plant foods during one of
the brief summer occupations. It is also possible, however,
that grinding implements were used to pulverize dried meat,
and, this activity could have taken place at any season.

Apparently, the population density during this period was
not great, especially in the conifer donimated forests to the
north. Many of the important cultural innovations developed
during the Middle Archaic period probably originated to the
south of the Great Lakes in the Carolinian biotic province.

The small and dispersed nature of Middle Archaic sites suggests that there was continuation of a band type level of socio-
political integration. The economics of these Middle Archaic
socities was importantly different from previous patterns in
the upper lakes area in that it was based upon the exploitation
of a great variety of resources. In short, diffuse economies were
developed during this period. This type of adaptation was not
possible during the Paleo-Indian or Early Archaic period simply
because this area was covered with a boreal forest and boreal
forests do not support a variety of resources.

If the term "Archaic" is used to refer to an adaptation based upon a balanced exploitation of both wild plant and animal foods, as opposed to Paleo-Indian hunting and Late Woodland agricultural patterns, then this term cannot be applied to the cultures of peoples who occupied areas where such an adaptation was not possible. The term "Boreal Archaic" as applied to the early cultures of the northeastern United States by Byers (1959), or to the Middle Archaic cultures of the Great Lakes by Quimby (1960) is clearly invalid. Properly, the term "Archaic" should not be applied to the Early Archaic cultures of the Great Lakes which seem to have had focal economic adaptation based upon hunting. It should be noted, however, the Early Archaic peoples farther south probably did develop diffuse adaptations much earlier than contemporary people of the Great Lakes. Because a greater variety of resources was available in those areas and because there was no game species large enough or abundant enough to support a focal adaptation, occupation of these areas required the development of a diffuse economy.

Theoretically, diffuse adaptation would develop in areas of ecological diversity. Since an adaptation of this type requires movement of the group or parts of the group from one seasonally available resource to another, the ease and efficiency with which these resources can be exploited varies directly with the geographic proximity of the resources. Thus, in areas of greatest ecological diversity, we may expect a great number of different kinds of available resources and consequently the possibility of greater population density and cultural diversity. Expansive natural communities would require such long distance movements from one resource to another, that these movements could not be correlated with the availability peaks of more than a few of the resources. This is probably the reason why diffuse economies developed most rapidly along the Atlantic and Gulf coasts and along the southern margin of the prairie peninsula in the eastern United States. Both are areas which offer access to a great number of different natural communities. Although the southern Upper Great Lakes area is also a region of ecological diversity (the northern margin of the prairie peninsula), diffuse adaptations did not flourish here as they did farther south. This can be attributed, in part, to the fact that there were fewer resources available at this more northern latitude. It must be noted here that ecological diversity, *per se,* does not produce cultural diversification or high populations. The availability of a variety of natural resources only provides a natural environment in which such developments can take place.

Whereas relatively uniform natural areas do not permit the development of diverse cultural adaptations, cultural uniformity may occur where such adaptations are possible.

A further aspect of the development of diffuse adaptations is the marked cultural localization which they produce. Since it is essential that people practicing this kind of adaptation be extremely well acquainted with a territory and be versed on the status of its resources at any particular time, they will tend to define and protect these resources and, therefore, a territory. Likewise, the common access to resources within this "territory" will reinforce and be reinforced by other bonds which unite the people who are jointly exploiting its resources. It is at this point that we can see the development of tribal groups and eventually, the flow of resources between producing groups within the tribe. Similarly, exchange of resources between tribes is not possible or feasible unless: (1) territories are established, and (2) there is production of different kinds of resources in adjoining territories. This more widespread flow of resources characterized only the later Late Archaic, Early Woodland, and early Middle Woodland societies of the Upper Great Lakes.

Finally, some mention must be made of the size of the territories. Size should relate to: (1) diversity of the natural environment, (2) kinds and frequency of resources available in each environmental zone, and most important, (3) number of resources which a particular culture has the ability or desire to exploit. As a consequence, territories would tend to be smaller in regions which contained a great many different resources within narrow geographic limits.

In summary, diffuse adaptations may develop in areas of ecological diversity but not in regions where natural communities are expansive. Since the type of adaptation practiced by a given society is culturally determined, ecological diversity does not require, but simply permits the development of smaller, more highly populated and culturally diverse societies within a given geographic area. This development seems to have characterized certain of the Middle Archaic cultures of the central and southern United States. The Middle Archaic cultures of the southern Great Lakes did not undergo a notable period of cultural diversification for causes which may have been due to cultural stability, the lack of ecological diversity in this area or a combination of both.

Late Archaic Cultures: 3,000 B.C. - 1,000 B.C.

With the cultures which we call Late Archaic i.e., Old Copper, Glacial Kame and Red Ocher, we have the earliest well documented evidence of regional ecological adaptation in the Upper Great Lakes basin. Late Archaic sites also furnish us with the earliest substantial collections of food remains.

Although most excavated Late Archaic sites have been burial localities, the Hart and Schmidt sites which have Lamokoid affinities and the Feeheley site with its Glacial Kame—Old Copper assemblage, have all yielded small amounts of identifiable plant and animal remains. Evidence from these sites indicates an economy which had two primary phases—summer fishing and winter hunting. Although we have little information on the other kinds of food sources which were being exploited, this type of adaptation is similar to the one practiced by people at a later time in the Carolinian biotic province. On the basis of the present evidence this adaptation has been labelled diffuse.

In addition to this seasonal pattern, there is evidence of the regional adaptation of Late Archaic cultures to broad biotic zones. Distributional studies of Old Copper materials by Griffin (1961c). Wittry (1957), and Fogel (1963); of Red Ocher by Ritzenthaler and Quimby (1962); and of Glacial Kame by Cunningham (1948) provide evidence that the distributions of these three fairly contemporary and very similar cultural manifestations are related to the natural environment. Although there is a certain degree of overlap in the geographic distribution of many cultural traits, it is interesting to point out that the Old Copper culture is, by and large, a culture of the Lake Forest while Red Ocher and Glacial Kame are largely confined to deciduous forest areas. Red Ocher occurs throughout the Illinois River valley into eastern Wisconsin and southwestern Michigan while Glacial Kame is distributed through northern Indiana, Ohio, and southcentral Michigan. Since most of the reported sites of these three cultural complexes are burial localities, we have very little information about their subsistence activities or adaptations.

We can, however, make a few observations on the Old Copper subsistence pattern based upon Old Copper technology and the resources of the Lake Forest. We know, for example, that the Lake Forest of the Canadian province does not support large game populations. Moose, woodland caribou, beaver, and black bear, are its only substantial meat resources and these are seldom, if ever, concentrated in local situations. Fish are fairly plentiful but not throughout the entire year. At the lati-

tude of the Lake Forest plant foods such as nuts and berries
are also fairly scarce. Given these available food sources, we
can predict that Old Copper subsistence patterns were based
upon the exploitation of these resources in direct proportion
to their seasonal availability. If we turn to the Old Copper
tool inventory, for a clue, it is apparent that both hunting and
fishing were of importance. Hunting implements include
socketed and stemmed copper spear points, and side and corner
notched flint points. Awls as well as knives, of both the cres-
cent and butterknife forms, probably were used in hide working.
Fishing implements include copper hooks, gorges, harpoons,
and gaffs. Other copper tools such as spuds, celts, gouges,
and chisels were no doubt used in wood working and perhaps,
employed in dugout canoe building.

The fish bone remains from both the Feeheley and Hart sites
indicate a seasonal village fishing pattern in the Saginaw area by
2,000 B.C. The widespread appearance of copper fishing gear
throughout the Upper and Lower Great Lakes indicates a substantial growth in the distribution of this pattern. Evidence
from the Schmidt site points to a contemporary seasonal pattern of hunting. Probably, these two seasonal subsistence activities were complementary in that summer fishing and winter
hunting constituted a single cycle. This type of adaptation
maximizes food resources by balancing productivity against the
seasonal availability of food. Thus, herbivores are easily
taken in the winter while fishing is relatively non-productive
in the same period. And in the spring, when large game animals are in poor condition, the fish begin to spawn and become
available in great quantity. During the late summer and fall
seasons hunting, fishing, fowling, and gathering activities are
together productive enough so that food is plentiful. The reduced return from gathering, fowling, and fishing in the late
fall leaves hunting as the only productive winter enterprise.

While this adaptation appears likely for the Saginaw Valley
and the Lake Forest zone to the north, we know little of the
adaptations of the Late Archaic people who lived in the deciduous forest areas of the Upper Great Lakes. Ground stone
mortars, pestles, nutting stones, and grinders associated with
Late Archaic cultures in southern Michigan and Wisconsin indicate an increased reliance upon gathered plant foods. Gathering was probably important in the Late Archaic subsistence
pattern of the deciduous forest, but evidence from the Durst
Rockshelter (Wittry 1959b:159-222) and Raddatz Rockshelter
(Wittry 1959a:55-69), in the ecotone of southern Wisconsin,

points to an emphasis upon deer hunting as a major subsistence activity (Parmalee 1959:83-90; 1960:11-17).

Both of these rockshelter sites are located on the Carolinian-Canadian forest edge. Since biotic transition zones, or ecotones, are characterized by greater concentrations in both kinds and numbers of plant and animal species, they are favorable hunting places for people who inhabit the larger biotic provinces which form them. Hickerson (1962:13-29) has shown the importance of the Carolinian-Canadian ecotone in historic Dakota-Chippewa Indian hunting conflicts in Minnesota and Wisconsin. If this ecotone was a contested hunting area in the historic period, it is probable that the conflict for the resources of this area has considerable antiquity. This argument is, of course, contingent on presence of competing groups within the biotic provinces which form the ecotone, i.e., the ecotone must be the boundary of two culture areas. It has been hypothesized that this factor was present during the Late Archaic with the Old Copper culture in the Canadian forests and Glacial Kame and Red Ocher cultures in the Carolinian forests.

Using as evidence the similarities in Archaic points from Raddatz Rockshelter, zone 6 Durst Rockshelter and Old Copper sites, and using the radiocarbon date from these, Wittry (1959a: 65) believes that these two rockshelter sites were probably occupation sites of the Old Copper culture. Parmalee (1959:89) reports that at least Raddatz, which, unlike zone 6 at Durst had large amount of well-preserved bone, was occupied by hunters who lived at the site during the winter months and occasionally at other times of the year (Appendix A, p. 98).

If Old Copper people were principally occupied with fishing during the spring and summer, and hunting during the winter, as it has been suggested, then the Raddatz Rockshelter and the Archaic levels of the Durst Rockshelter could have been occupied by Old Copper people who moved south to the Carolinian-Canadian ecotone during the winter to exploit its aboundant deer population. An alternative explanation is, of course, that these sites were occupied by Red Ocher peoples who were moving north for this same purpose during the hunting portion of their annual cycle.

Caldwell (1958:6) has argued that the culmination of the Late Archaic pattern in the deciduous eastern Woodlands (the Carolinian biotic province), was the establishment of a "primary forest efficiency" or the development of more stable populations through the gradual sophistication of hunting and gathering techniques within the forests. The fact is, however, that climax forest formations are notoriously poor in the major food items upon which Archaic peoples seem to have depended, i.e., deer, elk, waterfowl, molluscs, and plant seeds. This fact, as well as Caldwell's lack of empirical evidence for his argument of the importance of forest foods such as nuts and acorns casts doubt upon the whole concept of primary forest efficiency.

While Archaic peoples were undoubtedly developing more effective means of subsisting, this adaptation was not geared to the exploitation of forest products. Deer, the major meat source of Archaic peoples, are not forest animals. As Taylor (1956: 137) points out, "Forest lands in which the crowns of the trees produce virtually a closed canopy, and thereby shade the ground so that an abundance of low-growing shrubs and bushes cannot grow, make poor deer habitat." Similarly, seeds of the wild plants *Chenopodium, Amaranthus,* and *Iva* are not forest species but as Struever (1964:102) notes, "establish themselves only when some external factor has intervened to obliterate the potential competitors and open up a patch of raw soil. These genera do not belong to a stable plant association." Neither can molluscs, fish, nor waterfowl be considered forest species. On the other hand, Archaic peoples most certainly did exploit forest products such as hickory nuts, acorns, black bear, and turkey, to name the most important. But again, the exploitation of these foods represents only one phase of the year's subsistence cycle.

Not only does Caldwell misrepresent the nature of Late Archaic subsistence patterns, but he misunderstands the essence of their diffuse nature. Archaic people of the Carolinian province did not become more specialized but less specialized, not better adapted but more adaptable—they did become more efficient, but only at exploiting more kinds of resources rather than developing more efficient methods to exploit a few food sources. The secret of successful hunting and gathering is the ability to move between available resources in both time and space in such a way as to ensure a constant high level of productivity per unit of energy expended in collecting food. Such a diffuse adaptive pattern is possible only in areas where a large number of different kinds of resources are available within the temporal and spatial restriction of the efficient movement of people. As we have seen, where resources are too few or too scattered, diffuse adaptations are not possible.

In applying the diffuse-focal dichotomy of subsistence activity to the Late Archaic cultures and environments of the Upper Great Lakes two factors are immediately evident: (1) a diffuse economy is not now and never has been possible in the

Lake Forest of the Canadian biotic province because it lacks the variety of resources which makes this type feasible; (2) differentiation of Late Archaic cultural areas which correspond to the great environmental zones of the Upper Great Lakes signals the development of different adaptations in these natural areas.

During the time that the Early Archaic cultures occupied the Upper Great Lakes we have observed that these cultures occurred in both the Carolinian and Lake Forest formations. This implies that these people had a focal economy and we have speculated that it was based upon the hunting of medium sized game. The appearance of the ground stone technology in the Carolinian province during the Middle Archaic period is interpreted as an indication of the beginning of a diffuse adaptation in this region. It is also suggested that such a pattern probably developed in the southcentral United States at an earlier period and diffused northward into the southern Great Lakes area at a time which corresponded with the initial development of a deciduous forest environment in that area. During the Late Archaic we find a coterminous distribution of Old Copper culture with the Lake Forest and at the same time a hint of the development of a diffuse economy in the Saginaw Valley which lies in the Carolinian-Canadian province. We see two other cultural manifestations developing in the Carolinian province further south, Glacial Kame and Red Ocher. These do not extend north into the Lake Forest. The obvious conclusion is that Old Copper people within the Lake Forest were relying on a hunting-fishing focal subsistence pattern which had its origin in the Early Archaic, while the cultures of the Carolinian biotic zone had developed a diffuse economy which arose in this region during the Middle Archaic and closely paralleled the Late Archaic cultures further south.

Early Woodland Cultures: 1,000 B.C. - 300 B.C.

The distinction between Late Archaic and Early Woodland in the Great Lakes area is currently quite unclear. Frequently, there is an overlapping of traits usually considered definitive of both periods. Even interior-exterior cordmarked pottery is sometimes found on sites which are otherwise typically Late Archaic. Supposedly, the manufacture of pottery and the acquisition of domestic plants by Early Woodland peoples produced changes of such a magnitude as to warrant the classification of these cultures as an entirely different cultural pattern from that of their Late Archaic predecessors. The major weakness of such a classification is that it implies a closer relationship within the Woodland pattern than between Early Woodland and Late Archaic cultural manifestations.

In a recent survey of the distribution of Marion-Thick pottery in Michigan, Flanders (1963:48) found that this pottery occurred infrequently. The sites included in this survey are the Moccasin Bluff site in Berrien County, an unnamed site near the Norton Mounds in Kent County, the Spoonville Site in Ottawa County and the Andrews and Schultz sites in Saginaw County. It has recently been established, however, that the Early Woodland component at the Schultz site is quite extensive and this site has produced a huge sample of Marion-Thick pottery. All of these sites are located in the Carolinian biotic province or on the southern margin of the Carolinian-Canadian transition zone.

One of the most interesting Early Woodland sites in the Upper Great Lakes is the 20 SA 1 site reported by Wright (1964: 17-23) located near the Schultz site in Saginaw County, Michigan. Food remains from this small site include a few mollusc shells, unidentifiable bird, fish, turtle, and mammal bone as well as bones identified as beaver and muskrat. Also reported were acorns, hickory nuts, grape seeds, cherry or blueberry seeds, and two seeds of the squash family, *Cucurbita*. This site has been dated at 530±120 B.C. (M-1432; Crane and Griffin 1965). The occupation of the 20 SA 1 site most certainly took place during the summer and fall seasons.

The analysis of the fauna of the Early Woodland horizon at the nearby Schultz site presents an entirely different picture of subsistence activities (Appendix C, p. 117). Here we find almost exclusive hunting of mammals in both the medium and small game categories. Fishing was of little importance and only large fish were taken. In addition, the low frequency of species known to be available in the summer indicates that this was predominantly a winter occupation.

If we consider both of these Early Woodland occupations together it becomes apparent that these people were practicing a diffuse economy in the true sense of the word. Shellfish, fish, turtles, small mammals, nuts, berries, and some domestic plants supplied their summer and fall foods. The use of these foods required a variety of methods and techniques in order to gather, capture or cultiviate the resource and to prepare it for consumption. Winter was the season for hunting and unlike the hunting practiced by strongly agricultural peoples, these hunters did not place high selective pressure on a few species.

The total picture of the Early Woodland adaptation in the Saginaw Valley of Michigan is one based upon a diffuse adaptation.

In this respect, it is very similar to the economic adaptation hypothesized for the Late Archaic period. In fact, the introduction of the domestic squash and possibly the use of other domestic and wild plant seeds at that time only increased the margin of assurity within the diffuse economy. Early Woodland economics are, therefore, seen as an elaboration of those of the Late Archaic period and thus are more closely related to the diffuse Archaic pattern than to the focal argicultural adaptations of the Late Woodland period.

In another sense the adaptation of the Early Woodland period was extremely important in the development of later agricultural subsistence patterns. It was at this point, and in fact even earlier, that the social milieu and technology of agriculture was developed. Although the seeds of wild or domesticated plants were not yet of great importance, in the sense that people depended upon them, such a dependency now became only a matter of a shift of emphasis. The introduction of a more dependable and efficient inventory of domestic plants, notably corn and later beans, provided the reliability necessary to allow the gradual decline in the use of other food sources and the cultural implementation which made the exploitation of these resources possible.

Middle Woodland Cultures: 300 B.C. - A.D. 400

Sites of the cultures which we group under the somewhat nebulous term, Middle Woodland, are the earliest to have both wide geographic representation and documented faunal records. These include Rainy River aspect sites belonging to the Anderson and Nutimik foci of southeastern Manitoba (MacNeish 1958), the North Bay complex of Door County, Wisconsin (Mason 1966), the Saugeen focus of southwestern Ontario (Wright and Anderson 1963) and the Havana tradition complex in Michigan represented at the Spoonville site (Flanders 1965), and at the Schultz site. Wright and Anderson (1963:52) report that Rainy River aspect sites extend from the Manitoba border along the north shore of Lake Superior to Manitoulin Island along the north shore of Georgian Bay. Rainy River sites also occur in northern Minnesota (Wilford 1943, 1955). Sites of this aspect occur in the northern part of the Canadian biotic province. Near the southern border of this province, we find three other Middle Woodland manifestations. In Door County, Wisconsin, Mason (1966) has defined the North Bay complex on the basis of his excavations at the North Bay, Ports des Morts sites and lower and

intermediate levels of the Mero site. Fitting (n.d.) discusses
the Goodwin-Gresham site as a southern "Lake Forest Middle
Woodland" site located on the southern edge of the Canadian biotic province in eastern Michigan. Finally, Wright and Anderson
(1963) have defined the Saugeen focus on the basis of excavations
at a number of Middle Woodland sites in the southern Canadian
province of Ontario. These include the lowest levels of the
Burley site (Jury and Jury 1952), the Inverhuron/Lucas site (Kenyon 1959;Lee 1960), and the Donaldson site (Wright and Anderson
1963).

When we move southward in the Carolinian biotic province
of Michigan and Wisconsin, we find Middle Woodland cultures
closely related to those of the Illinois River Valley. However,
most reported sites have been burial mounds with little or no
information of economic activity. In Wisconsin, Cooper (1933)
discusses the Red Cedar focus, and McKern (1933) discusses
the Red Cedar focus, and McKern (1931) the Trempealeau focus.
In southern Michigan, Quimby (1941a, 1941b, 1943, 1944) has defined the Goodall focus while Greenman (1945) and Fitting (1965c)
have written on the Hopewellian occupations of the Detroit-Windsor
area. More recent excavations at the Spoonville site in Ottawa
County, by Flanders (1965), and at the Schultz site in Saginaw
County (Appendix C p. 117) have produced information about the
Middle Woodland village sites in these areas of Michigan.

The temporal positioning of these sequences is problemat-
ical. MacNeish estimates the age of the Nutimik focus material
at A.D. 500 - A.D. 1000, yet Wright and Anderson would place
closely related Saugeen material at about 500 B.C. (Wright and
Anderson 1963:52). The North Bay complex has been dated at
A.D. 160 (Mason (1966:125), the Spoonville site at A.D. 215 and
A.D. 110 (M-1427, M-1428;Crane and Griffin 1965:128), and a
Middle Woodland burial at the Juntunen site was dated at A.D.
50 (M-1392; Crane and Griffin 1965:129). Fitting (personal
communication) estimates the Middle Woodland occupations at
the Schultz site at 200 B.C. to A.D. 500. Based upon these
dates and MacNeish's estimates for the Rainy River aspect, it
would appear as though the 500 B.C. date for the Saugeen focus
is too early. The earliest Middle Woodland occupations seem
to have been in the Carolinian area of the Upper Great Lakes
during the first few centuries before Christ. Northern movements
of Middle Woodland concepts and perhaps people during the first
two centuries A.D. produced the Middle Woodland manifestation
of the Canadian biotic province.

If we examine the ethnozoological patterns of the Middle Woodland cultures of the Upper Great Lakes, we can distinguish the beginnings of two broad subsistence patterns, an agricultural-hunting complex in the south, and a fishing-hunting complex in the north, which became firmly established in the upper lakes area during the Late Woodland period. At the advent of the Middle Woodland period, hunting and fishing were important subsistence activities in each area. Fishing seems to have been more important in the north than in the south, which may be a factor of the later temporal positions of the northern cultures or of the scarcity of game in the Canadian biotic province.

In comparing his Rainy River aspect material with earlier foci in southeastern Manitoba, MacNeish (1958:178) tells us that the animal bones from Anderson focus sites show a further shift to aspen parkland but that, "the most noticeable change is the numerous fish bones." He also concludes that, "the occurrence of net-impressed pottery suggest that the fish were caught in nets," and that heavy reliance on fishing brought about less nomadism and made larger living groups possible. The Nutimik focus sites show a continuation of this trend. Fish bones constituted 47 percent of the identified bones from Anderson focus sites and 70 percent of the identified bone on Nutimik focus sites. However, it should be noted that if calculations of the total usable meat had been compiled, fish would not have appeared to be as important as they did when only the numerical frequency of bone types was used as the criterion.

Turning to sites of the Saugeen focus, we see the same general pattern. Bone preservation at the Donaldson site was excellent and Wright and Anderson (1963:42-43) report that mammal remains were relatively scarce. In contrast, fish bones seem to have been abundant. Unfortunately, fish bone quantities are presented by weight and are, therefore, almost meaningless for comparative purposes. Still, Wright and Anderson (ibid:49) do indicate the sites of this focus range in size from one to three acres and are located at favorable fishing locations. Since they are large sites and show rather homogeneous food remains, Wright and Anderson reason that they must be seasonal sites. If the fishing camps were occupied during the summer, small winter hunting camps should exist in other areas.

No quantification is provided for the faunal remains of the Saugeen horizon at the Inverhuron site, but Kenyon (1959:20) suggests that the presence of fish bone and scales indicates that the site was attractive because of the excellent fishing it afforded. Kenyon's field impression of the subsistence economy was that "these deposits contained only small amounts of fish refuse that would accumulate from day-to-day living." Kenyon, thus, implies that Saugeen peoples fished, but were not specialized fishermen. Both net sinkers and fish hooks are reported from this horizon.

Fitting (n.d.) reports that "some features" of the Goodwin-Gresham site in the southern part of the Canadian biotic province of eastern Michigan "contain, by weight, as much as 80 percent fish bone." This statement and the way in which the bone is quantified is extremely difficult to interpret, but the obvious implication is that the Goodwin-Gresham site was a fishing station.

Mason's (1966) North Bay complex is also located in the southern part of the Canadian biotic province, but these sites could not be characterized as fishing stations. The figures for the frequency of bone types as well as the amount of meat utilized by people at the two lower levels of the Mero site (Appendix D p. 145) indicate that fish provided about 20 percent of the meat represented. This is true in spite of the fact that fish bones represented about 70 percent of the sample. Nonetheless, fishing is considered important in these levels, although there is clear evidence that it became less important in succeeding horizons.

Essentially, the same subsistence picture is evident at the Schultz site located on the northern edge of the Carolinian biotic province in eastern Michigan. Here we have seen that fish bones were also extremely common, but that fish represented only about 20 percent of the total meat. As at the Mero site, hunting increased at the expense of fishing in later occupations. We have also seen that net fishing is indicated on the Middle Woodland occupations at the Schultz site, as it was in sites of the Rainy River aspect and the Saugeen focus farther north.

There is evidence for a different economy in the Middle Woodland sites in the Carolinian biotic province of Michigan. A small sample of faunal material from the Spoonville site (Table 2) and from the mound fill of the Norton Mounds (Table 3) indicates that the Middle Woodland peoples at these sites were exploiting the large game animals of this zone. Table 2 shows that 87.7 percent of the usable meat at the Spoonville site was either deer or elk. Aquatic mammals, waterfowl, and fish are insignificant. Because of the infrequent occurrence and unknown context of the bones in the fill of the Norton Mounds, it seems relatively meaningless to discuss them in terms of the meat they provided. Judging from frequency alone, it seems probable that deer were the important animal food source. Other faunal

TABLE 2

PERCENTAGE OF MEAT REPRESENTED BY THE ANIMAL BONES
AT THE SPOONVILLE SITE OTTAWA COUNTY, MICHIGAN

Species	Number of Bones	Approximate Number of Individuals	Live Weight in Pounds	Usable Meat / Individual	Usable Meat / Species	Percent
Deer	22	11	170	85	935	63.8 ⎤ 87.7
Elk	1	1	700	350	350	23.9 ⎦
Beaver	5	3	45	31.5	94.5	6.4
Raccoon	3	2	25	17.5	35	2.4
Muskrat*	62	7	3	2.1	15.2	1.0
Total Mammal	93	24			1,429.7	97.5
Sturgeon	2	1	45	36	36	2.5
Combine Total	95	25			1,465.7	100.0

*Muskrat bones from one refuse pit.

TABLE 3

FREQUENCY OF ANIMAL BONES IN THE FILL OF THE NORTON MOUNDS,
KENT COUNTY, MICHIGAN

Common Name	Scientific Name	Mounds					Totals
		H	D	K	I	C	
Deer	*Odocoileus virginianus*	2	1	4	4	12	23
Woodchuck*	*Marmota monax*	1		5		2	8
Striped skunk*	*Mephitis mephitis*				22		22
Raccoon	*Procyon lotor*	1					1
Muskrat	*Ondatra zibethicus*	3					3
Longtail weasel*	*Mustela frenata*	1					1
Elk	*Cervus canadensis*	1				1	2
Chipmunk*	*Tamias striatus*	4					4
Turkey	*Meleagris gallopavo*					1	1
Passenger pigeon	*Ectopistes migratorius*	3					3
Sturgeon	*Acipenser fulvescens*			1			1
Freshwater drum	*Aplodinotus grunniens*	1					1
Walleye	*Stizostedion vitreum*	1					1
Channel Catfish	*Ictalurus punctatus*					1	1
Unidentified mammal		59	5	47	43	111	265
Unidentified turtle			2	2	1	3	8
Unidentified fish		31	2	2	10	17	62
Total		108	10	61	80	148	407

*Intrusive.

remains which were placed in the burial pits as various kinds of artifacts included the bones of deer, elk, turkey, black bear, wolf, beaver, Blanding's turtle, and snowy owl (Flanders and Cleland 1964:302-309).

The faunal assemblage of both the Norton Mounds and the Spoonville site do not resemble those of other Middle Woodland sites in the Upper Great Lakes area. One reason is, of course, that they are located in a different biotic province. And, considering the fact that both of these sites are located in similar microenvironmental settings, i.e., bottomland, as is the Schultz site, but do not show an aquatically oriented subsistence economy, we can hypothesize a different ecological adaptation. In fact, there is a great deal of similarity between the assemblages of the Spoonville and Norton sites and those of Late Woodland villages of southern Michigan (see the Moccasin Bluff report, Appendix F, p. 211). Perhaps this similarity reflects not only common access to the same biota but a similar cultural adaptation and subsistence economy, one which was based to a large extent upon agriculture.

While all the Middle Woodland sites which have adequate faunal documentation show that hunting was a very important economic activity, it is possible to distinguish two broad adaptive complexes. The distinguishing feature of these complexes is the importance of other foods as secondary resources.

As previously shown, fish was very important as a secondary food source on the Middle Woodland sites of the Canadian province. The abundance of fish bone on the Rainy River, North Bay, and Saugeen sites is due, in part, to four factors: (1) the high availability of fish, (2) the relative scarcity of large game animals in conifer-dominated forests, (3) the relatively small number of plants which bear seeds and nuts at this northern latitude, and (4) the apparent introduction and use of nets in fishing. Fishing was probably more important than hunting during the spring, and at least as important as hunting during the summer. During the fall and winter, game animals probably supplied most of the food. This sort of economy seems to have resulted in an increase in the size and intensity of Middle Woodland occupations, especially those on lake shores. Although evidence of the Early Woodland economies of this region is generally lacking, there does not appear to be any earlier precedent for reliance upon fishing.

The second Middle Woodland adaptation has two variations depending upon the degree of reliance upon plant foods. The Schultz site, which represents one of the variants, is analogous

to that which Struever (1964:87-106) described as a riverine
adaptation. According to Struever, the subsistence activities of
riverine cultures were strongly oriented to exploitation of natural
plant food, although he points out that hunting may have been of
some importance. Hunting was certainly important at the Schultz
site, as was fishing. Fishing was probably a spring subsistence
activity, while hunting probably provided most of the winter
food. The large size and intensity of the Middle Woodland occupations at the Schultz site suggest the existence of another
important resource. In all probability, this resource was the
seeds of wild plants which were collected in the late summer
and fall. In addition, there is the strong possibility of the production of some crop plants—probably squash, pumpkins, and
sunflower. The decrease in the importance of hunting, accompanied by an increase in fishing from the Early to Middle Woodland horizons at this site, is seen as a movement toward a focal
economic pattern; a movement in which increased reliance on
plant foods is shifting emphasis away from hunting as the major
subsistence activity. The more secure subsistence base resulting from this shift produced an increase in population size and
residential stability.

The other variant of the southern Middle Woodland economy
is represented by the Spoonville site. This economy seems to
be similar to those of other Middle Wooldand village sites of
the Carolinian and Illinoian biotic provinces. The Havana Village
(McGregor 1952:53), Steuben Village (Morse 1963:115-125), and
the McGraw site (Parmalee 1965:115-118), all resemble the
Spoonville site in that large game animals appear in great abundance, whereas smaller mammals, birds, reptiles, and fish are
relatively less numerous. This type of faunal assemblage is
thought to signal the beginning of a new focal economy in which
heavy reliance is placed upon food production. The hunting of
large game animals becomes a secondary, and probably a seasonal subsistence activity. The evidence suggests that villages
were inhabited throughout the year by at least some people, a
condition made possible by higher production levels and storage
of agricultural products. This pattern is intensified in later
cultural developments in the same areas. Perhaps a date of
A.D. 200 would be a reasonable estimation of the earliest appearance of this kind of adaptive pattern, although it may have become established slightly earlier in the area south of the Great
Lakes.

The riverine and northern hunting-fishing adaptations seem to
begin somewhat earlier in time. The riverine adaptation seems

to be a result of the continual elaboration of a Late Archaic and Early Woodland adaptive pattern, while the more northern Middle Woodland adaptations seem to be a new and more diverse economy, resulting from the addition of fish as an important food source.

Late Woodland and Upper Mississippian Cultures:
A.D. 400-A.D. 1650

Although more is known about the cultures which occupied the Great Lakes area from the end of the Middle Woodland times until European contact than is known about the cultures of any other period, the depth of our knowledge is far from adequate.

In the Canadian biotic province near the western end of Lake Superior, we know that the Laurel tradition of Middle Woodland times gives way to a new cultural horizon which is called the Black Duck and Arvilla foci in Minnesota (Wilford 1955), and the Manitoba focus in Manitoba (MacNeish 1958).

We know very little about the Late Woodland sites to the east in the Upper Peninsula of Michigan and along the south shore of Lake Superior. Our sketchy knowledge suggests that the people who occupied sites of this area made pottery which is quite similar to the Black Duck pottery farther west. Black Duck traits have been found at least as far east as the Juntunen site in the Straits of Mackinac (McPherron 1963), and may reach even farther eastward and southward. In view of the distribution and the late temporal position of this ware, Griffin (1961c:11) has suggested that at least some of this pottery was made by Chippewa-speaking peoples. In the Straits of Mackinac area the Black Duck ware overlaps, to some extent, with Owascoid wares which presumably originate from the Canadian and Carolinian provinces of southern Ontario where Owasco culture, similar to that of New York, succeeds late Middle Woodland manifestations shortly before A.D. 1000. Fitting (1965c), in his study of the Late Woodland cultures of southeastern Michigan, defines the Younge tradition which he equates with the developmental Neutral sequence in southwestern Ontario. Fitting places the Younge tradition between A.D. 800 and A.D. 1500.

The Late Woodland cultures of central and western Michigan did not participate in the developments of Ontario and southeastern Michigan, but are more closely related to Late Woodland manifestations in Wisconsin. These cultures are somewhat obscure, but, have generally been referred to as Peninsular Woodland by Quimby (1960). Peninsular Woodland seems to

develop out of a late Middle Woodland base and is characterized
by cord-marked pottery with simple cord-wrapped stick im-
pressions on the rims of vessels, triangular projectile points,
and rather large village sites.

By about A.D. 1000, people with a Middle Mississippian
cultural complex moved northward into southern Wisconsin,
where they apparently stimulated the development of a number
of "peripheral Mississippian variants" which are called Upper
Mississippian. These cultures are represented in extreme
southwestern Michigan, northern Indiana and Illinois, and in
southern Wisconsin and Minnesota. They are neither Woodland
nor Mississippian, but a unique cultural development.

The adaptations of the Late Woodland cultures of the Upper
Great Lakes are the best defined of the prehistoric period. This
fact is a result of fairly adequate site representation, the recovery of preserved organic material on these sites and historic
documentation of many of these cultures.

There is ample evidence from sites of the period from
shortly before A.D. 1000 to the early 18th century to document
three distinct regional adaptations within the Upper Great Lakes
area. The first adaptation is characterized by large agricultural
villages, with both patrilineal and matrilineal social systems and
fairly stable residential units. This adaptation is limited by the
perimeters of effective corn agriculture, and is largely confined
to the Carolinian and Illinoian biotic provinces.

The second type is based upon marginal corn agriculture,
fishing and hunting. Sites of this type are distributed throughout the Carolinian-Canadian transition zone. Here, we find
lakeshore villages occupied by relatively large patrilineal bands
during the summer season. These villages were not stable, but
fragmental, due to the seasonal reduction of fish and vegetal
foods. The winter social groups were small hunting bands.

The final adaptive pattern is exhibited by people who occupied the Canadian biotic province. Here, we find people who
were strictly hunters and gatherers, except that they would be
more accurately described as fishermen and hunters. Population
density, and the size and composition of residential units varied
greatly with both geographic location and the season of the year.
Typically, small patrilineal bands gathered on lake shores in the
summer to fish and collect wild plant foods, then with the winter,
they scattered over wide areas to hunt moose, woodland caribou,
beaver and hare.

One of the interesting features of these three adaptive patterns is that it is possible to trace their development in time.

What appear to be new adaptations to the environments of the
Great Lakes by Late Woodland cultures are, in fact, only inten-
sifications of the adaptations which we saw in formative stages
during the Middle Woodland period.

Turning first to the Canadian biotic province, we have ample
evidence of the importance of fishing in the Late Woodland cultures of that area. In discussing the faunal remains of his Selkirk focus of southeastern Manitoba, MacNeish (1958:178) reports
that:

The bone fragments from the Selkirk Focus are little different from
those of the previous horizon [Manitoba focus], except that moose bones
and teeth occur. This is good evidence that much of southeastern Manitoba during this time period was covered by a pine forest as it is at
present. The subsistence at this time was definitely based on fishing,
with the hunting of moose, deer, buffalo, bear, and wolf; the trapping of
hare, beaver and muskrat; and food-gathering of shells, plums, and wild
rice being of secondary importance. Such a subsistence pattern would
allow for larger, more sedentary groups. This is confirmed by sites
that are uniformly large, even though the depth of refuse is not great.
It is interesting to note that many of these larger camps are at spots
along waterways that even at present yield great quantities of fish. Perhaps large seasonal fishing bands may be considered characteristic of
Selkirk times.

The Juntunen site on Bois Blanc Island in the Straits of
Mackinac shows that this same fishing village pattern was established in this area by at least A.D. 800. McPherron (1965)
summarized the external relationships of Juntunen site pottery.

Pottery of the earlist, or Mackinac, phase (A.D. 800-1000) shows broad
generic similarities to many other early Late Woodland wares but has
closest ties to that pottery of the upper Lake Michigan basin orginally
called "Lake Michigan ware" by McKern (1931). Bois Blanc-phase pottery (A.D. 1000-1200) marks the appearance in the Upper Great Lakes
of more definite regional traditions. It is similar to both Wisconsin
and Black Duck pottery. In the latest, or Juntunen phase, which flour-
ished about A.D. 1300, pottery shows a break with traditions in the
Lake Michigan basin and most closely resembles Barrie-Uren-pottery
of southern Ontario.

Moving eastward, the same summer fishing village pattern
appears on the shores of the Canadian biotic province of Ontario. At the Inverhuron site both the Late Woodland occupation
(which has "push-pull" Black Duck motifs similar to those dated
at A.D. 1330±100 years (M-1391) at the Juntunen site) and the
Iroquoian occupation represent fishing stations. Kenyon (1959)
equates this latter occupation with Wintemberg's (1948) Middleport site and Ridley's (1952) Lalonde material. Kenyon (ibid:31)

tells us that "the Irquois site excavated at Inverhuron probably represented not a village, but a fishing station occupied only during spring and early summer." By this, Kenyon presumably means that these Iroquois had a permanent village elsewhere, and only visited Inverhuron to fish.

The Late Woodland people who occupied the Canadian biotic province were adapted to much different environmental conditions than neighboring cultures of the Carolinian province. Not only were there striking differences in the fauna, which required the application of different hunting techniques, but most important, efficient corn agriculture was not possible in all but the extreme southern edges of the Canadian province. As a consequence, we find great differences in residential stability and in the division of labor within these societies. In addition, there are major differences in material culture, and in social and political systems.

In Ontario, we see a clear cut division between the Algonquin speakers of the Canadian province, and the Irquoian speakers of the Carolinian province. At the time of French contact, these two cultural areas stood in a symbiotic relationship. Tooker (1964:25) notes that "Corn, fishing nets, wampum, and other objects were traded to the Algonquin for fish and for animal skins (JR 13:249; 27:27; 31:209; 33:67)" and that "This trade made Huronia 'the granary of most of the Algonquins' (JR 8:115)." Tooker (ibid:25) explains that this trade rested, not on Algonquin lack of knowledge of agriculture, nor on Huron lack of knowledge of hunting and fishing, but rather on the amount each could conveniently practice.

Jerome Lalemant, S.J., (JR 21:239) describes the Nipissiriniens, or Nipissing, who lived well within the Canadian biotic province: . . .[they] form a Nation of the Algonquin tongue which contains more wandering than settled people. They seem to have as many abodes as the year has seasons, . . ." Lalemant notes that these people spend the spring fishing, and that in the summer they gather together on the borders of the large lake which bears their name, where they fish and cultivate a little land, "more for pleasure and that they may have fresh food to eat, than for their support." Finally, these peoples spend the winter to the south in the land of the Hurons, where they trade for corn, and probably hunt.

In 1615, Samuel de Champlain (Bourne (1922(2):101) visited the Ottawas or Cheveux Réleves who occupied the Bruce Penninsula on the southern margin of the Canadian biotic province. Champlain comments that this is a tribe of great warriors, hunters and fishers, but that "most of them plant Indian corn." All descriptions of the Huron who occupied the Canadian-Carolinian edge, and the Neutral and Tobacco who lived within the Carolinian biotic province, make it quite clear the these people were sedentary agriculturalists.

Trigger (1962), in an excellent article, considers the historic location of the Huron in reference to both their cultural and natural environment. He observes that the Huron were located in a very small area which was near the northern limits for practical corn agriculture. Yet, these people are characterized by an extremely high population density. Noting the striking ecological changes of this region, Trigger (ibid:139) outlines the affect of the Carolinian-Canadian edge on the cultures of the Huron and their northern Algonquin neighbors.

The region to the south [of the Canadian province] yielded abundant harvests which permitted large numbers of Indians to live together in towns throughout the whole year. The Indians to the north were able to grow only small amounts of corn in the best years, and were dependent on fishing, hunting animals such as deer, bear, and rabbits, and collecting plants. These Indians were few in number, and did not live for the whole year in one village as they had to keep on the move in order to stay alive.

Trigger concludes that the location of Huronia, and the large size of its population, was the result of the agricultural productivity of this region and the existence of a flourishing pre-Columbian Algonquin-Huron trade. This trade relationship gave both groups access to the resources of both the Carolinian and Canadian biotic provinces.

Most of the historic descriptions of the aboriginal peoples of the peninsulas of Michigan are of a much later date than those of Ontario. Nonetheless, we have clear indications of the same fundamental relationship between the natural areas and the adaptation of their aboriginal populations. Speaking of the Sauteur (Ojibwa) at Sault Sainte Marie, as he observed them in the last part of the 17th century, La Potherie (Blair 1911:276-77) describes them as a nonsedentary tribe.

This tribe is divided: part of them have remained at home to live on this delicious fish [whitefish] in autumn, and they seek their food in Lake Huron during the winter; the others have gone away to two localities on Lake Superior, in order to live on the game which is very abundant there.

La Potherie also notes also notes a curious summer movement to the south which brought the Ojibwa into areas where corn agriculture was possible.

Those who have remained at the Saut, their native country, leave their villages twice a year. In the month of June, they disperse in all directions along Lake Huron, as also do the Missisakis and Otter people [apparently, other Ojibwa bands]. (Blair 1911:279)

Here, on small islands, these groups collected blueberries, speared sturgeon, and planted corn. When the corn was ripe, they returned home to the rapids at Sault Sainte Marie where they fished during the autumn. At the approach of winter, they again resorted to the shores of the lake to kill beaver and moose, but did not return to the islands until the spring, in order to plant their corn. Nicolas Perrot visited the Indians on the south shore of Lake Superior in the middle 17th century. He reported that,

. . .[they] hunt the beaver and the moose. They also go fishing and catch excellent fish; and they harvest some Indian corn, although not in so great quantity as do the tribes on the shores of Lake Huron, who live in open or prairie country (Blair 1911:109).

Raudot (Kinietz 1940:370,371) described the economy of the two Chippewa bands, the Amiquories and Mississague. Of the former, he says,

The Amiquorués, otherwise Nation of the Beaver, are small in number. In summer they live along the shores of Lake Huron, where they live well on fish. They make fields on the islands in this lake, where they sow Indian corn, which ordinarily they gather green. The fogs keep it from becoming entirely ripe. In the fall they make provision of a quantity of blueberries which they conserve for winter. . . . The Mississagué live on a river bearing their name, which comes into the lake [Huron] on the north side. It is abundant with fish, especially with sturgeon. The members of this tribe all come together in the spring on the bank of this river to plant corn, which ripens little. They have forty-five to sixty warriors and are almost all thieves.

The Ottawa, as well as the Ojibwa who occupied the southern edge of the Canadian biotic province and the Carolinian-Canadian transition zone of Michigan and Wisconsin, were semi-sedentary people. That is, they had permanent villages from which people went out to hunt at least twice a year (Kinietz 1940:236). In addition, people probably left the village at other times to fish, and to collect blueberries, wild rice, and other seasonal plant foods. Their adaptation to this ecological zone was neither a simple one, nor marginal to the more highly agricultural societies farther south. When the Ottawa were expelled from their homeland by the Irquois, they moved westward, but stayed within the same ecological transition zone which they occupied on the Bruce Peninsula. Their new settlements at Mackinac, Thunder Bay, Manitoulin, Green Bay, and L'Arbre Croche are all in areas where some crops could be cultivated so that their mixed economy and semisedentary existence could be maintained.

It has already been mentioned that the tribes of the Carolinian biotic province of Ontario were agricultural. Although these people probably depended almost entirely upon crop plants, they also engaged in seasonal hunting and fishing activities. Perhaps the most frequently mentioned of these secondary subsistence activities is Champlain's description of a Huron deer drive in October, 1615, which yielded 120 deer.

The same seasonal hunting pattern was followed by the agricultural people living near Fort Detroit in 1761. Noting the military implications of this activity, Captain Donald Campbell reported to Colonel Henry Bouquet at Fort Sandusky that, "All the Indian Nations have gone to their Hunting and by that means will be quiet here till Spring" (M.P.H.C. 1892:121).

The Grand River valley of Michigan was apparently near the southern boundary of the Carolinian-Canadian transition zone, a fact noted by Dwight Goss who wrote about the Indians of the Grand Valley.

> The Chippewas took possession of the northern portion of the peninsula, the Ottawas of the valleys of the Muskegon and the Grand, while the Potawatomies took possession of the Kalamazoo Valley and beyond [south]. The Indians always gathered about the waters of a country, for by their canoes they traveled, fished, hunted and transported their game. In autumn an entire family, and sometimes two or three families together, would leave the villages and wander up the smaller streams into the forests of the interior for their winter's hunt, and they would generally camp in or near a bunch of maple trees in order that they might make sugar in the spring. (M.P.H.C. 1906:172)

This ecological boundary is placed farther south by George Willard (M.P.H.C. 1891:298) who says that "the river [Kalamazoo] which divides your county unequally as it runs through it toward the lake, was the separating line between the Pottawattamis and the Ottawas who, thus shared between them, the greater part of the Lower Peninsula at the time of American settlement."

Perhaps the most perceptive of early Michigan pioneer writers was Edward Foote, who wrote of the Indians of Eaton County:

The oak opening land in the south part of the county seemed better adapted to the Indian [probably Pottawattami] mode of living than the dark and heavily timbered forests north of here. . . . During the sugar-making season, they would move into the heavy timber and camp among the great sugar maples. After this they would come out and remain in the oak openings in the south part of the county, cultivating corn, pumpkins, and gathering berries. In Walton [township], they had 100 acres in scattered patches, under cultivation. (M.P.H.C. 1881:379)

Hickerson (1962:2) gives us an excellent summary of the settlement pattern of the Chippewa who occupied the Lower Peninsula of Michigan and neighboring Ontario in the 18th century:

. . .[They] were farmers, hunters, and fishermen. They made little use of wild rice, but harvested maple sugar in quantity. In the late 18th century, those whose winter hunting grounds were in the heart of the lower peninsula appeared to have been organized for the winter season in extended family hunting bands. These aggregates were larger than the family territorial units of the northern Chippewa and appear to have constituted temporarily detached segments of large, permanent summer villages on the lakes Huron and Michigan shores to the north.

The extreme southwestern parts of Michigan, and adjacent areas of Indiana and Illinois, were probably occupied by the Miami. This was an area of open forests and frequent small prairies. The Miami were even more intensely agricultural than their northern neighbors, the Pottawattomi. They lived in large and rather permanent villages which were inhabited by at least some people throughout the year (Kinietz 1940:171). In the autumn, the Miami undertook large communal bison hunts on the prairies of Illinois. They also hunted elk, deer, bear, and beaver (Kinietz ibid:174). According to Charlevoix (Kellogg 1932:112), the Miami preserved corn and other fruit in large storage pits which were dug in the ground and lined with bark; these pits preserved the grain in exceedingly good condition.

The southern portions of Wisconsin, as well as southwestern and western Minnesota, were occupied by Siouan and Algonquian speaking agriculturalists, who were probably as economically dependent upon the products of the land as the Miami. The tribal identification of these people is unclear, but this area was probably originally occupied by the Winnebago, Ioway, and Santee Sioux.

In his classic study of the southwestern Chippewa, Hickerson (1962) makes note of the fact that the way of life of the Chippewa of northern Wisconsin and Minnesota was in sharp contrast to the settled agriculturalists to the south. Hickerson attributes these differences to the adaptation of these cultures to very different environmental factors. The Chippewa occupied the northern conifer forest (the Canadian biotic province) and were hunters and fishermen. The Siouan tribe was one of farmers who occupied the open deciduous forest (Carolinian and Illinoian biotic provinces) to the south. Unlike the Huron and their northern Algonquian neighbors who were adapted to similar bordering ecological communities in Ontario, the Sioux and Chippewa came into open conflict over intermediate ground. Hickerson attributes this intertribal conflict to the high game population of the very narrow Carolinian-Canadian edge zone which divided these two unrelated cultural groups. This game, particularly deer, drew the Chippewa hunters south and Siouan hunters north so that the edge zone became a contested area.

The historically documented adaptations of the Upper Great Lakes area may be clearly traced into the prehistoric period. The Juntunen site is an example of the adaptation of peoples of the Canadian biotic province. Because of the modifying effect of the lake waters in the Straits of Mackinac area, this site could also be considered as one of the Carolinian-Canadian transition zones. We have seen that, although it basically represents a summer encampment of fishermen, some corn was also produced. The relative stability in the kinds and the frequency of fish and game animals represented at the site, both before and after the introduction of corn, indicates, however, that agriculture never became important in the total subsistence economy. Juntunen people obtained most of their food during the summer by spearing sturgeon and other large fish. Hunting was not unimportant in the summer, although it was basically a winter activity. In addition, Yarnell (1964:143) has shown that these people collected at least sixteen varieties of seeds, nuts, and berries. We can hypothesize that the winter sites of these people were small, inconspicuous hunting camps probably located in the interior of either the Upper or Lower Peninsula of Michigan. Juntunen summer subsistence activities were specialized (fishing) as were the winter hunting activities of these people. The adaptation, as a whole, is to be classified as focal.

This pattern, which began in the Canadian province during the Middle Woodland period, is based upon high availability of fish at certain localities during the spring, summer, and fall seasons. The apparent introduction of the use of nets during

Middle Woodland times, and the subsequent evolution of the social system geared to the exploitation of this resource, produced
the inland shore fishery of the Late Woodland period. To some
extent, the development of this adaptive pattern produced population changes which paralleled those produced by the appearance of
the intensive agricultural pattern farther south. These changes
include a higher level of population density, larger sites, and
more stable residency. Unlike similar changes in the agricultural societies, these changes were not as permanent or as
dramatic. They were, in fact, only related to summer occupations. The increase in human carrying capacity in the Canadian
province, during the Late Woodland period, was probably due
almost entirely to the exploitation of spring fish runs. Since
food is otherwise scarcest at this season, due to the expenditure of food stores, and the poor condition of game, the amount
of food available in late winter and early spring determines the
population level. Given the proper technological and cultural
system which can exploit this resource, we would expect a higher
population level. The larger size of these Late Woodland fishing
sites is due not only to increased food supply, but also to the
temporary nature of the great abundance of fish. During the
spring runs, a great deal of intergroup cooperation was probably
required to both catch and process fish. Ethnographic sources
do not tell us precisely at what level this cooperation occurred
or how the fish were subsequently distributed. Hickerson (1962:
49) notes that "the village, the largest segment of southwestern
Chippewa society not based on kin affiliation, had certain economic functions, i.e., the allotment of sugarbush, the maintenance
of gardens, and fishing and ricing areas,..." Presumably, villages were made up of a number of extended patrilineal families
which cooperated economically while in the summer encampment,
but fragmented into economically independent hunting bands during the winter.

When we examine the adaptation of the cultures in the Carolinian-Canadian transition zone, there is a noticeable shift toward reliance upon crop plants, but also important secondary
subsistence activities based upon one or more other resources.
These are truly mixed economies which may also be classified as
diffuse. The Late Woodland occupation at the Schultz site is
typical of the transition zone. The faunal analysis of this occupation produced evidence that both hunting and fishing were important subsistence activities at this time. The trend toward
more exclusive hunting of large herbivores, and a slight decrease
in fishing from the Middle Woodland occupations, is thought to

indicate greater reliance upon crop plants as a food source.   In
addition, we know from historic sources that the Indians of the
Saginaw Valley were village farmers who hunted and fished.
This way of life stands in strong contrast to more northern
peoples who were primarily fishers and hunters, but who occasionally farmed.   It also implies larger populations and more
residential stability, and perhaps even more important, a new
role for women as producers of food.   The seasonal subsistence
round probably included several phases, but most important were
summer villages and relatively smaller winter hunting camps.
La Potherie (Blair 1911:281-283) says that there were also
summer hunts near the villages in addition to the winter hunting,
but that these were less important.   There is reason to believe
that the winter hunting camps were not nearly as small as the
ones of the Algonquin hunters of the Canadian province.   This
fact is primarily due to the much larger game populations of
the transition zone.   As we have seen, the transition zone was
also a zone of intertribal contention simply because it was a
favorable hunting area.   This is especially true where the transition zone is narrow and separates two groups with different
adaptations, such as the Chippewa and Sioux in Wisconsin and
Minnesota.

    Where this zone is wide, these areas are usually occupied
by people who are adapted to the resources of that zone.   The
Ottawa, Huron, Pottawattomi, Fox, Sauk, and Kickapoo were all
occupying the Carolinian-Canadian transition zone at the time of
European contact.   Except in the case of the Huron and their
northern Algonquian neighbors (who had apparently reached a
mutually beneficial, though perhaps tenuous, trading relationship
across the southern Canadian forest boundary) these groups
came into constant conflict with their neighbors and each other.
Raudot (Kinietz 1940:382) writing in 1710, reported that:

These Outagamis [Fox] as well as the Sakis [Sauk] are so savage that
the others cannot stand them, but as they are numerous, mustering
nearly five hundred warriors, they fear them and let them make war
without interference on the Scioux.

Also, (Knietz ibid:382)

These Kicapous are almost all crippled with wounds and covered with
scars, being always at war.

Champlain (Bourne 1922:100-101) worte of the Ottawa,

In the first place, they are at war with another tribe of savages called
Asistaguerouon which means Fire People [Pottawattomi], who live ten
days' journey from them.

Kinietz (1940:262) writing on Ottawa warfare says that:

The Ottawa had disputes with practically all of the rest of the tribes around them, with the exception of the Chippewa and Menominee. Their quarrels with the Huron, however, never broke into open warfare. Their major engagements with their foes, aside from the Sioux and the Iroquois, during the contact period were follows: Winnebago, about 1640; Miami, 1690, 1706, 1712; Flatheads (Cherokee, Chickasaw, Catawba, etc.), 1700 et seq.; and Fox, 1712, 1716, 1723.

Although all of this warfare is obviously not a result of simple competition across ecological zones, the evidence indicates that the occupation of a relatively well endowed ecological community, bordered by and containing other societies all competing for these resources, will lead to conflict.

The Moccasin Bluff site represents a society of sedentary agriculturalists. The faunal analysis of the food refuse shows a very selective hunting pattern, almost exclusively for deer and elk. About the only bird these people hunted was the turkey, and, aside from sturgeon, they did not engage in fishing to any extent. The fauna also indicates that the site was not seasonal, but occupied on a year-around basis. Sturgeon fishing and hunting were probably seasonal activities which supplemented the staple dietary elements obtained from agriculture.

At Verchave II site (Fitting 1965c:120), Feature 2 was a stratified refuse pit which illustrated the presence of seasonal subsistence actvities on a Late Woodland site in southeastern Michigan. The basal layer of this feature was largely composed of bone of the yellow walleye *Stizostedion vitreum*. At least 21 individual fish of large size, between 375 and 465 mm in length, were represented; their size indicates that they were probably taken by harpoon during a spring spawning run. Above the lens of fish bone, was dark brown layer containing hickory nuts, walnuts, hazelnuts, hawthorn, grape seeds, and corn. Richard Yarnell, who identified this material, believes that this lens was deposited in the fall season. Above this lens was another layer of fish bone, again representing a spring deposit of fish refuse.

The Silver Lake site is also representative of groups which relied principally upon agriculture. The cultural and faunal material from the Silver Lake site was collected by George Davis and Edward Gillis of Grand Rapids who discovered the site as it was being eroded from a sand dune along Lake Michigan in Oceana County, Michigan. The pottery from this site could be described as Lake Michigan ware and it probably dates between

A.D. 1200 and A.D. 1600. As at the Moccasin Bluff site, the faunal material shows a great deal of hunting selectivity. Deer and elk provided about 82 percent of the meat, and, mammals as a group, provided almost 95 percent of the total meat represented by the sample. Fish and beaver were the only other food species which also provided a significant amount of meat. (Table 4)

Unfortunately, we have no way of determining the importance of game in the total diets of prehistoric agricultural peoples because we do not know how much vegetal food was consumed. Ethnographic sources tell us that hunting was a seasonal activity among the agricultural groups of the Upper Great Lakes, and that hunts were often an activity in which most of the men participated as a cooperative enterpise. It was the common practice among such groups as the Iroquois, Huron, Miami, Illini, and the Siouan tribes for the hunters to leave the villages for extended periods during the winter season. These parties often traveled hundreds of miles to hunt deer, elk, and bison in areas where one or more of these species were abundant. Presumably, most of the meat was dried and taken back to the villages which were occupied, even during the winter season, by all those who were not hunting.

More is known of the developmental sequence of the agricultural societies of southern Wisconsin. Griffin (1960b) suggests that Oneota in Wisconsin is the result of a cultural transition from a Middle Mississippian base to a simpler Upper Mississippian socio-economic pattern. He hypothesizes that the climatic deterioration which reduced the reliability of agriculture in central Wisconsin during the period from A.D. 1200 to A.D. 1700 was the primary contributory cause of this transition. In brief, Griffin cites evidence for a movement of Middle Mississippian peoples, with an Old Village economic, social-political, and ideological system, into southern Wisconsin by about A.D. 700-A.D. 800. Griffin (personal communication) now believes this movement to have taken place at about A.D. 1000. These people occupied sites of the Rock River focus, such as Aztalan and, like their relatives at Cahokia, probably practiced intensive agriculture. This northern movement coincides with a warm climatic phase which Griffin (1961) places between A.D. 700 and A.D. 1200. The onset of cooler weather at the close of this period is thought to have shortened the growing season, reduced the reliability of agriculture, and generated a new mixed economy based upon agriculture and hunting. This new economic orientation would have been accompanied by a deterioration of ceramic styles and social-political organization. These are Upper the

TABLE 4

FAUNAL REMAINS FROM THE SILVER LAKE SITE, OCEANA COUNTY, MICHIGAN

Species	Number of Bones	Minimum Number of Individuals	Pounds of Usable Meat/ Individual	Pounds of Usable Meat/ Species	Per- cent
Deer	104	14	85	1,190	51.7
Elk	5	2	350	700	30.4
Beaver	22	7	31.5	220.5	9.6
Woodchuck	7	4	5.6	22.4	
Raccoon	3	1	17.5	17.5	
Dog	4	1	15	15	
Muskrat	8	4	2.1	8.4	
Fox	1	1	4.5	4.5	
Mink	3	1	1.4	1.4	
Eastern chipmunck	1	1			
Red squirrel	1	1			
Peromyscus spp.	1	1			
Total Mammal	160	38		2,179.7	94.4
Passenger pigeon	6	3	0.7	2.1	
Common loon	1	1	4.2	4.2	
Canada goose	2	2	5.6	11.2	
Anas spp.	2	2			
Total Bird	11	8		17.5	0.8
Walleye	19	5	4.8	24	
Sturgeon	1	1	36	36	
Longnose gar	2	2	1.6	3.2	
Drum	10	4	2.96	11.8	
Northern pike	6	1	2.4	2.4	
Channel catfish	4	1	3.2	3.2	
Total fish	42	14		80.6	4.8
Combine Total	213	60		2,271.5	100.0

Mississippian manifestations of Wisconsin which we know as
Oneota. Griffin (1961b) attributes sites of the Oneota aspect to
the ancestors of the Chiwere-Siouan and Winnebago speakers of
the historic period.

Baerreis contends, on the basis of new radiocarbon dates
from Aztalan, and a date of A.D. 800 for the beginning of the
Old Village occupation at Chokia, that Aztalan was occupied between A.D. 1100 and A.D. 1300 (Baerreis and Bryson 1965).
Baerreis (n.d.) also interprets the animal remains from evolving
Oneota sites, such as Carcajou Point, as evidence that the economic shift from a strongly agricultural economy to one of mixed
agriculture and hunting had already been established by A.D.
1000. If such is the case, Griffin's proposed "cool phase" at
A.D. 1200 to A.D. 1700 could not possibly be a causative factor
in the new economic orientation. Baerreis agrees with Griffin
that Oneota cultures do not display the ceremonial intensity which
characterized Middle Mississippian manifestations to the south,
yet Baerreis is reluctant to accept Griffin's degeneration hypothesis. If, as Baerreis points out, the size and density of population is an indication of cultural efficiency, then the fact that
some Oneota sites are larger than Aztalan indicates an increase
rather than a decline in population during the period of Oneota
dominance. While this may be the case, inferences about population density from the size of archaeological sites are likely
to be incorrect, especially when the temporal spans of these
sites are not equivalent.

According to Hall's (1962) developmental sequence for Wisconsin Oneota, Aztalan is recognized as a Middle Mississippian
outpost of the Old Village aspect at Cahokia. This complex is
followed by Carcajou Point, a site showing both evolved Old
Village and the new Oneota traits. Hall interprets Carcajou
Point as an early site within the Oneota aspect.

If Carcajou represents the inception of the Oneota cultural
pattern, its economy should reflect a considerable shift away
from the strongly agricultural pattern of Old Village and Aztalan.
Since mammalian species usually represent the important source
of meat, both in agricultural and in hunting and gathering societies, the frequency of mammal bone on archaeological sites
should reflect the intensity with which species of this class were
exploited. Table 5 shows the frequency of various mammalian
game animals on a number of sites of the Oneota tradition and
at Cahokia. These figures indicate that there is no substantial
change through time in the frequency of mammal bones reported
by Adams (n.d.) at Cahokia, Parmalee (1960a) at Aztalan, or

TABLE 5

PERCENTAGE OF MAMMALIAN SPECIES IN SITES OF THE ONEOTA
TRADITION COMPARED WITH CAHOKIA

		Deer	Elk	Bison	Bear	Beaver	Mammals
A.D. 1700	Bell	35.5	0.92	2.27	7.4	26.41	27.7
A.D. 1200	Lasley's Point	65.15	5.15	1.57	2.36	4.11	21.66
A.D. 1100	Carcajou Point	88.05	2.56		0.51	1.53	7.35
A.D. 1100– A.D. 1200	Aztalan	88.17	2.03		0.17	1.69	7.94
	Cahokia	88.47	0.07				11.46

those represented by the present survey of faunal remains at
Carcajou Point. At all three sites deer is the single most important source of meat, and in all cases, the percentage of
deer bone compared with other mammal bone is exactly 88 percent of the total. At Lasleys Point, a Lake Winnebago focus of
the Oneota site, deer represents only 65.2 percent of the total
mammal bone. This percentage drops even further at the historic period Bell site (Parmalee 1963), where deer bone represents a mere 36.2 percent of the total. Table 5 also indicates
that the frequency of other large herbivores, such as elk and
bison, remain relatively constant through time. The decrease
in the frequency of deer is balanced by a concomitant increase
in the frequency of smaller animals such as raccoon, muskrat,
and beaver. Beaver becomes especially frequent at the Bell
site, perhaps as Parmalee (1963) supposed, a reflection of fur
trading activities.

The shift in economy from one based upon agriculture, as
illustrated by Cahokia, Aztalan, and Carcajou Point, to one
based to a large extent upon hunting, like that of the Bell site,
does not precede the appearance of developed Oneota at about
A.D. 1200. Evolving Oneota economies, if the one at Carcajou
Point is typical, were similar in all respects to those at Cahokia
and Aztalan and, therefore, primarily agricultural.

It may be argued that the data presented in Table 5 does
not represent a shift in subsistence activities through time, but
are a reflection of the natural availablility of mammalian species
on a north to south axis. This argument is effectively countered
by the fact that Cahokia is located over three hundred miles
south of Carcajou Point, and that the two sites lie in different

biotic provinces. Yet, the faunal proportions on these sites are more similar than those of Carcajou Point and Lasley's Point which are only fifty miles apart and occur in nearly identical ecological situations. Similarly, Lasley's Point and the Bell site are only a few miles apart, but their faunal assemblages do not reflect their close geographic proximity. In addition, all of these sites are considered to be located in deciduous forest edge habitats which would be nearly equally favorable for deer populations. Similarities and differences in the faunal assemblages of these five sites are almost surely attributable to cultural selection of food species.

In societies where the stable dietary elements are agricultural products, hunting becomes a supplemental subsistence activity. Though meat is important as a source of protein, hunting is not a full time occupation. Hunting, therefore, tends to become a specialized activity in that emphasis is placed on harvesting the one or few species whose size and density most efficiently reward the energy expended in their capture. In the eastern United States, the species which most perfectly meets these requirements is the white-tailed deer. Economic systems which do not place primary reliance on agriculture cannot afford this often unreliable specialized hunting pattern. While deer may remain the choice game species for these societies, small and less common mammals, birds, and fish are also important food sources.

The increase in the numbers and variety of these small animal species, in addition to the drop in the percentage of deer bone on Oneota sites in central Wisconsin, marks a mixed agricultural and hunting economy. While the time of the shift to this new economy seems to agree with the onest of Griffin's A.D. 1200-A.D. 1700 cool climatic phase, there is still no good evidence to indicate that climatic change initiated the shift. An alternate explanation may be that the appearance of the Oneota foci of Wisconsin are the result of several distinct regional adaptations to ecological situations which share a limited potential for agriculture. The climate of this northern region probably would not permit an intensive agricultural subsistence base, but as Baerreis has pointed out, the large size and density of Oneota sites suggests that these people had made a favorable economic adjustment to this condition. The fact that Oneota sites are found in different micro-environments, all supporting different food sources, would mitigate against a single Oneota adaptation. It is suggestive that the known distributions of the five Oneota foci of Wisconsin all correspond very closely to small areas of ecological homogeneity.

TABLE 6

FAUNAL REMAINS FROM THE LASLEY'S POINT SITE,
WINNEBAGO COUNTY, WISCONSIN

Species	Number of Bones	Approximate Number of Individuals	Live Weight in Pounds	Percent of Usable Meat	Pounds of Usable Meat/ Individual	Pounds of Usable Meat/ Species	Percent
Deer	331	44	170	50	85	3,740	40.2
Elk	28	10	700	50	350	3,500	37.6
Bear	12	6	300	70	210	1,260	13.5
Beaver	21	12	45	70	31.5	378	4.1
Dog	28	16	30	50	15	240	2.6
Raccoon	7	6	25	70	17.5	105	1.1
Muskrat	37	20	3	70	2.1	42	0.4
Otter	7	2	18	70	12.6	25.2	0.3
Fisher	1	1	7	70	4.9	4.9	
Marten	2	2	3	70	2.1	4.2	
Woodchuck	2	1	8	70	5.6	5.6	0.2
Mink	3	3	1.5	70	1.05	3.15	
Cottontail	1	1	3	70	2.1	2.1	
Fox	2	1	9	50	4.5	4.5	
Shorttail shrew	3	3					
Red squirrel	1	1					
Least chipmunk	8	2					
Eastern chipmunk	2	1					
Microtus spp.	4	2					
Bison	8	7					
Total Mammals	508	141				9,315.00	100.0
Pintail	61	30	2	70	1.4	42	17.7
Canada goose	7	7	8	70	5.6	39.2	16.5
Blue and/or green wing teal	154	54	1	70	0.7	37.8	15.9
Hooded merganser	31	13	3	70	2.1	27.3	11.6
Baldpate	25	13	1.5	70	1.05	13.65	5.8
Redhead	38	13	1.5	70	1.05	13.65	5.8
Great blue heron	3	3	5	70	3.5	10.5	4.4
Common mallard	7	6	2.5	70	1.75	10.5	4.4
Red-breasted merganser	5	4	2.5	70	1.75	7.0	2.9
Greater scaup	19	5	2	70	1.4	7.0	2.9
Common merganser	5	3	3	70	2.1	6.3	2.7
American coot	11	8	1	70	0.7	5.6	2.4

TABLE 6--Continued

Species	Number of Bones	Approximate Number of Individuals	Live Weight in Pounds	Percent of Usable Meat	Pounds of Usable Meat/ Individual	Pounds of Usable Meat/ Species	Percent
Wood duck	16	5	1.5	70	1.05	5.25	2.3
Lesser scaup	10	6	1.0	70	0.7	4.2	1.8
Surfscoter	7	4	1.5	70	1.05	4.2	1.8
Passenger pigeon	2	2	1.0	70	0.7	1.4	0.6
Pied-billed grebe	1	1	1.0	70	0.7	0.7	0.3
Yellow billed cuckoo	1	1	0.5	70	0.35	0.35	0.15
Yellow shafted flicker	1	1	0.5	70	0.35	0.35	0.15
Mergus spp.	1	1					
Songbird	2	1					
Total Birds	407	181				237.00	100.0
Ranidae	36	6					
Softshell turtle	2	2	50	20	10	20	45.45
Snapping turtle	2	2	50	20	10	20	45.45
Wood turtle	1	1	20	20	4	4	9.1
Total Frogs and Turtles	41	11				44	100.0
Sturgeon	20	13	45	80	36	468	76.5
Walleye	17	12	6	80	4.8	57.6	9.4
Bowfin	22	11	2.5	80	2	22	3.6
Drum	7	7	3.7	80	2.96	20.7	3.3
Northern pike	8	6	3.0	80	2.4	14.4	2.4
Lake trout?	1	1	18	80	14.4	14.4	2.4
Channel catfish	3	3	4	80	3.2	9.6	1.6
Northern yellow bullhead	5	4	0.75	80	0.6	2.4	0.4
Northern black bullhead	5	4	0.5	80	0.4	1.6	0.3
Shorthead redhorse sucker	4	2	0.5	80	0.4	0.8	0.1
Sucker	3	2					
Bass	2	2					
Catfish	10	10					
Total Fish	107	77				612.0	100.0
Combined Total	1,063	410				14,408.0	

The Lake Winnebago focus is restricted to an area of ecological transition between the grasslands of the Central Plains province and the woodlands of the Eastern Ridges and Lowlands province. It is evident from the faunal remains at Lasley's Point that these Oneota peoples were exploiting a great number of aquatic animal species and fish. Nearly seventy percent of the species at this site are either aquatic animals or animals closely associated with the habitat (Table 6).

Carcajou Point, representing the Koshkonong focus, is located in the prairie area of the southern Eastern Ridges and Lowlands province. This region currently enjoys 160 frost-free growing days per year. All other Oneota foci are situated in regions with little more than 140 frost-free growing days. If this ratio of growing days prevailed during the period of Oneota occupation, the people who resided at Carcajou Point would have found agriculture more productive than their neighbors who resided further north. As we have seen, the frequency of deer bones on this site indicates that these people were indeed primarily agricultural. As at Lasley's Point, the aquatic faunal element is well represented — a reflection of similar microenvironments. The difference between the two faunal assemblages is in the intensity with which various animal species were exploited.

The Grand River focus is confined to the rolling hills of the eastern part of the Central Plains province. This area was one of ecological transition between grasslands and woodlands and could perhaps be characterized as open woodlands. This situation is ideal for large herbivores. Although we have no faunal studies for Grand River focus sites, their economy was probably based upon agriculture and hunting large herbivores. If such was the case, we could expect refuse pits on Grand River focus sites to yield numerous remains of herbivorous species. Elk and bison, which prefer grasslands and open woodland, may surpass deer as a meat source.

Little is known of the Oneota peoples who occupied the wooded regions of the Door Peninsula but here again, we could expect a different ecological adaptation based on the resources which are unique to this region. In all probability, the subsistence activities of these people were oriented toward the rich aquatic resources of Green Bay and Lake Michigan.

The last defined Oneota focus in Wisconsin is the Orr focus (McKern 1945). Sites of this focus are found on the terraces and flood plains of the lower stream valleys of the Western Uplands province. A preliminary analysis of the fauna of the

Midway site indicates that the people who occupied this site of the Orr focus had an economic pattern based upon hunting large and small woodland mammals, and catching some of the larger fish typical of the Mississippi River drainage. The number of frost-free days approaches a 160-day growing season in this region so that agriculture was also probably quite important. The water birds and small aquatic animals so common on eastern Oneota sites are poorly represented.

A survey of the faunal remains from a limited number of sites of the Oneota tradition, as well as the location of the various Oneota foci in relation to the natural ecological zones, permits several hypotheses on the origin and nature of Oneota subsistence economies. It now appears that people with an Old Village cultural assemblage and a predominantly agricultural economy moved into southern Wisconsin at about A.D. 1000. These people settled in areas where the growing season was of sufficient length to permit the continuation of this subsistence pattern. Further northward and eastward, movement of predominantly agricultural peoples with a developing Oneota culture brought them into areas marginal for dependable agricultural production at about A.D. 1100. The result was a series of new regional adaptations with economies based upon agriculture and some other food resources. By about A.D. 1200, the internal cultural cohesion resulting from adaptation to the resources of several distinctive ecological zones in southern Wisconsin produced those foci which we recognize as Oneota. The possibility of climatic deterioration at A.D. 1200 would have strengthened the position of such a mixed economy.

Unlike the diffuse adaptations of the Canadian biotic province and the Carolinian-Canadian transition zone, those of the Carolinian province may be classified as focal. These are specialized societies geared to the production of plant foods. The population level, residential stability, technological implementation, matrilinial social systems, and higher levels of political structure of these societies are all based upon their ability to produce food. Failure in this end would prove disastrous simply because there are no alternate means of procuring a similar or nearly similar quantity of food. There are, of course, degrees of economic specialization and adaptive focalization, and it is necessary to add that even the most highly specialized agriculturalists of the Upper Great Lakes did not, in this regard, approach the societies of the midwestern and southeastern regions of the United States. Probably, the reason for this was the fact that crops could not be staggered to great advantage where there were many

less than 200 frost-free days, whereas corn may be grown with
assurance where there are at least 140 frost-free days. Yarnell
(1964:136) calculated the present average frost-free period for the
localities of several classes of archaeological sites in the northeastern United States. He found that the average frost-free
period was 153 days for Iroquoian sites, 168 days for Upper
Mississippian sites, 178 days for Fort Ancient sites, and 190
days for Middle Mississippian sites. People living in all of
these localities could successfully produce single crops of corn,
but probably only those living in areas with more than 190 days
could successfully stagger at least two crops. The ability to do
this adds a tremendous margin of safety to the successful
harvest of at least one crop since it lessens the chance of a
disaster to one of the plantings by such factors as late or early
frost, drought, wind damage, or insect infestations. The Iroquoian
and Upper Mississippian cultures of the Upper Great Lakes region could not stagger crop plantings and could, therefore, not
match the level of productivity achieved by the Middle Mississippian cultures to the south.

Variation within the focal agricultural economies ranges from
cultures which probably relied almost exclusively on food production, such as the Neutral and Tobacco, to some of the Oneota
groups which also counted quite heavily upon other resources.
Nonetheless, the year-to-year maintenance of all of these societies
was dependent upon their ability to successfully produce food
crops, and to store some of these foods for winter use. In the
societies where secondary foods were important, the failure of
even these supplementary resources could lead to a serious
disruption of social units. The failure of crops in just one
season would surely result in famine and a drastic reduction in
population density. Given these alternatives for failure, and the
facts of climatological and ecological transition in the Upper
Great Lakes area, it is not difficult to see that each cultural
group became adapted to its particular environment. Given the
presence of agriculture as a means of providing food, the degree
of dependency on other resources, measured both in quantity and
in variety, varied directly with the probablility of a successful
agricultural yield. However, this does not mean that any one
agricultural society could move indiscriminately across ecological
zones simply by varying its emphasis on the acquisition of one
or another food resource. On the contrary, each cultural group
became adapted to a particular environment to such a degree
that alternative methods of production were not possible within
the structural framework of that society. Here we find one of

the principal differences between diffuse and focal adaptations. It would be conceivable, for instance, that some of the southern Chippewa or Ottawa, who had diffuse adaptations, could move into areas favorable for really efficient corn agriculture and become agriculturalists simply by relying more upon the farming part of their subsistence cycle and less upon hunting. Conversely, they could become hunters and gatherers simply by emphasizing these subsistence activities. In fact, we know that the historic Chippewa did switch back and forth when necessity or opportunity presented these alternatives. On the other hand, agricultural groups such as the Miami could not have been successful in northcentral Michigan without a significant revision of their cultural system. Here, where corn could not be produced with assurance, Miami residential units would be too large, since the lack of external marriage ties in the presence of matrilineal marriage patterns would limit accesible hunting territory. The Miami seasonal hunting pattern would not produce a constant supply of meat, and failure to use, or the lack of ability to use, available fish resources would be a fatal shortcoming. In this regard, Miami culture could not provide the flexibility necessary to meet environmental instability because it did not contain the variation necessary to provide alternate means of production. It was, in the environment to which it was adapted, a highly efficient, specialized, and successful adaptation—yet the high degree of production resulting from this cultural specialization was wagered against the unlikelihood of environmental change and won at the expense of flexibility.

IV

SUMMARY AND CONCLUSIONS

This study has been presented in two parts; a discussion of the prehistoric ecological sequence of the Upper Great Lakes, and a description of the ways in which the prehistoric cultures of this area utilized available food resources. Properly, these two aspects should be related, in so far as it is possible, to establish some direct relationship between the changing natural environment and the ways in which prehistoric cultures were adapted to these environments. This has been done to some extent in the chapter on ethnozoology and in the reports on the fauna of various Upper Great Lakes sites which appear as appendices. Breifly, the relationships between man and the natural environments of the Upper Great Lakes can be summarized as follows:

Paleo-Indian Cultures 12,000 B.C. - 9,000 B.C.

The climate of this period was cold and this factor played a major role in the determination of the composition and distribution of floral and faunal communities. Animal remains and pollen analysis indicate that the earliest forest of the southern part of the Great Lakes region was open spruce-fir forest. Following the retreat of glacial ice, the northern area was rapidly colonized by dense conifer forests which by this time, were already well established to the south.

Paleo-Indian occuaption probably began by at least 11,000 B.C. when small bands of hunters entered this area from the south. The focal hunting economy of these people must have been supported by a large and plentiful species although small and less numerous species were probably also hunted with regularity. It has been hypothesized that the barren ground caribou was probably the staple element of the Paleo-Indian economy of the Great Lakes. This and other large herbivores, such as the mammoth and musk-ox, preferred well-drained areas, which at that time supported open boreal woodland. These were also the areas favored by Paleo-Indian hunters.

Continued conifer forestation produced a very dense boreal forest throughout the Upper Great Lakes area by about 8,000 B.C. This event led not only to the gradual extinction of the grazing herbivores, but greatly reduced the carrying capacity for most game species as well. Such climatic and ecological changes would, of course, have a disastrous effect on a focal hunting economy. The Paleo-Indian specialized hunting adaptation was no longer compatible with the new environment and passed out of existence in the Great Lakes area.

Early Archaic Cultures 9,000 B.C. - 7,000 B.C.

The climate of the Great Lakes was becoming more moderate, but in relative terms it was still quite cool. The forests were of the dense conifer type and similar to the boreal forest of the modern Canadian subarctic. Both the pine and deciduous elements became increasingly frequent in the southern part of this area by the end of this period. Important forest game species probably included moose, woodland caribou, beaver, and hare. The small amount of empirical evidence at our disposal points to a focal hunting adaptation based upon large and medium sized game. Perhaps some fishing was also practiced during the summer season. Although this adaptation could support small numbers of people in all areas of the Upper Great Lakes, the heaviest Early Archaic occupations took place in the southern part of the region. Here, warmer weather and the increasing deciduous forestation produced a more favorable habitat for game species, particularly the whitetail deer. Deer hunting became the major subsistence activity of the Early Archaic cultures which occupied areas favorable to this species.

Middle Archaic Cultures 7,000 B.C. - 3,000 B.C.

Continued amelioration of the climate during the Altithermal climatic episode, brought about a gradual replacement of conifer forest by deciduous forest in all but the most northern parts of the Upper Great Lakes area. Probably, peoples living in these northern areas continued in the focal hunting tradition of earlier Archaic cultures. In the southern part of the region Middle Archaic peoples had developed a more diffuse economy based principally upon deer hunting. This new way of life was now possible due to the significantly greater variety of resources available in deciduous forest regions as opposed to relatively impoverished conifer-dominated terrain. The appearance of a ground stone technology in the southern Upper Great Lakes area at this time is the first evidence of divergent adaptive patterns within the region, and supports the theory that the more southern Middle Archaic cultures were beginning to utilize more plant resources.

Late Archaic Cultures 3,000 B.C. - 1,000 B.C.

The expansion of deciduous forest reached its most northern limit at about 2,000 B.C., during the peak of the Altithermal climate episode. At this time the weather was warmer than it is at present. During this period we see the first solid evidence of regional adaptations in the Upper Great Lakes. Old Copper peoples with a winter hunting—summer fishing focal adaptation occupied the conifer dominated forests of what is now the Canadian biotic province, while the Red Ocher and Glacial Kame cultures of the more southern Carolinian forests had developed a diffuse adaptation. This adaptation had its beginning in the Middle Archaic societies of the same area. The diffuse economy of the Glacial Kame and Red Ocher cultures was based upon winter deer hunting, spring and summer fishing and the collection of substantial quantities of wild plant foods including nuts, berries and probably most important, the seeds of wild plants. Familiarity with local food resources and regularity of movement between these resources is essential for this type of economy. As a result of these movements, it has been theorized that tribal territories were established. In addition, the extent of such territories were defined by the loci of resources that were exploited on a regular basis by a particular society. Differentials in the distribution of some resources was one of the factors which led to the widespread intergroup and intragroup exchange of the Late Archaic period.

Early Woodland Cultures 1,000 B.C. - 300 B.C.

The climate and distribution of biotic communities during this period was not unlike that of present time. Although we have no real evidence for the type of adaptation practiced at this time in the Canadian biotic province, we can safely assume a continuation of a focal hunting-fishing economy which so often characterized this area. In the Carolinian province, and in the Carolinian-Canadian transition zone there is evidence for the continuation of the Late Archaic diffuse adaptation. The introduction of some domestic plant species did not result in a cessation of the diffuse pattern, but in fact, strengthened it by adding a new, more reliable source of food to the "wild seed" phase of the economy. It is suggested that the classification of cultures of this period within the Woodland pattern is improper, despite the presence of pottery and domestic crop plants. In actuality, the total adaptations of Early Woodland cultures in the Great Lakes area most closely resemble those of the Archaic. Nonetheless, the introduction of domestic plant species into societies which were already preadapted to the collection, processing and consumption of plant seeds had important consequences for the later development of focal agricultural societies.

Middle Woodland Cultures 300 B.C. - A.D. 400

There has been some argument whether the climate of the Middle Woodland period was slightly warmer or cooler than at present. It was, at any rate, very nearly like the modern climate. Also, it has been argued that the effect of climate upon Middle Woodland cultures was practically negligible.

Evidence points to two distinct adaptive patterns in the Upper Great Lakes at this time. In the Canadian biotic province we see the development of lakeside villages, which are believed to be the result of greater reliance upon spring and summer fishing. Probably, the use of fish nets was one of the most important factors in this new adaptation. Winter hunting for moose, woodland caribou, bear, beaver, and hare was still very important.

In the Carolinian province we find the Middle Woodland period the time of an extremely important revolution in subsistence economics. Early within this period there is evidence for the continuation of the diffuse subsistence pattern of the Late Archaic and Early Woodland periods. Hunting, fishing, and collecting, but particularly the collecting of plant seeds were important subsistence activities. The location of early Middle Woodland sites on alluvial bottoms, their relatively large size, and the kinds and quantities of secondary resources being exploited indicate that the use of plant seeds, both wild and domestic, had become the principal subsistence activity of these societies. The presence of an abundant and storable food resource produced a social and technological milieu suitable for a new focal adaptation. Presumably, the arrival of corn, sometime late within the Middle Woodland period, provided the catalyst for this new adaptation. The successful utilization of this crop did not require major cultural changes. It merely added the necessary margin of reliability to the existing economy so that other, less productive subsistence enterprises could be discontinued.

One of the effects of this new focal economy was the breakdown of the territories of the Late Archaic, Early Woodland, and early Middle Woodland times. Concentration on one subsistence activity negated the necessity of social control over widely scattered resources, and as a result, intragroup contact was reduced to a minimum. Neutral or even competitive relationships replaced the once thriving reciprocal trade networks of earlier times. No doubt, the so-called "Hopewellian decline" which was characterized by such features as a cessation in the flow of exotic burial goods and raw materials and a breakdown in the communication of stylistic design motifs was the result of newly established focal agricultural economies.

Late Woodland and Upper Mississippian Cultures
A.D. 400 - A.D. 1650

There were several periods of climatic fluctuation during the time that Late Woodland and Upper Mississippian cultures occupied the Upper Great Lakes area. Although these climatic episodes did not have any drastic effect upon the biota of the region, from time to time they did influence the type and distribution of environmental adaptation of Upper Great Lakes cultures which practice agriculture.

During this period we find three basic kinds of adaptations —fishermen and hunters of the Canadian biotic province, who practiced no agriculture; peoples of the Carolinian-Canadian transition zone, who practiced agriculture to varying degrees, but who could not depend upon this resource alone; and finally, strongly agricultural societies in the Carolinian biotic province.

The subsistence pattern and adaptation of the cultures of the Canadian province can be classified as focal. Because of the abundant fish resources of the Great Lakes and the inland fishing complex which these people had developed, the population density and summer residential stability was far greater than that normally found in cultures with focal economies. This pattern was broken only during the late winter when short food resources necessitated a temporary reversion to a family-band hunting economy.

In the Carolinian-Canadian transition zone we find diffuse economies which were strongly oriented toward the production of domestic food plants. The amount of food produced in this manner depended upon their geographic position in the zone, climatic episodes, and yearly fluctuations in the length of the growing season. During the Neo-Atlantic period of A.D. 800 - A.D. 1200, for instance, we find people practicing effective corn agriculture farther north than in preceding or subsequent periods. In fact, the desirability of corn as a food resource led to continued pressures on the northern periphery of corn production. This practice resulted not only in occasional abundant years and in the quick follow-up of warm climatic phases by a northward movement of agricultural peoples, but also to the continued breeding of cold resistant races of corn. Despite these facts, agriculture was not in itself reliable enough to warrant the expenditure of full scale subsistence effort. Hunting, some gathering, but particularly fishing were also important. In short, the adaptations of the cultures of the Carolinian-Canadian transition zone were as transitional as the fauna and flora of the region in which they developed. Agricultural activities, for whatever additional food they provided, were simply superimposed over the inland fishing complex of the Canadian biotic province. It has also been pointed out that the transition area was very favorable for hunting, and that where the zone was narrow and bordered on two sides by different cultural adaptations it became an unoccupied zone of conflict. More frequently, the transition was wide enough to support its own unique cultural adaptation, but even in this case, agricultural pressure from the south and hunting pressure by northern people made it a zone of intra-group conflict.

The occupation of the transition zone of southern Wisconsin by Upper Mississippian peoples, and the later differentiation of several distinct regional adaptations within this area has been seen as a process in the establishment of a new diffuse economic pattern. These developments took on exactly the opposite kind of manifestations that were observed in the formation of focal agricultural economies during the late Middle Woodland period. Here we see diffuse economies developing from the focal agri-cultural economies of more southern Middle Mississippian so-cieties. Such a change is thought to be the result of the north-ward push of the agricultural complex into areas which would not support a focal agricultural economy. These people were thus, not only forced to switch the emphasis they had placed on various resources, but to arrive at a significantly new cul-tural adaptation. As we recall, it is much easier to move from a diffuse to a focal economic adaptation than the reverse. As a result of these major changes, Upper Mississippian cul-ture became much different from the Middle Mississippian culture from which it had developed. These changes affected the technological and economic aspects of these societies as well as their social, political, and ideological phases. The readaptive process eventually brought about the differential

utilization of secondary resources which were available in varying quantities in different microenvironmental situations. As a
result, there was again a period of territorialization, and while
this was not as intense as the same phenomenon as observed
in the diffuse adaptations of the Late Archaic, it was strong
enough to inspire the appearance of several recognizably different
Upper Mississippian foci.

During the Late Woodland period the cultures of the Carolinian biotic province occupied territory which was well within
the limits of reliable agriculture. These societies became more
and more dependent upon the production and utilization of domestic plant foods. In every respect these were focal economies.

Although this pattern is essentially an intensification of the
focal pattern established in late Middle Woodland times, we see
the gradual development of larger and more stable residential
units. This series of events was probably due both to increased
sophistication of agricultural techniques, and the introduction or
development of more productive races of corn. In addition, the
bean was probably introduced at some time during this period.
Secondary subsistence activities became less and less important
until seasonal hunts, devoted almost exclusively to either deer,
elk or bison, became the only other key to economic security.
These hunts were cooperative and undertaken by the males of
one residential complex. Usually hunting took place during the
period when it would not interfere with agricultural activities,
i.e., during early summer and especially late winter. These
hunts were usually undertaken at some distance from the village
and often lasted several months.

The most favorable areas for this type of economy were
fertile areas where the forest was relatively open, although, the
openness of the forest could be and was controlled by periodic
clearing and burning. Culture areas within the Carolinian biotic
province seem to have been determined, to a large part, by the
presence of natural barriers such as large lakes, blocks of
climax forests, and the convolutions of isothermic boundaries of
agricultural potential.

APPENDIX A

RE-ANALYSIS OF FAUNAL REMAINS FROM
RADDATZ ROCKSHELTER, SAUK COUNTY, WISCONSIN

The Raddatz Rockshelter which is located in Sauk County,
Wisconsin, was excavated by Warren L. Wittry in 1957. Wittry's
excavations reached twelve feet below the surface and produced
cultural material to a depth of ten feet below the surface. The
lowest levels of the shelter have been dated at 9652±300 B.C.
(M-812). In the Raddatz Rockshelter report, Wittry (1959a) recognized three distinct cultural horizons. The earliest human
occupation occurs in stratum R which is estimated to date between 9000 and 8000 B.C. Unfortunately, no diagnostic artifacts
were recovered from this stratum. Overlying this deposit, including those levels below level 12 or stratum I, are Early
Archaic materials which Wittry dates at 4500 B.C. Then, overlying
these are Middle Archaic depostis, stratum I through D, or levels
12 through 5. Here Wittry recovered Raddatz side notched
points which he places in an Old Copper context. One radiocarbon date from Feature 3 of level 10 is 3241±300 B.C. (M-813).
This occupation is assumed to have spanned the Altithermal
period. Levels 3 and 4 contain projectile points similar in most
respects to those from the nearby Durst Rockshelter (Wittry
1959b). Wittry believes Durst Points to be Late Archaic. The
most recent deposits of the shelter levels 1 and 2 were disturbed by modern activities.

The Raddatz shelter is an important site for Great Lakes
archaeology because it is the only excavated site in this area
with a relatively unbroken cultural sequence throughout the
Archaic period and because it is one of the few Archaic sites
in the Upper Great Lakes region where organic materials are
preserved. Fortunately, the shelter is located in a strategic
position for recording ecological changes as these changes are
reflected by vertebrate fauna. Since the site is situated on the
southern margin of the present Canadian biotic province, we
would expect a higher incidence of Canadian and Hudsonian
species if the prehistoric climate was cooler, while a warmer

98

prehistoric climatic phase should eliminate Canadian and Hudsonian species from the faunal assemblage. The site is also
located near the prairie areas of southern Wisconsin so that
grassland introgressions should be apparent from the appearance of prairie fauna.

The fauna from the Raddatz Rockshelter was identified by
Paul W. Parmalee of the Illinois State Museum who reported
the results of his analysis in the Wisconsin Archeologist
(Parmalee 1959). Faunal analyses underaken by different investigators are often incomparable because of the varying techniques
applied by these investigators. Such was the case with the fauna
from the Raddatz site. Because this is an important site in the
study of Upper Great Lakes paleoecology and ethnozoology, Dr.
Parmalee kindly consented to loan his laboratory notes to me
for re-evaluation. It is hoped that this study combined with the
excellent one which Dr. Parmalee has already published will
be useful as a guide to the climate and subsistence patterns of
the Archaic period in southern Wisconsin.

In the original analysis of the Raddatz fauna, Parmalee
identified over 5200 bones representing some 50 species. Although most of these remains have been considered in the re-
analysis, the number of both identified bones and species has
been slightly reduced by the necessity of eliminating a small
number of species which came from unclear or mixed provenience
units. The stratigraphic origin of each species and the number
of bones representing each species is shown in Table 7. Deer
occur in all of the defined levels from the surface to level 15.
Ruffed grouse appear in 93 percent of the levels, passenger
pigeons and chipmunks appear in 80 percent and gray squirrels
appear in 73 percent. In addition, woodchuck, raccoon, beaver,
flying squirrels, elk and turkeys appear in at least one half of
all levels of the site. All other species appear less frequently.
Deer bones comprise 85.7 percent of the stratigraphic sample;
while the next most common vertebrate remains were those of
the passenger pigeon which make up only 2.6 percent of the
total bone sample; chipmunks and ruffed grouse are the only other
species which comprise more than 1.0 percent of the total sample.
The frequency of the remaining species is but a fraction of 1.0
percent of the total bone count.

A cursory survey of Table 7 will indicate that some species
in the Raddatz deposit have a rather intermittent pattern of
occurrence. Some appear only in upper or lower levels while
others appear only in the intermediate levels. In order to facilitate more precise observations on the changes of the natural

TABLE 7

STRATIGRAPHIC OCCURRENCE OF ANIMAL REMAINS FROM THE RADDATZ ROCKSHELTER
SAUK COUNTY, WISCONSIN

Species								Levels								13,14,15	Below 15	Total	Percent
	1	2	3	4	5	6	7	8	9	10	11	12	13	14	15				
Deer	109	163	250	354	527	536	414	296	144	117	79	46	34	31	19	21	5	3,145	85.7
Cottontail		2							1	1	2	1				1	1	11	0.3
Canis Spp.	1															1		4	0.1
Passenger pigeon				1	1	1		2	6	7	7	10	8	16	14	20	2	96	2.6
Screech Owl	1				1	1					1					1		5	0.1
Ruffed grouse	1	7	2	3	1	1		6	5	8	9	2	2	5		4		57	1.6
Turkey	1	1		1	1	1			1	1		1			1			9	0.2
Painted turtle	1		2	2		6	2	2									2	17	0.4
Elk		1	2	1	2	1	4	5	1	1	1					1		18	0.5
Gray squirrel		1	2				1	1	3	3	2					1		18	0.5
Sheep*		4	2															6	0.2
Wolf		2	4	1	3	3	6	1						2	1			20	0.5
Gray wolf		1				1												2	0.055
Box turtle	1	1	1	1	2	2	1				1							9	0.2
Woodchuck			5	1	1	1	1	2	1	8	1			1	1	3		25	0.7
Raccoon			1	1	1	12	3	1		2				1				22	0.65
Flying squirrel			2	1		3	1	1	3	3	3	1	1	1		6		22	0.65
Chipmunk			1	1	2	3	3	3	7	5	1		1	4	2	2	1	36	1.0
Flicker			1			1		1		2								6	0.2
Chicken*			1		1	1	1										1	1	0.03
Sharp-tailed grouse			1										1	1			1	4	0.1
Wood duck			1			1		1										1	0.03
Barred owl			1															1	0.03
Passerine birds			1	2		1	1	2	1			2						2	0.055
Snake		1	1		1	2	1	1		1		1		4	2			13	0.4
Frog		1	1	1						1	1	1	1	4	1			7	0.2
Emys, Clemmys, Graptemys spp.			4								1				1	1		10	0.3
Beaver				1	3			5	1	1	5	1	1					5	0.1
Turkey vulture				1				1										18	0.5
Woodpecker				1							1							2	0.055
Red-tailed hawk				2												1		2	0.055
Mountain Lion					1													1	0.03

TABLE 7--Continued

Species										Levels									
	1	2	3	4	5	6	7	8	9	10	11	12	13	14	15	13,14,15	Below 15	Total	Percent
Mole										1	1	1		2	1	1		9	0.2
Coot						1												1	0.03
Dog							1											2	0.055
Crow							1											1	0.03
Canada goose							1											1	0.03
Snapping turtle							1	11								1		18	0.5
Rodent								1	1		1	1		1	1	1		7	0.2
Short-tail shrew									1									1	0.03
Big brown bat									1	2						1		5	0.1
Red squirrel										1	1	4	1	1	1	3		9	0.2
Myotis spp.										1	2	1						6	0.2
Microtus spp.										1	1							3	0.08
Red fox										1								1	0.03
Mallard duck										1								1	0.03
Marten											1							1	0.03
Squirrel												1						1	0.03
Sora rail												1						1	0.03
Red-headed woodpecker												1						1	0.03
Redwing blackbird												1						1	0.03
Weasel														1				1	0.03
Peromyscus spp.																	1	1	0.03
Totals	117	181	286	374	551	575	442	344	179	170	125	82	49	69	44	67	12	3,668	100.00
Percent	3.1	4.9	7.8	10.3	15.0	15.7	12.1	9.5	4.9	4.6	3.4	2.2	1.4	1.8	1.1	1.9	0.3		

*Intrusive

environment which must have in part determined the nature and magnitude of faunal change, it was necessary to qualify the habitat preferences of the species involved. A scoring system was devised that weighs habitat preference according to type of habitat(s) in which a species is most frequently encountered. If a species is found exclusively in one habitat, that habitat was scored two points. If, however, a species occupies habitats other than the preferred one, these were scored one point. Thus, a score was obtained for the habitat types occupied by the faunal assemblage of each level. Only those species with a definable habitat preference were scored. Since an animal such as the wolf occupies all of these types, scoring this species would simply increase the score of each habitat by a constant amount. The scoring of the habitat preferences of each rated species is shown in Table 8.

TABLE 8

SCORING OF THE HABITAT PREFERENCES OF THE SPECIES
AT THE RADDATZ ROCKSHELTER, SAUK COUNTY, WISCONSIN

Species	Habitat Types				
	Deciduous Forest	Conifer Forest	Deciduous Forest Edge	Grass-lands	Aquatic
Deer	1		2		
Cottontail			2		
Passenger pigeon	2				
Screech owl			2		
Ruffed grouse		1	2		
Turkey	2		1		
Elk			1	1	
Gray squirrel	2				
Woodchuck	2		1		
Raccoon	2		1		1
Flying squirrel	2				
Chipmunk	1		2		
Sharp-tailed grouse		2	1		
Barred owl	2				
Beaver					2
Vulture			1	2	
Woodpecker	2				
Flicker	2		1		
Red-tail hawk			1	1	
Red squirrel	1	2			
Red fox	1	2	1		

Figure 2 is a diagram of the changes in the percentage of the
habitat preferences of the assemblages of each level of the Raddatz Rockshelter.

The results of this analysis are very interesting, and, although differences between levels are probably not statistically
significant, they do show interesting climatic trends.   These
changes in habitat correspond very well to the climatic changes
which are thought to characterize these periods (Griffin 1961a;
1961b; 1965).

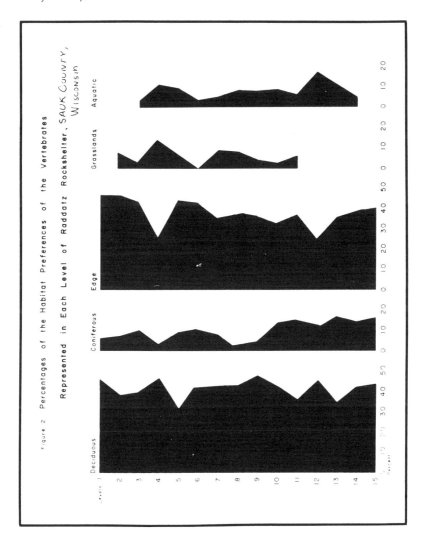

First of all, the faunal assemblage is dominated from the lowest to the highest levels by species which occupy deciduous forest and deciduous forest edge. Other habitat types make only small inroads into these habitats, but even these changes are useful in tracing ecological and climatic fluctuations. The conifer forest and aquatic habitats are most strongly represented in the lowest levels of the site. Thus, a cooler and wetter climate is indicated at that time. The lack of grassland species reinforces this interpretation. This trend reaches a climax in level 13 and from this point in time, both conifer forest and aquatic habitats generally decrease at the expense of deciduous forest and deciduous forest-edge. Wittry dates the levels below level 13 at more than 9000 years before Christ, and his supposition is supported by the radiocarbon date of 9650 B.C. for level 15. The animal species in these levels are not indicative of the conifer forest which must have grown in this part of Wisconsin at 9000 B.C. It is, therefore, suggested that level 14 and 13 probably date from a later time, perhaps 5000-6000 B.C. The forest of southern Wisconsin at this late time must have been of mixed deciduous-coniferous compostion and much like the one represented by the provinces shown in the habitat reconstruction of Figure 1. Levels 12 through 8 show a prolonged climb in the deciduous forest type and a decline in conifer forest habitat. This change is marked by several fluctuations. Level 11, for instance, shows a decline in deciduous forest habitat accompanied by a sharp decrease in the aquatic habitat, a rise in edge habitat and the sudden appearance of grasslands. These changes are thought to mark the onset of the warm-dry climate of the Altithermal period. Wittry (personal communication) estimates the date of level 12 at 4500 B.C.; the evidence presented here would tend to substantiate this estimation. The further decrease in aquatic species, an increase in grassland species, as well as the continual advance of deciduous forest habitat at the expense of conifer habitat seems to reach a maximum at level 8. Wittry dates this level at 2300 B.C. an estimation which is, in part, based on the radiocarbon date of 3241 B.C. for level 10. This estimation for level 8 would place its occupation at the height of the Altithermal period, and the faunal habitat analysis supports this hypothesis.

Habitat interpretation of levels 8 to 6, which represent the period from about 2500 B.C. to 1000 B.C., is somewhat confusing. Clearly, there is a slow decrease in deciduous and grassland habitats and a corresponding increase in aquatic and conifer forest habitats indicating a return to cooler and moister climatic conditions. The increase in edge habitat also indicates that forests were more open. At 1500 B.C., in level 5, there was a sudden decrease in deciduous forest which is accompanied by a slight decrease in conifer forest and a slight increase in edge, grassland, and aquatic habitat. No reasonable climatic explanation can be produced to explain this change nor for the continued increase in both grassland and aquatic habitat in level 4. In this level, however, we see a striking increase in deciduous forest and an equally notable drop in both edge and conifer forest habitats. Perhaps these changes reflect a warm but wet climatic phase for the period of about 1000 B.C. After this time, there is a strong decrease in deciduous forest habitat, an increase in the conifer and edge habitat and a decrease in both the grassland and aquatic habitat. This is strong evidence for a cool-dry phase in the period shortly after 1000 B.C. Subsequently, there is a gradual increase in deciduous forest and deciduous forest edge habitats at the expense of the conifer habitat, changes which signal a climatic recovery some time following the cool-dry phase of level 3.

In most respects, the environmental sequence reconstructed from the habitat preferences of the faunal assemblages of each level seems to correspond with those generally recognized in the Eastern United States. The cool period represented by the decrease of deciduous forest habitat in levels 5 and 6 probably corresponds to that which Griffin (1961a:714) postulated for the period of 1800 to 1300 B.C. Similarly, the increase in deciduous forest and decrease in conifer forest represented in level 5 probably corresponds to Griffin's 1300-800 B.C. warm stage. This analysis also tends to substantiate another cool then warm phase, perhaps relating to those Griffin hypothesized for the periods between 800 and 300 B.C. and between 300 B.C. and A.D. 300 respectively. Since the last two levels of the Raddatz Rockshelter are disturbed, we cannot be sure of the dates of these levels nor to which climatic phases they belong.

Aside from consideration of the paleoecology of the Raddatz Rockshelter, we must also investigate the animal species as food sources. In order to do this, it is necessary to speak of these remains in terms of the meat represented by the animal remains. Table 9 is a tabulation of the percentage of meat represented by the important food animals in the three major cultural horizons at the site. It is immediately apparent that deer were far and away the most important source of food in all levels. The only other species of consequence is the elk which became important in both the early and late levels of the site. These two species as a class — large herbivores — comprise between 94.9 and 97.7 percent of the meat in all cultural horizons. These species and

TABLE 9

AMOUNT OF MEAT REPRESENTED BY THE ANIMAL REMAINS OF RADDATZ ROCKSHELTER
SAUK COUNTY, WISCONSIN

Species	Late Archaic Levels 3 & 4		Middle Archaic Levels 5-12		Early Archaic Level 12		Total pounds of Meat	Percent of Total
	Pounds of Meat	Per-cent	Pounds of Meat	Per-cent	Pounds of Meat	Per-cent		
Deer	6,200	60.3	20,300	93.3	3,600	80.8	30,100	82.5
Elk	3,850	37.4	350	1.6	700	15.7	4,900	13.4
Woodchuck	16.8	0.2	56	0.3	28	0.6	100.8	0.3
Raccoon	35	0.3	140	0.6	17.5	0.4	192.5	0.5
Wolf	100	0.9	225	1.0			325	0.9
Beaver	31.5	0.3	346.5	1.6	31.5	0.7	409.5	1.1
Other Mammals	4.7	0.05	79.1	0.4	22.4	0.5	106.2	0.3
Total Mammals	10,238	99.5	21,496.6	98.8	4,399.4	98.7	36,134	99.0
Birds	23.8	0.2	126.7	0.6	46.9	1.1	197.4	0.5
Turtles	28	0.3	130	0.6	10	0.2	168	0.5
Total	10,289.8	100.0	21,753.3	100.0	4,456.3	100.0	36,499.4	100.00

other mammals represent more than 98.7 percent of all meat. Meat derived from birds and turtles is insignificant while no fish bones are represented in the deposit. The fact that a wide variety of smaller animal species is represented serves to point out the fact that these Archaic hunters had a diffuse economy. Unlike hunters of the Woodland period, who also preferred deer, these people did not hunt deer to the virtual exclusion of other species.

There are some very interesting gaps in the faunal assemblage of Raddatz which may be due to either the lack of these species in the neighborhood of the site or to the fact that they were not selected as food animals. These species include the fox squirrel, gray fox, black bear, mink, badger, striped skunk, and otter. At least the mink and black bear were taken by Late Archaic people living at the Durst Rockshelter located only a mile from the Raddatz site (Parmalee 1960b). The most mystifying is the absence of the black bear. Perhaps this can be explained by the presence of a taboo against the killing of bears, or perhaps bears may not have been available if the site was occupied during the winter hibernation period.

One interesting faunal record from this site is the occurrence of the box turtle. Neither the eastern species, *Terrapene carolina*, nor the western species, *Terrapene ornata*, presently occur in Wisconsin (Conant 1958). The western species has been occasionally reported from some counties in southern Wisconsin and does occur in northern Illinois. This species prefers a dry grassland habitat and is probably the one represented at Raddatz. The appearance of box turtles in the Raddatz strata appears to correspond with the appearance of the prairie habitat, i.e., level 11, and again between levels 7 and 2. Unfortuantely, this species could not be included in the habitat reconstruction since it is not known whether *T. ornata* or *T. carolina* was represented.

Parmalee believes, on the basis of his analysis, that the Raddatz shelter was occupied most frequently during the winter. This suppostion is based upon the absence of deer antler as well as the presence of male deer skulls from which antlers had been dropped. In addition, Parmalee points to the paucity of the water fowl remains in support of his theory. Despite the fact that every level of the Raddatz shelter contains some species which would be available only during the warm months of the year, Parmalee is probably correct in his assumption. If the shelter had been occupied most frequently in the summer, we would certainly expect many more migratory birds and deer antler. In addition, many of the species which are indicative of a summer occupation such as passerine birds, turtles, chipmunks and woodchucks could have entered the shelter of their own accord. Probably, the Raddatz Rockshelter served mainly as a winter habitation or hunting site but was visited periodically in the summer months.

In summary, the stratigraphic analysis of the faunal remains of the Raddatz Rockshelter has produced new evidence on both the paleoecology and ethnozoology sequence at this important site. An analysis of the habitat preferences of the faunal assemblage of each level, shows a remarkable correspondence with those hypothesized for the Upper Great Lakes area produced by pollen analysis. The earliest levels of the shelter show the presence of a relatively cool-moist climatic phase which is believed to date near the end of the Pine period. A gradual decrease in conifer and aquatic habitat and an increase in deciduous forest, forest edge and grasslands, characterizes the intermediate levels of the site. These changes are believed to reflect the increasing warmth and dryness of the Altithermal climatic phase. A decrease in grasslands and deciduous forest and an increase in both aquatic and conifer forest at the end of this period indicates a return to a climate reminiscent of the modern period. This stage is followed by habitat changes indicating a warm-moist period at about 1000 B.C., a subsequent cooling and finally a return to a warm-dry climate.

The subsistence economy of the Raddatz site is undeniably based upon the exploitation of deer and elk. All other food species occur much less frequently, although the consistency with which these species appear is indicative of a diffuse subsistence pattern. In short, small mammals, birds and turtles, were not the major food source and, although these Archaic hunters preferred to kill deer or elk, they did not ignore other food sources. Neither can it be said that these small species were not important since they probably acted as vital dietary supplements when larger game was not available. Faunal evidence indicates that the site was principally occupied as a winter shelter but that it was also visited periodically during the warmer months of the year.

APPENDIX B

THE ANIMAL REMAINS FROM THE
FEEHELEY, HART AND SCHMIDT SITES,
SAGINAW COUNTY, MICHIGAN

The Feeheley Site

The Feeheley site (20-SA-128) is located on a sand ridge
in the southeast quarter of Section 1, Range 4E, Township 11N
in Saginaw County, Michigan. The site is at an elevation of 608
feet above sea level. This sand ridge is a remnant of a sand
spit or dune, most likely formed shortly after the maximum rise
of the Lake Nipissing stage of the development of the Great Lakes.
The rise of Nipissing waters to a height of about 605 feet has been
dated from two localities in the immediate area of the Feeheley
site. A white cedar log recovered at an elevation of 572 feet
from a Nipissing marl deposit a short distance west of the site
was probably drowned by the rising waters of this stage and has
been dated at 3330±150 B.C.; M-1138 (Crane and Griffin 1961).
A spruce log associated with a pre-Nipissing burial at the Andrews
site, located 2 miles northeast of the Feeheley site was dated at
3350 150 B.C.; M-941 (Crane and Griffin 1960). As the lake level
of Nipissing fell, wind action must have formed much of the ridge
upon which the Feeheley site is located. Since some of the burial
pits extend below the level of Nipissing waters (605 feet) the site
must have been occupied after the fall of Nipissing to lower levels.
This evidence is substantiated by the radiocarbon date for the
Feeheley burial complex at 1980±150 B.C., M-1139 (Crane and
Griffin 1962). Thus the site was occupied at about 2000 B.C.
at a time when the lake level was between the Nipissing maximum of 605 feet and the Algoma stand at 595 feet dating approximately 1200 B.C. This water level (and in fact even a slight
rise above the present lake level) would make the Saginaw Valley
area one extensive swamp and probably a swamp with a good
deal of open water. Botanical remains from the Feeheley site
indicate that the site was covered with mixed mesophytic forest
with oak, beech, hickory, basswood, maple, pine, ash, elm,
butternut, walnut and sycamore all represented (Harnell 1964:28).

109

Animal bone from the Feeheley site was recovered by two techniques. Most of the sample was collected by fine screening (window screen) fire pits and burial debris. The remaining sample was collected during the trowelling process. The bones collected by screening were usually very small flakes in the 2 mm. to 10 mm. sized class, while the larger fragments (none over 30 mm.) were obtained in trowelling. Approximately 90 percent of the bone was in the smaller size class. All animal bone was calcined and in an extremely poor state of preservation.

Poor preservation limited the identification of most of the bone to the class level, that is, it was identified as fish, turtle, bird or mammal, on the basis of the distinct bone structure of each of these classes. The number of bones in each class is given in Table 10. Only five species were identified, the fresh water drum *(Aplodinotus grunniens)*, the brown bullhead *(Ictalurus nebulosus)*, the yellow perch *(Perca flavescens)*, the muskrat *(Ondatra zibethicus)*, and an intrusive chipmunk *(Tamias striatus)*, Of the total bone recovered 60.7 percent was fish, 22.3 percent was mammal, 9.6 percent was turtle and the remaining 7.4 percent was bird.

TABLE 10

NUMBER AND PERCENT OF THE TOTAL NUMBER OF BONES OF
EACH OF THE FOUR CLASSES OF ANIMALS
RECOVERED FROM THE FEEHELEY SITE,
SAGINAW COUNTY, MICHIGAN

Class	Number of Bones	Percent of Total Number of Bones
Fish	540	60.6
Mammal	199	22.3
Turtle	86	9.7
Bird	66	7.4
Total	891	100.0

The remains of the fresh water drum indicate a size range from individuals less than a half pound to several others that probably were as large as four pounds. The other fish remains were very small and none probably exceeded six inches in length. The bird and mammal bones were also very small and probably came from species of the small to medium rodents and songbird size classes. The only other larger animal was of course the muskrat.

No specific occupation levels were apparent from concentrations of animal bone. As a general rule these species were recovered from all areas and all levels of the site. It is important to note, however, that the areal distribution of animal bone corresponds in all details to the concentration of cultural refuse. Several test pits on the western slope of the site produced neither animal bone nor cultural materials.

The animal remains of the Feeheley site are interesting in several respects. There are, first of all, very few remains and these remains are all from small species. There is a very limited variety of species represented and fish remains are more numerous than are those of mammals. The fact that there are so few food remains is no doubt in part due to poor preservation. There are, however, other probable reasons. The scarcity of animal bone may simply indicate a relatively short occupation. Or, the variety of plant remains recovered may indicate that subsistence was primarily based on the collection of plant foods. The fact that all the bones recovered were from small species is quite interesting, since if any large game had been killed at least a few fragments of larger bone would surely have been preserved. Such is not the case and we can report with assurance that there is no evidence for the exploitation of big game.

The absence of large mammals, particularly deer, could indicate two things: either the site was not occupied for long and no deer were taken during its occupation; or that these people were not hunting deer but were concentrating on the resources of a particular microenvironment. There is support for the latter supposition in the lack of variety of species present and in the fact that fish remains are more numerous than mammal remains. All the species recovered prefer very similar ecological conditions. The brown bullhead is commonly found in deeper waters of weedy shallows; the drum occurs in the shallow waters of lakes, ponds and streams where it is a bottom dweller and prefers turbid conditions. Yellow perch, of the size recovered, are usually found in shallow water of shore areas. The muskrat requires shallow water with marsh vegetation, and turtles are also usually associated with moist or wet habitats. It seems to be apparent, therefore, that the occupants of the Feeheley site were exploiting the resources of a very local area and that these resources were from the shallow water marshes which surrounded the site when it was occupied. It is a moot question as to whether they were living on the site to exploit these resources or whether these resources were exploited because they were readily available in that area.

In additon to the animal bone, several species of terrestrial gastropods were recovered from the site and were identified by Barry Miller of the Museum of Paleontology of the University of Michigan Museums. These species were identified as *Polygyra albolabris*, ten individuals, *Zonitoides arborea*, one individual, and *Helicodiscus parallelus*, two individuals. In addition, five shells were identifiable only as *Polygyra* (Table 11). All these land snail are common in the area today. Fourteen of the eighteen specimen

TABLE 11

TERRESTRIAL GASTROPODS FROM THE FEEHELEY SITE

Species	Number of Shells	Excavation Unit	Depth in Feet from Surface
Helicodiscus parallelus	1	50-275	2.0
	1	60-110	4.6
Zonitoides arborea	1	60-110	4.6
Polygyra albolabris	1	10-305	0-1.4
	1	70-130	.4-1.0
	1	70-130	1.0-2.2
	1	80-80	1.6
	1	70-120	1.6-2.0
	1	65-125	2.5
	1	90-140	2.5
	2	40-350	3.6-3.8
	1	60-110	4.6
Polygyra	1	60-150	0- .7
	1	60-110	0-1.1
	1	70-120	1.6-2.0
	1	90-110	2.5
	1	60-110	2.6

were recovered from the general burial area of the site and although none were associated directly with the burials some were apparently associated with refuse pits. They occur here probably not as food remains but as a result of their propensity for areas containing organic debris. Although all these species exhibit a wide habitat preference, Ruthven (1911:142-148) records these species as occurring together in three of the many habitats he studied--drywood, wood flats and on the borders of lakes and swamps. Only in the last habitat were Polygyrids more abundant than *Zonitoides* or *Helicodiscus* and at the Feeheley site the Polygyrids compose 83 percent of the gastropods recovered (Table 11). Thus as with other animal species the gastropods indicate wet marshy conditions at the time of the site's occupation.

In summary, the Feeheley site was a short term, summer occupation and burial site on the shores of an extensive swamp. The people who occupied the site were primarily gatherers who also apparently spent some time fishing for small shallow water species. The small size of the fish remains indicates the use of a tight meshed seine. Birds, turtles and small mammals were also exploited but there is no indication of big game hunting.

The Hart Site

The Hart site (Wright and Morlan 1964:49-53) is located in James Township of Saginaw County. This "Dustin Lamoka" occupation took place on a sand beach which has a geological history similar to that described for the Feeheley site. Although the temporal position of this site has not been precisely determined, it is probably somewhat later in the post-Nipissing, pre-Algoma sequence than the Feeheley site. Perhaps a guess date of 1500 B.C. would be fairly accurate. The food remains from the Hart site are not unlike those of Feeheley and in fact Wright and Morlan have called it a summer fishing camp. Identified species include only drumfish *(Aplodinotus grunniens)* but the identification of bone fragments to class indicates a high frequency of fish bone (Table 12). As at the Feeheley site, no bone was derived from mammals larger than a muskrat. The subsistence activities of these two sites seem to be identical.

The Schmidt Site

The Schmidt site, located in Section 19 of Bridgeport Township, Saginaw County, Michigan, yielded a cultural assemblage like that of the Hart site but differs from both the Feeheley and Hart sites in the subsistence activity.

TABLE 12

COMPARISON OF THE FREQUENCY OF CLASSES OF ANIMAL BONE
AT THE FEEHELEY, HART AND SCHMIDT SITES,
SAGINAW COUNTY, MICHIGAN

	Feeheley		Hart*		Schmidt	
	Number	Percent	Number	Percent	Number	Percent
Mammal	199	22.3	22	21.2	4,576	79.3
Bird	66	7.4	1	0.9	1,003	17.4
Turtles	86	9.6	14	13.5	192	3.2
Fish	540	60.7	67	64.4	3.0	.1
Total	891	100.0	104	100.0	5,774.0	100.0

*Corrected for unidentifiable bone after Wright and Morlan (1964:52)

The animal bone sample from the Schmidt site consisted of 5,774 very small calcined bone fragments. Only 271 fragments could be identified to genera or species. All the bone, however, was identified as to class on the basis of bone structure. Seventy-nine percent of the total sample was mammal bone, 17.4 percent was bird, .1 percent was reptilian and 3.1 percent was fish.

Remains of 4 species of mammal, 8 bird, 2 reptile and 11 fish species were identified. Of the mammals, deer were the most important food species. Table 13 shows that this species provided 77.4 percent of the total amount of meat represented by the animal remains of the site. Of the remaining 22.6 percent of the meat, other mammals represent 5.7 percent, fowl represent 5.5 percent, reptiles 2.4 percent and fish apporximately 9 percent. This evidence indicates that mammals and particularly deer were by far the most important source of animal food.

The Schmidt site faunal assemblage is overwhelmingly dominated by animal species which are closely associated with the aquatic habitat. In fact, of the 26 identified species, only the deer and dog are not aquatically oriented. The obvious implication is that the Schmidt site was located near a body of water.

It is possible to discover some of the salient features of this body of water by examining the habitat preferences of the fish which occupied it. The most frequent fish remains were those of the bowfin *(Amia calva)*. This fish prefers clear water with an abundance of rooted aquatic vegetation. It avoids habitually turbid water with clayey silt (Trautman 1957). Small members of the catfish family were also common and these are probably the remains of the northern yellow bullhead *(Ictalurus*

TABLE 13

AMOUNTS OF MEAT IN POUNDS FROM THE DIFFERENT SPECIES
FOUND AT THE SCHMIDT SITE, SAGINAW COUNTY, MICHIGAN

Species	Number of Bones	Per-cent	Minimum Number of Individuals	Pounds of Usable Meat	Per-cent
Deer	60	22.1	12	1,020	77.4
Dog	3	1.1	3	45	3.4
Raccoon	1	0.4	1	17.5	1.4
Muskrat	8	2.9	6	12.6	0.9
Canid	1	0.4	1		
TOTAL MAMMAL	73	26.9	23	1,095.1	83.1
Hooded mer-ganser	25	9.3	16	33.6	2.5
Blue and/or green wing teal	49	18.2	26	18.2	1.4
Baldpate	20	7.5	10	10.5	0.8
Pintail	3	1.1	2	2.8	
Ruddy duck	4	1.5	4	2.8	
Wood duck	2	0.7	2	2.1	0.8
American coot	1	0.4	1	0.7	
Common mallard	1	0.4	1	1.75	
Anas spp.	1	0.4	1		
TOTAL BIRD	106	39.1	63	72.45	5.5
Soft shell turtle	2	0.7	2	20	1.6
Snapping turtle	1	0.4	1	10	0.8
TOTAL TURTLE	3	1.1	3	30	2.4
Sturgeon	1	0.4	1	36	2.7
Drum	9	3.3	7	20.7	1.6
Walleye	4	1.5	3	19.2	1.5
Largemouth bass	7	2.6	6	14.4	1.1
Bowfin	25	9.3	8	14	1.0
Channel catfish	3	1.1	3	9.6	0.7
Longnose gar	1	0.4	1	3.2	
Yellow perch	3	1.1	3	1.2	0.4
Northern yellow bullhead	1	0.4	1	0.4	
Catfish	31	12.6	13		
Bass	4	1.5	3		
TOTAL FISH	89	32.9	49	118.7	9.0
COMBINED TOTAL	271	100.0	138	1,316.25	100.0

natalis). This fish prefers ponds, lakes or streams where the gradient is basic or low, the water is clear and aquatic vegetation is profuse. The next most frequent fish species is the largemouth bass *(Micropterus salmoides)*. Unlike the smallmouth bass, the largemouth prefers nonflowing waters with much aquatic vegetation but where the water is clear (Trautman 1957). In fact, all the fish in the Schmidt site assemblage prefer shallow, clear water with an abundance of aquatic plants. Most avoid situations where there is current, silty water or a muddy bottom.

The presence of the remains of a large number of migratory water birds at the Schmidt site gives us some evidence for determining the season of occupation. The teal *(Anas carolinensis* or *discors)*, the bird most frequently represented, is a summer resident in the Schmidt site locality. The hooded merganser *(Lopnodytes cucullatus)* is a year-round resident of the area. All other less common bird species are summer residents except the baldpate or American widgeon *(Mareca americana)*. The latter species is a spring and fall visitant to the area. These bird remains indicate that the Schmidt site was occupied during at least the late summer and fall seasons. Thus, the fauna from the Schmidt site indicates that the Archaic peoples who occupied it were camped near a shallow weedy pond or small lake during the warmer months of the year.

The economy of these people seems to have had a wide base, to judge from the large number of fish, bird and animal species present. However, the hunting of deer and fowling were the major subsistence activities. Deer were the preferred game species and may have been hunted at some distance from the site. Aquatic species which occurred in close proximity to the site served as a handy supplementary food source.

While all three of these Late Archaic sites were located near the shallow post-Nipissing Saginaw embayment and the people of all three sites were exploiting the resources of this embayment, the Schmidt site is divergent both in the variety of species utilized and the high frequency of bird and mammal remains (Table 12, p. 114). It is important to note that Late Archaic people of the Saginaw Valley had developed a subsistence pattern which included both specialized fishing sites and hunting camps. It seems likely that fishing and gathering was a summer activity while deer hunting and fowling provided food during the fall and winter months. The Schmidt site is thought to represent a fall and perhaps early winter camp, while the Feeheley and Hart sites are summer fishing stations.

APPENDIX C

ANALYSIS OF THE
ANIMAL REMAINS AT THE SCHULTZ SITE,
SAGINAW COUNTY, MICHIGAN

The Schultz site is located in Saginaw County, Michigan on the north bank of the Tittabawassee River immediately above its junction with the Saginaw River. This large stratified site was occupied intermittently over a period of approximately 2000 years by people with Early, Middle and Late Woodland cultures. Since these occupations took place on natural levees and backswamps formed by the river, the progressive deposition of alluvial soils has expanded the vertical distribution of cultural material in such a way as to permit its recovery in discrete geological and cultural units.

Fortunately, the preservation of organic materials has been excellent in these alluvial soils, so that archaeological excavations by the University of Michigan Museum of Anthropology in 1962, 1963 and 1964 recovered large quantities of bone and plant refuse. Fitting (n.d.) gives the following brief summary of the archaeology of this important site.

To briefly summarize the stratigraphy, we have four major depositional layers. The lowest represents a lacustrine deposit. This is overlain by three major culture bearing horizons, each with two or more subdivisions. The earliest major cultural horizon is an Early Woodland living floor with many sherds of Marion thick pottery and distinctive stemmed projectile points and ovate bifaces. Overlying this is a horizon which contains Havana-like ceramics. This gives way, with ceramic overlap between geologically distinct levels, to a horizon which is predominantly Havanna but contains Hopewell and Baehr-like ceramics. The lithic sequence is quite continuous with side notched points of the larger size giving way to smaller forms through time. Sub-triangular bifaces are popular in the early Havanna levels replacing the ovate bifaces of the Early Woodland level but they tend to disappear through time.

The Late Woodland horizons are also geologically distinct and contain ceramics which resemble those of southeastern Michigan and adjacent Ontario.

The Saginaw Valley lies well within the Carolinian-Canadian Transition zone. It presently receives about 28 inches of

117

precipitation per year while the average January temperature is between 70 and 71 degrees Fahrenheit. This area is well suited to agriculture since it has slightly more than 160 frost-free growing days each year (Senninger 1964:5-8). The original forest cover (Hudgins 1961:60), was composed of mixed hardwoods on well drained higher ground, cedar, balsam, and tamarack in the low poorly drained areas and open expanses of marsh and wet prairie. The latter formations were probably of particular importance in the low lying areas near the confluences of the Shiawassee, Tittabawassee, Cass, Flint and Bad Rivers south and southeast of the city of Saginaw. Here these rivers enter a low flood plain ten miles in diameter known as the Shiawassee Flats. The elevation of the Shiawassee Flats is 590 feet above sea level or only about five feet above Saginaw Bay. Water from the Saginaw Valley discharges into the bay by way of the Saginaw River. Before modern drainage projects, the Shiawassee Flats area was marsh land and was probably open to human occupation only on natural river levees and on sand ridges produced by the beaches of former high lake levels. Wright (n.d.) concludes that the Schultz site occupations took place on a stabilized natural levee whose elevation is 587 feet. Cultural material was deposited on the crest of the levee and along its back slope. The site was thus located between the Tittabawassee River and a low swampy area behind the levee produced by seasonal floodwater which periodically swamped the levee.

The remains of forty-nine animal species were recovered from the eight occupation strata at the Schultz site. These include sixteen mammals, eleven birds, three turtles and twenty species of fish. These species are listed in Table 14. Table 15 is a more detailed stratigraphic record of the provenience of these species showing their order of appearance in the deposit. Because Table 1 records only those species which could be assigned to one of the recognized stratigraphic units, and because it was necessary to omit certain unassignable provenience units, there has been a reduction in both the numbers of species and frequency of species which could be assigned to these units.

Mammals

The mammals from the Schultz site fall within several habitat types. The largest group includes those closely associated with an aquatic habitat including muskrat, beaver, otter, mink, the bog lemming, meadow vole, and the raccoon. These species all frequent locations with open water or damp conditions, as along stream and river banks. The provenience of the mink, bog lemming and mea-

TABLE 14

FREQUENCY OF OCCURRENCE OF ANIMAL SPECIES FROM THE SCHULTZ SITE, SAGINAW COUNTY, MICHIGAN

Common Name	Scientific Name	Provenience Units												Total			
		20x20B		20x20C		500E600		510E500		Trench 6		Trench 7		Total			
		Number of Bones	Number of Individuals	Number of Bones	Number of Individuals	Number of Bones	Number of Individuals	Number of Bones	Number of Individuals	Number of Bones	Number of Individuals	Number of Bones	Number of Individuals	Number of Bones	Percent of Total Mammals	Number of Individuals	Percent of Combined Total
Deer	Odocoileus virginianus	161	22	56	11	21	9	26	6	288	21	67	10	619	40.1	79	4.9
Muskrat	Ondatra zibethicus	122	42	48	16	19	9	12	9	248	40	8	6	457	29.6	122	7.5
Beaver	Castor canadensis	69	23	18	14	8	5	12	9	37	14	2	2	146	9.5	67	4.1
Raccoon	Procyon lotor	7	6	3	3			2	2	23	11			35	2.3	22	1.3
Bear	Ursus americanus	18	15	2	2	1	1	3	3	11	6			35	2.3	27	1.6
Dog	Canis familiaris	5	5	3	3					16	9	3	3	27	1.78	20	1.2
Elk	Cervus canadensis	5	3	1	1	2	1	1	1	4	4	3	3	16	1.03	13	.8
Otter	Lutra canadensis	1	1	1	1	2	2	1	1	4	4	1	1	10	0.6	10	.6
Meadow vole	Microtus spp.	171	20											171	11.1	20	1.2
Marten	Martes americana	1	1							2	2			3	0.2	3	.18
Woodchuck	Marmota monax	1	1							1	1			2	0.1	2	.12
Fisher	Martes pennanti				1					6	3			7	0.5	4	.24
Mink	Mustela vison									4	3			4	0.4	3	.18
Southern bog lemming	Synaptomys cooperi	5	2											5	0.3	2	.12
Skunk	Mephitis mephitis									2	2			2	0.1	2	.12
Carnivore		1	1											1	0.06	1	.06
Deer mouse	Peromyscus spp.	2	1											2	0.1	1	.06
Total		569	143	133	52	53	27	57	31	646	120	84	25	1,542		299	24.28

TABLE 14 (Continued)

Common Name	Scientific Name	20x20B Number of Bones	20x20B Number of Individuals	20x20C Number of Bones	20x20C Number of Individuals	500E600 Number of Bones	500E600 Number of Individuals	510E500 Number of Bones	510E500 Number of Individuals	Trench 6 Number of Bones	Trench 6 Number of Individuals	Trench 7 Number of Bones	Trench 7 Number of Individuals	Total Number of Bones	Total Percent of Total Birds	Total Number of Individuals	Total Percent of Combined Total
Common mallard	*Anas platyrhynchos*	2	2							4	4	1	1	7	23.3	7	.43
Common loon	*Gavia immer*			1	1					5	5			6	20	6	.37
Whistling swan	*Olor columbianus*									4	4			4	13.3	4	.24
Hooded merganser	*Lophydytes cucullatus*	2	1							2	2			4	13.3	3	.18
Blue winged teal	*Anas discors*									1	1			1	3.3	1	.06
Great blue heron	*Ardea herodias*									1	1			1	3.3	1	.06
American bittern	*Botaurus lentiginosus*	1	1							1	1			2	6.7	2	.12
Crane	Gruiformes									1	1			1	3.3	1	.06
Common crow	*Corvus brachyrhynchos*	1	1											1	3.3	1	.06
Canadian goose	*Branta canadensis*											1	1	1	3.3	1	.06
Passenger pigeon	*Ectopistes migratorius*					2	2							2	6.7	2	.12
Total		6	5	1	1	2	2			19	19	2	2	30		29	1.76

TABLE 14 (Continued)

Common Name	Scientific Name	20x20B Number of Bones	20x20B Number of Individuals	20x20C Number of Bones	20x20C Number of Individuals	500E600 Number of Bones	500E600 Number of Individuals	510E500 Number of Bones	510E500 Number of Individuals	Trench 6 Number of Bones	Trench 6 Number of Individuals	Trench 7 Number of Bones	Trench 7 Number of Individuals	Total Number of Bones	Total Percent of Total	Total Number of Individuals	Total Percent of Combined Total
Spiny soft Shell turtle	*Trionyx ferox*	2	2	8	2					21	8			31	62	12	.73
Snapping turtle	*Chelydra serpentina*	1	1							15	6	1	1	17	34	8	.49
Blanding's turtle	*Emys blandingi*			1	1					1	1			2	4	2	.12
Total		3	3	9	3					37	15	1	1	50		22	1.34
Walleye	*Stizostedion vitreum*	397	101	37	14	122	41	48	25	2,164	382	44	19	2,812	55.1	582	35.6
Sturgeon	*Acipenser fulvescens*	198	22	15	6	68	22	34	18	476	34	23	10	814	15.9	112	6.8
Channel catfish	*Ictalurus punctatus*	41	17	14	7	23	9	2	2	121	36	15	7	216	4.2	78	4.8
Northern black bullhead or Northern yellow bullhead	*Ictalurus melas or natalis*	3	2			2	2	1	1	124	45			130	2.5	50	3.1
Bowfin	*Amia calva*	20	6	1	1	1	1	1	1	96	28	3	3	121	2.4	39	2.4
Longnose gar	*Lepisosteus osseus*	4	3	1	1	1	1	1	1	98	14	1	1	106	2.1	21	1.3
Northern pike	*Esox lucius*	1	1					1	1	37	15			39	0.8	17	1.0
Smallmouth bass	*Micropterus dolomieui*	1	1							20	10			21	0.4	11	.67

Provenience Units

TABLE 14--Continued

Common Name	Scientific Name	20x20B		20x20C		500E600		510E500		Trench 6		Trench 7		Total			Total	
		Number of Bones	Number of Individuals	Number of Bones	Number of Individuals	Number of Bones	Number of Individuals	Number of Bones	Number of Individuals	Number of Bones	Number of Individuals	Number of Bones	Number of Individuals	Number of Bones	Percent of Total Fish	Number of Individuals	Percent of Combined Total
Largemouth bass	*Micropterus salmoides*	1	1							20	9			21	0.4	10	.61
White bass	*Roccus chrysops*									3	3			3	0.06	3	.18
Rock bass	*Ambloplites rupestris*									1	1			1	0.02	1	.06
Shorthead redhorse	*Moxostoma aureolum*									9	4			9	0.2	4	.24
Silver red-horse sucker	*Moxostoma anisurum*					2	2	1	1					3	0.06	3	.18
Golden red-horse sucker	*Moxostoma erythrurum*									1	1			1	0.02	1	.06
Longnose sucker	*Catostomus catostomus*					3	1			1	1			4	0.08	2	.12
Common white sucker	*Catostomus commersoni*							1	1					1	0.02	1	.06
Sucker	*Moxostoma* spp.	1	1			3	1			19	9			23	0.5	11	.67
Yellow perch	*Perca flavenescens*							1	1	1	1			2	0.04	2	.12
Drum	*Aplodinotus grunniens*	80	49	49	28	31	14	25	18	538	120	47	4	770	15.1	233	14.2
Lake trout	*Salvelinus namaycush*			1	1									1	0.02	1	.06
Catfish	*Ictalurus* spp.					2	2	4	4					6	0.12	6	.37
Total		747	204	118	58	258	96	119	73	3,732	713	133	44	5,107		1,188	72.6
Combined Total		1,326	339	260	113	313	125	176	104	4,435	968	220	72	6,726		1,637	99.98

TABLE 15

THE ORDER OF APPEARANCE OF ANIMAL SPECIES IN THE SCHULTZ SITE HORIZONS PRESENTED IN THE FREQUENCY OF BONE REPRESENTING EACH SPECIES

| Species | Early Woodland | | | Middle Woodland | | | Late Woodland | | Total | Per- |
	IIb	IIc	IId	IIIa	IIIb	IVa	IVb	IVc	Bones	cent
Deer	13	39	4	73	76	18	11	3	237	15.8
Beaver	6	2		33	8	6	1	4	60	4.0
Muskrat	1	13	2	88	16	2	16		138	9.2
Channel catfish	3	3		34	18	14	7		79	5.2
Northern pike	1					1			2	.1
Drum	1	2	2	27	7	16	10	4	69	4.5
Bear		2		6	1	1	2		12	.8
Raccoon		1		5		1			7	.5
Dog		1		3	3				7	.5
Fisher		1							1	.1
Marten		1							1	.1
Mallard		1		1	1				3	.2
Walleye		26	2	305	87	42	74	2	538	36.1
Sturgeon		6	2	156	38	24	38	3	267	18.0
Bowfin		3		17	3	1			24	1.6
Elk				1	3			1	5	.3
Otter				2	1	1			4	.3
Woodchuck				1					1	.1
Hooded merganser				1					1	.1
American bittern				1					1	.1
Crow				1					1	.1
Loon				1					1	.1
Snapping turtle				1	3				4	.3
Soft shell turtle				1					1	.1

TABLE 15--Continued

Species	Early Woodland			Middle Woodland			Late Woodland		Total	Per-
	IIb	IIc	IId	IIIa	IIIb	IVa	IVb	IVc	Bones	cent
Northern black bullhead or Northern yellow bullhead				2		1	1		4	0.3
Lake trout				1					1	0.1
Longnose gar				4	1				6	0.4
Largemouth bass				1					1	0.1
Smallmouth bass				1					1	0.1
Northern red-horse				1		1	1		3	0.2
Passenger pigeon					1	1			2	0.1
Canada goose					1				1	0.1
Silver redhorse sucker					1				1	0.1
Yellow perch					1				1	0.1
White sucker						1			1	0.1
Longnosed sucker									1	0.1
Total	25	101	12	768	270	132	162	17	1,487	
Percent	1.7	6.8	0.8	51.6	18.2	8.9	10.9	1.1		100.0

dow vole is undetermined. The raccoon appears in the Early and Middle Woodland horizons, otter appears only in Middle Woodland context, while beaver and muskrat appear throughout the deposit.

Another group of mammals prefer mature forest habitats. These include black bear, fisher, deer mouse, and the marten. The bear has a wide distribution within both deciduous and conifer forests and is infrequently found in other habitat types, while the fisher and marten are seldom encountered far from mature conifer forests. The bear, fisher and marten all appear in the Early Woodland horizon; the fisher and marten do not appear in other contexts.

Finally, there is a group of mammals which prefers open woodland with low brush and some clearings. These include deer, elk, woodchuck and striped skunk. The provenience of the striped skunk is undetermined, the deer occurs throughout the deposit woodchuck occurs in Middle Woodland context while elk come from both Middle and Late Woodland horizons.

Considering the fact that some 1,500 mammal bones were identified from the Schultz site, it is remarkable that so few as sixteen species were recovered. If the three rodent species, which may be intrusive, and the dog are subtracted from the total, then these 1,500 bones represent only 12 species. This lack of variety can only be explained by hunting selectivity. The list of mammal species which were surely present in the Saginaw Valley at this time, but do not appear in the Schultz sequence, is a long one and includes many smaller rodents, weasels, foxes, the wolf, bobcat, mountain lion, squirrels, and the cottontail rabbit.

The habitat preference of the several mammal species points to a mature forest on or near the site during the Early Woodland period. This is indicated by the presence of bear, raccoon, fisher and marten. The latter two species are definitely northern in distribution and may indicate that the climate was cooler during the Early Woodland phase at about 500 B.C. The appearance of open woodland species such as the elk and woodchuck in the Middle and Late Woodland horizons indicates a change in forest cover, perhaps a clearing of forest in conjunction with agricultural activities. This sequence of forest types is also hypothesized by Brose (n.d.) who studied the mollusca of the Schultz site. Brose reports a sharp decline in the percentage of molluscan species which occur in original timber and woodland clearing during the time of the Middle Woodland occupation (levels IIIa, IIIb, IVa). These species decline while those species which occur near large rivers and inland lakes increase. This situation raises the possibility that the change in forest cover at this time may not be result of clearing by fire but the result of thinning of the forests due to extensive and repeated flooding of the alluvial valley.

Birds

The remains of eleven species of birds were identified from all of the Schultz deposits. These species were represented by only 30 identified bones. With the exception of the crow and passenger pigeon, all species are aquatic. The crow occupies a wide range of habitats and the passenger pigeon formerly occurred in great numbers in mature, deciduous forests. The crow, loon, and hooded merganser, and occasionally the mallard and Canada goose, winter in the Saginaw Valley area. The whistling swan, blue winged teal, great blue heron, American bittern and passenger pigeon are only summer visitants. We can see from Table 15 that at least th Middle Woodland occupations must have taken place during the warmer months of the year.

Not only are there few species of birds from the Schultz site, but there are also very few bird bones. This infrequency is not a result of differential preservation since bird bone was well preserved and since fish bone which is more delicate was preserved in great quantity. The lack of bird remains is especially noticeable in the Early Woodland deposits, a fact which suggests a placement of these horizons in a winter context.

Reptiles are represented by three species: the soft shell turtle, the snapping turtle and Blanding's turtle. All occurred infrequently and only the latter two species could be assigned stratigraphic provenience, i.e., Middle Woodland. These species are aquatic and all occur in the Saginaw River today. Since turtles are available only during the warm months of the year, they are indicative of a summer occupation.

Fish

Unlike the other classes of vertebrates, the fish appear in great variety and abundance. Twenty species represented by 5,107 identified bones were recovered from the Schultz site. The fish fauna is typically riverine as would be expected from the location of the site on the Tittabawassee River. Although this river presently has a slow to base current with a silt and muck bottom and carries a great deal of suspended silt and organic material, the habitat preference of the fish species from the Schultz site indicates that the river had different characteristics in the aboriginal period. While most, if not all the species recovered prefer shallow and slow or non-flowing water, it is also true that most avoid waters with muck bottoms and a lot of suspended material. A great many of these species also prefer an abundance of rooted aquatic vegetation. The catfish, bowfin, perch, northern pike, gar, and largemouth bass can be included in this category. Other species such as the suckers, sturgeon, walleye, drum, and smallmouth bass prefer situations with few aquatic weeds. Many of the species from the Schultz site including the sturgeon, walleye, channel catfish, suckers and yellow perch are essentially lake fish which ascend large rivers in the spring to spawn. In most instances, spawning takes place in shallow flooded areas during the spring and early summer, late March to early June. The abundance of spawning walleyes is recorded in "Personal Reminiscences" by Ephraim S. Williams (M.P.H.C., 1886:256), an early settler who lived in Saginaw from 1828 to 1840.

In the spring of the year, in high water, the ice being gone, the walleyed pike would run up the Saginaw in great numbers, running on to the Saginaw in great numbers, running on to the Shiawassee meadows which were over-flowed for miles from three to six feet deep. One beautiful, warm spring morning, Major William Mosely and myself purposed to go up the Shiawassee River about four miles and have a little sport, spearing in the evening by torch light. I took a large canoe, one man, our lunch basket, blankets, etc., expecting to stay overnight. Arriving at the Indian Camps, the water for miles was like a mirror in the hot sun. We went out a short time and found the water alive with fish. We speared a good many, with much sport. The Indians purposed if I would buy fish, they would all go out and spear enough to fill our canoes. I agreed to do so, and in an hour or two, they came in alongside my canoe. I would count the fish, taking each Indian's name and number of fish in a pass book. We loaded our canoe, and I engaged two others, loaded all and got home before dark, when we set men to work cleaning and packing for market. Next morning, the result of our days sport was thirty barrels, then worth and sold for five dollars per barrel. These fish were in schools and the water was black with them. An Indian stood in the bow with a spear, while one in the stern would hold the canoe still on one of these schools, and the spearman would fill his canoe, often brigning in 3 or 4 fish at a time, averaging from three to six and eight pounds each.

Those species which were most numerous at the Schultz site deposit are those which apparently ascended the Saginaw River to spawn. These are lake fish which prefer clean, cool, weed-free water. Other species seem to be those which prefer clean, slow moving or quiet water with an abundance of aquatic vegetation. The habitat preferences of the fish in the latter category seem to accurately reflect the aboriginal condition of the Tittabawassee River.

The Schultz site bone sample consited of 86,242 bone fragments. Of this total, 21.4 percent were mammal, 0.2 percent
bird, 0.9 percent reptiles, and 77.4 percent were fish (Table 16).
These identifications were made on the basis of bone structure.
Fifteen thousand three-hundred sixty nine bones from the total
sample were assignable to stratigraphic units of the site, of these
6,730 bones were identifiable to species. Of the total identified
bones, 22.9 percent were mammal, 0.5 percent were bird, 0.7
percent were reptile, and 75.9 percent were fish. These percentages come extremely close to the original percentages of
mammal, bird, reptile, and fish bone and thus lend a great deal
of confidence in the accuracy obtained in evaluating these species
as food sources.

When the amount of meat provided by the identified animal
bone at the Schultz site was calculated, the results were not consistent with the original percentages. Of 35,046.9 pounds of meat
represented by the sample, 76.8 percent was mammal, 0.3 percent bird, 0.2 percent reptiles, and 22.7 percent fish. These differences are, of course, simply due to the fact that the average
mammal weighs more than the average fish (Table 17). These
results however are consistent with the percentages obtained for
pounds of meat represented by each class in the stratigraphic
computations. Table 18 shows a total of 13,690.3 pounds of meat
of which 79.5 percent is from mammals and 20.5 percent from
fish, birds and turtles having been dropped as insignificant.

When the percentages of meat obtained from mammal and
fish are plotted by stratigraphic units, an interesting change in
the importance of these meat sources can be noted through time
(Figure 3). Mammals are, in all periods, the most important
source of meat During the earliest occupation of the site, fish
were of little importance in the total economy, but during the
late Early Woodland period, they began to increase in importance.
This trend continued through the late Middle Woodland period. In
the Late Woodland horizons, there is a slight upsurge in the importance of mammals, but this trend does not reach an intensity
equal to the Early Woodland period. While there is no way of
evaluating the importance of plant foods and therefore the importance of meat in the total diet, the decreased importance of
hunting in the Middle and Late Woodland horizons is likely the
result of an economy which utilized more wild or domestic plant
foods. In other words, after the Early Woodland period, hunting
was given up as a subsistence specialty and became a secondary
subsistence activity. On the other hand, fishing, which was of

TABLE 16

FREQUENCY OF IDENTIFIED AND UNIDENTIFIED BONE FROM SIX
PROVENIENCE UNITS OF THE SCHULTZ SITE, SAGINAW COUNTY, MICHIGAN

| | Unidentified | | | | | | | | Identified | | | | | | | | Total | |
| | Mammal | | Bird | | Turtle | | Fish | | Mammal | | Bird | | Turtle | | Fish | | | |
Provenience Units	Number of Bones	Percent of Total	Number of Bones	Percent of Total	Number of Bones	Percent of Total	Number of Bones	Percent of Total	Number of Bones	Percent of Total	Number of Bones	Percent of Total	Number of Bones	Percent of Total	Number of Bones	Percent of Total	Combined Total	Percent
20 x 20 B	4,441	5.1	30	0.03	161	0.2	3,822	4.4	570	0.7	6	0.007	3	0.003	747	0.87	9,780	11.3
20 x 20 C	948	1.1	3	0.003	26	0.03	386	0.4	132	0.15	1	0.001	9	0.01	118	0.1	1,623	1.9
500 E 600	1,623	1.9	25	0.028	88	0.1	2,849	3.3	53	0.06	2	0.002			258	0.3	4,898	5.7
510 E 500	1,491	1.7	38	0.04	58	0.07	1,116	1.3	57	0.07					119	0.1	2,879	3.3
Trench 6 - Area B	8,036	9.3	107	0.12	381	0.4	53,104	61.6	647	0.75	19	0.022	37	0.04	3,732	4.3	66,063	76.6
Trench 7	354	0.4	3	0.003	46	0.05	376	0.4	84	0.1	2	0.002	1	0.001	133	0.15	999	1.2
Total	16,893	19.6	206	0.240	760	0.90	61,653	71.5	1,543	1.8	30	0.030	50	0.06	5,107	5.90	86,242	100

TABLE 17

TOTAL AMOUNT OF MEAT PRODUCED FROM EACH CLASS OF
ANIMALS AT THE SCHULTZ SITE, SAGINAW COUNTY, MICHIGAN

	Number of Individuals	Total Pounds of Meat	Percent of Total	Average Weight
Mammals	377	26,901.4	76.8	71.4
Birds	29	104.0	0.3	3.6
Turtles	41	60.6	0.2	1.5
Fish	1,165	7,980.9	22.7	6.9
Totals	1,612	35,046.9	100.0	

TABLE 18

MEAT DERIVED FROM MAMMALS AND FISH IN EACH STRATIGRAPHIC LEVEL OF THE SCHULTZ SITE

Species	IIb	IIc	IId	IIIa	IIIb	IVa	IVb	IVc	Total	Percent
Deer	400	700	200	1,400	1,500	500	600	200	5,500	40.2
Beaver	126	315		441	189	126	31.5	63	1,291.5	9.4
Muskrat	2.1	16.8	4.2	56.7	25.2	4.2	10.5		119.7	0.9
Bear		420		1,050	210	210	420		2,310	16.9
Raccoon		17.5		70		17.5			105	0.8
Dog		15		45	45				105	0.8
Fisher		4.9							4.9	.04
Marten		2.1							2.1	.02
Elk				350	700			350	1,400	10.2
Otter				25.2	12.6	25.2			63	0.5
Woodchuck				5.6					5.6	0.04
Total Mammals	528.1	1,491.3	204.2	3,443.5	2,681.8	882.9	1,062	613	10,906.8	79.80

TABLE 18--Continued

Species	IIb	IIc	IId	IIIa	IIIb	IVa	IVb	IVc	Total	Percent
Channel catfish	3.2	9.6		44.8	28.8	16.0	9.6		112.0	0.8
Northern pike	2.4					2.4			4.8	0.4
Drum	2.96	5.92	5.92	68.08	20.72	44.4	29.6	5.92	183.5	1.3
Walleye		78.4	11.2	324.5	207.2	95.2	123.2	5.6	845.3	6.2
Sturgeon		120	24	504	432	216	216	72	1,584	11.6
Bowfin		4.0		8.0	6.0	2.0			20	0.1
Northern black or yellow bullhead				1.0		0.5	0.5		2.0	0.01
Lake trout				14.4					14.4	0.1
Longnose gar				4.8	1.6	1.6			8.0	0.06
Largemouth bass				2.0					2.0	0.01
Smallmouth bass				1.6					1.6	0.01
Northern redhorse				0.4		0.4	0.4		1.2	0.01
Silver redhorse					0.4				0.4	0.00
Yellow Perch					0.4				0.4	0.00
White sucker						1.2			1.2	0.01
Longnose sucker							2.4		2.4	0.02
Total Fish	8.6	217.9	41.1	973.6	697.1	379.7	381.7	83.5	2,783.2	20.27
Combined Total	536.7	1709.2	245.3	4417.1	3378.9	1262.6	1443.7	696.5	13,690.0	100.07

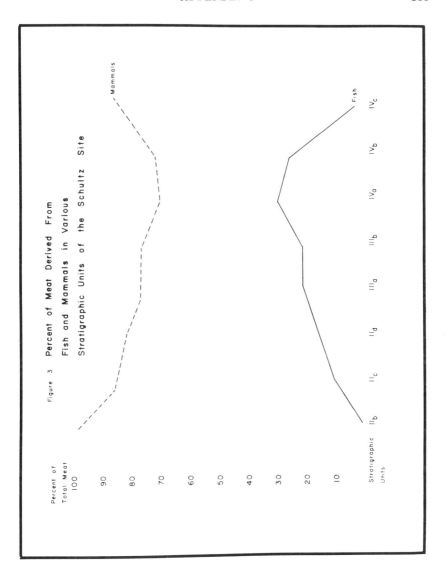

Figure 3   Percent of Meat Derived From Fish and Mammals in Various Stratigraphic Units of the Schultz Site

minimal importance in Early Woodland times, became an important economic pursuit by the Middle and Late Woodland periods.

When we consider the importance of individual species as sources of food (Tables 19 and 20), it is apparent that deer was the most important single game animal. Deer supplied 40 percent of the total meat represented by the Schultz sample, 52 percent in the Early Woodland and 37 percent in both Middle and Late Woodland periods. Other significant mammal food sources include bear, 16.8 percent, elk, 10.2 percent and beaver, 9.4 percent. All bird and reptile species were insignificant, but several fish species were relatively important. Sturgeon represented 11.5 percent of the total meat, and walleye, 6.2 precent of this total. All other fish were insignificant both as individual species and as a group.

It is interesting to note that the meat supplied by small mammals decreases rather markedly through time. These species yielded 20.2 percent of the Early Woodland meat, 11.9 percent of Middle Woodland meat and only 4.5 percent of the Late Woodland meat. This decrease is thought to be a function of increased agricultural activities resulting in more and more specialization in the hunting of large game animals on a seasonal basis. Agricultural Indians hunted these species extensively and apparently did not concern themselves too much with small game.

Using 3,000 calories per day as a minimum caloric intake for an adult male, Hinsdale (1932:9) calculated that a man would require 2.6 pounds of lean meat or 6.7 pounds of fish per day. If we consider that the animal remains from the excavated portions of the Schultz site represent 35,046 pounds of meat, then this amount of food would represent 11,829.4 subsistence days. This estmate is extremely conservative since American Indians could probably survive on a lower caloric intake than the 3,000 calories estimated by Hinsdale and since women and children, who do not require as many calories per day, would also be included in a given population. Probably, less than one-tenth of the Schultz site has been excavated so that a rough figure of 118,290 subsistence days is represented by the meat of this site. Assuming a population density of 100 souls, these people could subsist on this amount of meat for 1,182 days. Of course, we know that the size of occupation must have varied greatly from year to year and season to season and that at least Late Woodland and probably Middle Woodland peoples obtained most of their food from plants. In addition, we know that the Schultz site was occupied from time to time over a period of two thousand years. Such uncontrolled

TABLE 19A

PERCENTAGES OF MEAT REPRESENTED BY THE FAUNAL REMAINS OF THE EARLY WOODLAND HORIZONS AT THE SCHULTZ SITE, SAGINAW COUNTY, MICHIGAN

Species	Number of Bones	Approximate Number of Individuals	Live Weight / Individual	Percent of Usable Meat	Usable Pounds / Individual	Usable Pounds / Species	Percent of Total
Deer	56	13	200	50	100	1,300	52.1
Beaver	29	14	45	70	31.5	441	17.7
Bear	2	2	300	70	210	420	16.8
Raccoon	1	1	25	70	17.5	17.5	
Dog	1	1	30	50	15	15	
Muskrat	16	11	3	70	2.1	23.1	2.5
Marten	1	1	3	70	2.1	2.1	
Fisher	1	1	7	70	4.9	4.9	
Carnivore	1	1					
Total Mammal	108	45				2,223.6	89.1
Common mallard	1	1	2.5	80	2.0	2.0	
Total Bird	1	1				2.0	0.1
Sturgeon	8	6	30	80	24	144	5.8
Walleye	28	16	7	80	5.6	89.6	3.6
Drum	5	5	3.7	80	2.96	14.8	
Channel catfish	6	4	4	80	3.2	12.8	1.4
Bowfin	3	2	2.5	80	2.0	4	
Northern pike	1	1	3.0	80	2.4	2.4	
Total fish	51	34				267.6	10.8
Combined Total	160	80				2,493.2	100.0

TABLE 19B

PERCENTAGES OF MEAT REPRESENTED BY THE FAUNAL REMAINS
OF THE MIDDLE WOODLAND HORIZONS AT THE SCHULTZ SITE,
SAGINAW COUNTY, MICHIGAN

Species	Number of Bones	Approximate Number of Individuals	Live Weight/ Individual	Percent of Usable Meat	Usable Pounds /Individual	Usable Pounds /Species	Percent of Total
Deer	167	34	200	50	100	3,400	37.3
Bear	8	7	300	70	210	1,470	16.2
Elk	4	3	700	50	350	1,050	11.5
Beaver	47	24	45	70	31.5	756	8.3
Raccoon	6	5	25	70	17.5	87.5	
Muskrat	106	41	3	70	2.1	86.1	3.6
Dog	6	6	30	50	15	90	
Otter	5	5	18	70	12.6	63	
Woodchuck	1	1	8	70	5.6	5.6	
Microtus spp.	5	3					
Total Mammal	355	129				7,008.2	76.9
Common mallard	2	2	2.5	80	2.0	4.0	
Passenger pigeon	2	2	1.0	80	0.8	1.6	
Hooded merganser	2	1	3.0	80	2.4	2.4	
Canada goose	1	1	8	80	6.4	6.4	0.3
Common loon	1	1	5	80	4.0	4.0	
American bittern	1	1	6	80	4.8	4.8	
Common crow	1	1	3	80	2.4	2.4	
Total Bird	10	9				25.6	0.3
Snapping turtle	2	2	50	20	10	20	0.3
Soft shell turtle	1	1	50	20	10	10	
Total Turtle	3	3				30	0.3
Sturgeon	214	4	30	80	24	1,152	12.6
Walleye	434	112	7	80	5.6	627.2	6.9
Drum	50	45	3.7	80	2.96	133.2	1.5
Channel catfish	66	28	4	80	3.2	89.6	1.0
Bowfin	21	8	2.5	80	2.0	16.0	
Longnose gar	6	5	2.0	80	1.6	8.0	
Northern black bullhead	2	2	0.5	80	0.4	0.8	0.5
Northern yellow bullhead	1	1	0.75	80	0.6	0.6	
Northern pike	1	1	3.0	80	2.4	2.4	

TABLE 19B--Continued

Species	Number of Bones	Approximate Number of Individuals	Live Weight/ Individual	Percent of Usable Meat	Usable Pounds /Individual	Usable Pounds /Species	Percent of Total
Northern redhorse sucker	2	2	0.5	80	0.4	0.8	
Silver redhorse	1	1	0.5	80	0.4	0.4	
Common white sucker	1	1	1.5	80	1.20	1.2	
Yellow perch	1	1	0.5	80	0.4	0.4	
Lake trout	1	1	18	80	14.4	14.4	
Smallmouth bass	1	1	2.0	80	1.6	1.6	
Largemouth bass	1	1	2.5	80	2.0	2.0	
Sucker	1	1					
Catfish	4	4					
Total Fish	808	219				2,050.6	22.5
Combined Total	1,176	360				9,114.4	100.0

variables make these calculations relatively meaningless—none-the-less they point out the tremendous quantity of food represented by the animal remains.

Seasonal hunting patterns have been noted for most of the Late Woodland cultures of Michigan in the historic period. Kinietz (1940:237) mentions that the Ottawa hunted in the Saginaw Valley every other year where they sought deer, bear, and beaver. The fact that Late Woodland animal remains from the Schultz site rank deer, bear and beaver as the three most frequently occuring species supports this statement. In the winter of 1675-1676, Father Nouvel, S.J., visited the Saginaw Valley on December 2, and proceeded a few miles up the Tittabawassee River where he found a deserted Indian village.

I arrived at the hut-group of the Indians I was looking for, and with whom I was to spend the winter had just left. I saw evidences of the good hunting they had had, the remains of the bears, the deer, and turkeys they had killed, pike and other fish they had caught, that caused our people to rejoice, but I was grieved to see a large dog hanging from the top of a painted pole, which was a sacrifice made to the sun. (Guta 1957:76)

TABLE 19C

PERCENTAGES OF MEAT REPRESENTED BY THE FAUNAL REMAINS
OF THE LATE WOODLAND HORIZONS AT THE SCHULTZ SITE,
SAGINAW COUNTY, MICHIGAN

Species	Number of Bones	Approximate Number of Individuals	Live Weight/ Individual	Percent of Usable Meat	Usable Pounds /Individual	Usable Pounds /Species	Percent of Total
Deer	14	8	200	50	100	800	37.4
Elk	1	1	700	50	350	350	16.4
Bear	2	2	300	70	210	420	19.6
Beaver	5	3	45	70	31.5	94.5 ⎫	
Muskrat	16	5	3	70	2.1	10.5 ⎭	4.9
Total Mammal	38	19				1,675.0	78.3
Sturgeon	41	12	30	80	24	288	13.5
Walleye	76	23	7	80	5.6	128.8	6.0
Drum	14	12	3.7	80	2.96	35.52 ⎫	
Channel catfish	7	3	4	80	3.2	9.6 ⎪	
Catfish spp.	2	2				⎬	2.2
Norther yellow bullhead	1	1	0.75	80	0.6	0.6 ⎪	
Redhorse sucker	3	1				⎪	
Longnose sucker	3	1	3	80	2.4	2.4 ⎭	
Total Fish	147	55				464.92	21.7
Combined Total	185	74				2,139.92	100.0

Hinsdale (1932:30-31) says that the

Saginaw Valley was the most populous part of the state [Michigan].
There have been identified 120 old villages, in addition to other sites
in Saginaw County. Almost 30 percent of all the Indians of Michigan
frequented the counties of Bay, Saginaw, Genesee, Shiawassee and
Tuscola.

The high frequency of archaeological sites in the Saginaw Valley
as well as the frequent mention of the area as a favorite hunting
ground in historic texts leaves little doubt that this place was
favorable for prehistoric man. In fact, the Saginaw Valley was
a favorable place for man because it was also favorable for animals and the cultivation of plant foods.

TABLE 20

PERCENTAGES OF POUNDS OF MEAT REPRESENTED IN THE THREE MAJOR
CULTURAL HORIZONS AT THE SCHULTZ SITE,
SAGINAW COUNTY, MICHIGAN

Species	Early Woodland		Middle Woodland		Late Woodland	
	Pounds	Percent	Pounds	Percent	Pounds	Percent
Deer	1,300	52.1	3,400	37.3	800	37.4
Elk			1,050	11.5	350	16.4
Beaver	441	17.7	756	8.3	94.5	4.4
Bear	420	16.8	1,470	16.2	420	19.6
All other mammals	62.6	2.5	332.2	3.6	10.5	0.5
Sturgeon	144	5.8	1,152	12.6	288	13.5
Walleye	89.6	3.6	627.2	6.9	128.8	6.0
All other fish	34.0	1.3	271.4	3.0	48.12	2.2
All birds	2.0	0.1	25.6	0.3		
All turtles			30	0.3		
Total	2,493.2	100.0	9,114.4	100.0	2,139.92	100.0

Ecologically, the Saginaw Valley lies in the Carolinian-Canadian ecotone and by virtue of this fact, seems to have harbored species of both provinces—the edge effect. In addition, it is an area of diverse habitat types; extensive lowland marshes and wet prairies, pine forests on the numerous sand ridges formed by ancient lakes, extensive upland oak-hickory forests and fine broad alluvial valleys. Each of these habitats offered distinctive resources. All of the resources of all these habitats were available within this one relatively small area. In addition, the Saginaw River and its large tributaries—the Flint, Cass, Shiawassee, and Tittabawassee all converge in the Saginaw Valley. All were filled with fish but especially the walleye and sturgeon which ascended these rivers in great numbers in the spring to spawn. Aside from its fish resources, the wide flood-scoured alluvial valleys of these rivers provided excellent places for primitive agriculture and for gathering wild plant seeds. While the Saginaw Valley is located on the southern margin of the Carolinian-Canadian transition zone, it is nestled within an isothermal pocket where there are 160 frost-free growing days per year. Considering the natural resource of this valley, there is little wonder that aboriginal peoples found it a favorable place to live.

There is very little evidence concerning the method by which the people of the Schultz site hunted game. Drives for deer and elk were employed by most hunters of the northern deciduous woodlands and in the historic period this technique was probably used by the people living at the Schultz site. Both the stalking of individual deer, a southern hunting technique, and the trapping of large game, a northern Algonquin hunting practice, may also have been employed.

More can be said about the techniques used to catch the fish represented at the Schultz site. We, of course, already know from records such as the Williams Reminiscences that historic Indians speared walleye pike during the spring spawning runs. One harpoon fragment from the Schultz site shows that this technique was also employed in the aboriginal period. There is, however, good evidence to suppose that other fishing techniques were being employed. Unlike the hypothesized harpoon fishery at the Juntunen site, where the fish remains were large individuals of the larger species (Appendix E), very small fish are often represented in some horizons at the Schultz site locality. Not only do we find small fish, but the smaller species are well represented along with the medium and large sized species.

Small and medium sized species appear most frequently in Middle Woodland horizons, less frequently in Late Woodland context, but not at all in the Early Woodland period, when fishing was not a major subsistence activity, may partially account for the absence of small species. However, another more reasonable explanation is forthcoming, namely, change in fishing techniques and the importance of fishing through time. It has been mentioned that the peoples of the Early Woodland component at Schultz were primarily hunters, fishing being of secondary importance and geared to the larger varieties of fish. Probably these were speared or harpooned. With the advent of Middle Woodland influence from the south, fish became a more important subsistence item and a new technique was employed to catch them, either nets or weir traps. The use of this technique is indicated by the fact that the fish remains of this horizon more nearly represent a random sample of both the species and sizes of fish which were in the river. When one employs a seine or builds a fish weir, large as well as small fish are caught; these are non-selective fishing techniques. Rostlund (1952:98) is of the opinion that the historic northern distribution of the use of nets as a fishing device indicated a general southward diffusion of this technique from the Canadian subarctic into the Carolinian woodlands where it never became popular. He also points out the temporal precedence and abundance of net sinkers in the archaeological sites of the middle south and speculates that the use of nets once may have been popular in that area but had been lost by the contact period. The use of harpoons is clearly a boreal forest and arctic fishing technique which was also used in the waters of the Canadian province. Harpoons first appeared in a Late Archaic context in the Saginaw Valley and continued to be used as a major piece of fishing gear in that area well into the historic period.

Faunal evidence from the Schultz site indicates that the use of nets was essentially a Middle Woodland characteristic. As such, it may have been a trait of the Middle Woodland riverine adaptation that Struever (1964:87-106) hypothesizes for the Havana traditions of the Illinois Valley. The pottery and other artifacts of the Middle Woodland component at Schultz shows strong and persistent cultural communications with contemporary cultures in the Illinois Valley.

In summary, we are fortunate to be able to make certain deductions about the economy and subsistence techniques of the three cultural horizons represented at the Schultz site. These observations are possible only because of the excellent preservation of animal remains and because these remains have been subjected to painstaking quantitative and qualitative analysis.

EARLY WOODLAND

The Early Woodland component at the Schultz site took place on the crest of a natural levee of the Tittabawassee River and is estimated by Taggart (n.d.) to have covered approximately one half acre. However, a more recent estimate by Fitting (personal communication) is at least ten acres. This occupation has been dated at 500 B.C. (M-1433, 530±120 B.C.; M-1524, 540±130 B.C.; M-1525, 530±150 B.C.).

The habitat preferences of the mammalian species of these occupations indicate that the area was surrounded by a mature forest which may have had a strong conifer element. The appearance of several typically northern species indicates that the climate may have been somewhat cooler than present.

Hunting of large game was the primary subsistence activity of these people and emphasis was placed upon deer as a meat source. Unlike later occupations of the site, Early Woodland peoples did not disregard smaller animal species and as a group these beasts were a fairly important source of protein. Fishing was not very important and those fish which are represented are rather large, indicating the use of harpoons or spears as a fishing technique. Although the faunal sample from this occupation was relatively small, the absence of waterfowl and turtles may indicate that these were winter occupations. Additional evidence presented by Wright (1964) indicates that at least one Early Woodland occupation took place in the fall season. At this season wild nuts were evidently an important subsistence item. In addition, Wright reports the presence of squash seeds signalling at least incipient use of domesticated plants at this time. Nonetheless, the Early Woodland people of the Schultz site would be most accurately described as hunters and gatherers with a diffuse economy.

MIDDLE WOODLAND

The Middle Woodland occupations of the Schultz site are believed to date between 200 B.C. and about A.D. 400 (Fitting, personal communication). During this period people were living on both the old natural levee occupied by Early Woodland groups and the former river channel which was opened for habitation by a shift in the course of the river. Taggert (n.d.) estimated that the size of this occupation approached ten acres and Fitting suggests about sixteen acres.

The appearance of species which prefer open woodland conditions and their persistence in later horizons in addition to the disappearance of species preferring dense forests indicate a change toward a more open forest at this time. It has been suggested that this change may be a local phenomenon associated with either alluvial disturbances on the flood plain or purposeful clearing for agricultural activities. Except for the negative evidence presented by the disappearance of two typically northern species, there is no evidence for hypothesizing a warm climatic phase at this time.

Hunting was again concentrated upon large game and particularly deer and elk. Small game became much less important during these and later occupations. It has been suggested that the hunting of big game may have been a seasonal activity. The appearance of quantities of turtle and migratory waterfowl remains in strata IIIa shows that at least some of the Middle Woodland occupations took place during the summer period, while the great quantity of spring spawning fish in IIIa and IIIb point out occupation during that period.

Fishing was an important subsistence activity for Middle Woodland people and the presence of small as well as large sized fish produced by this activity indicates the use of nets as a new fishing technique. Net fishing is usually a communal enterprise because of the temporary nature of the abundance of fish and the need to cordinate the harvest, preparation and distribution of the catch. Cooperative subsistence activities often require more social and political control than do individualized or family oriented subsistence efforts.

The importance of plant foods cannot be evaluated from the food remains at the Schultz site, but the large size of the Middle Woodland occupations indicates that they did play an important subsistence role. Struever has recently re-emphasized that the closely related Havana tradition sites of the Illinois Valley were adapted to a riverine environment and this would be an accurate description of the adaptation of the Middle Woodland cultures of the Schultz site. Speculating on the data presented in this study, we can project the following subsistence and settlement patterns. Middle Woodland people who occupied this site lived in a large and fairly permanent village. During the early spring and summer, they fished in the river and subsisted primarily upon their catch through the early summer. Local hunting, fishing, collecting berries, and perhaps planting crops occupied these people during the summer. In late summer and fall, plant foods probably became the main source of food, especially the seeds of wild plants which grew on the flood plain of the river. Nuts and perhaps a few crop plants may have also been important. During the winter, these people probably lived on stored vegetable foods and meat obtained from the winter big game hunts. There is a good possibility that some people left the village during the winter to hunt in other localities. With spring, people returned to the site for the fishing season.

LATE WOODLAND

The Late Woodland occupation of the site was probably nearly as large as the one of the Middle Woodland period. Age estimations place this occupation at about A.D. 400 to A.D. 900.

Mammals which appear with these occupations point to a rather open forest habitat near the site. Big game hunting, particularly deer, elk and bear, supplied most of the meat. The hunting of small game became even less important than during Middle Woodland times, but reliance on larger species undergoes a slight increase at the expense of fishing. Even though fishing seems to be less important, the appearance of some small fish implies continued use of nets or weir traps. We know from historic sources, that the Late Woodland Indians of the Saginaw Valley used spears to take fish and also that they were agricultural people. The increase in the quantity of big game associated with a drop in small game and fishing is probably closely related to an agricultural way of life. Here again, we find the use of fish and products of the hunt to be supplemental to the diet instead of a staple resource.

Reconstructing, from both historic reports and the faunal remains from the Schultz site, the yearly subsistence round of Late Woodland peoples in the Saginaw Valley was something as follows. These peoples lived in rather large villages on the banks of rivers during the spring and summer season where they fished, hunted and planted their crops. After the fall harvest, the village broke up into small family groups and each group went into the interior where they established small winter hunting camps. In these camps people lived on stored plant foods and game animals. In the spring, families returned to the Saginaw Valley in time for the fish runs and the planting of crops.

FAUNAL REMAINS FROM THE
MERO AND HEINS CREEK SITES,
DOOR COUNTY, WISCONSIN

The Mero Site

The Mero site, located in Door County, Wisconsin, is a multicomponent site which was occupied by Middle and Late Woodland peoples. The fauna sample of 822 bones was recovered from stratified area III. The lower and intermediate middens of this area are short, late Middle Woodland occupation by people of the North Bay culture, while the upper midden represents occupations by Late Woodland people who were being influenced by Mississippian culture. The North Bay occupation at Mero is very similar to the one at the Porte des Morts site which has been dated at A.D. 173±100.

The mammals recovered at the Mero site (Table 21) are essentially those which are found in or near Door County today. These include the deer, beaver, porcupine and less frequently the otter. The only exception is the marten, which no longer occurs in Wisconsin. The northward retraction of the range of the marten is probably the result of the disappearance of mature timber in all parts of the state as well as extensive modern trapping. The presence of the marten and porcupine indicates that the forest around the Mero site may have had a high percentage of conifers. Yet the presence of deer, a deciduous forest edge species, and the absence of other species commonly associated with coniferous forest habitat indicate that the forest was probably of mixed composition.

Identifiable bird remains appear only in the upper midden, and with the exception of the robin, these are aquatic species. The loon and horned grebe are both residents of the area in all seasons of the year, the pintail duck and robin are both summer visitants, while the whistling swan occurs in Door County only as a transient during its migration period. This information is, of course, important in determining the seasons during which the site was occupied. The people who left the upper midden debris must have occupied the Mero site at least during early April and late October.

TABLE 21

ANIMAL SPECIES FORM THE MERO SITE, DOOR COUNTY, WISCONSIN

Species	Number of Bones	Minimum Number of Individuals	Pounds of Meat
Upper Midden			
Deer *Odocoileus virginianus*	4	1	100
Beaver *Castor canadensis*	3	1	38
Porcupine *Erthizon dorsatum*	6	1	10
Marten *Martes americana*	1	1	3
Otter *Lutra canadensis*	4	1	12.5
Dog *Canis familiaris*	2	1	10
Common loon *Gavia immer*	1	1	5
Horned grebe *Podiceps auritus*	1	1	1
Whistling swan *Olor columbianus*	1	1	10
Pintail duck *Anas acuta*	3	2	1.5
Duck *Anas*	2	1	1
Robin *Turdus migratorius*	1	1	–
Sturgeon *Acipenser fulvescens*	13	1	36
Catfish *Ictalurus*	1	1	3
White sucker *Catostomus commersoni*	1	1	2
Smallmouth bass *Micropterus dolomieui*	2	1	2
White bass *Roccus chrysops*	1	1	1
Wallye *Stizostedion vitreum*	3	1	2
Drum *Aplodinotus grunniens*	1	1	1
Total	51		
Intermediate Midden			
Deer *Odocoileus virginianus*	5	1	100
Beaver *Castor canadensis*	2	1	38
Sturgeon *Acipenser fulvescens*	10	1	36
Channel catfish *Ictalurus punctatus*	2	1	3
Largemouth bass *Micropterus dolomieui*	2	1	2
Walleye *Stizostedion vitreum*	15	4	2
Total	36		

TABLE 21--Continued

Species	Number of Bones	Minimum Number of Individuals	Pounds of Meat
Lower Midden			
Deer *Odocoileus virginianus*	2	1	100
Beaver *Castor canadensis*	1	1	38
Sturgeon *Acipenser fulvescens*	10	1	36
Channel catfish *Ictalurus punctatus*	2	1	3
Smallmouth bass *Micropterus dolmieui*	1	1	2
Walleye *Stizostedion vitreum*	3	1	2
Drum *Aplodinotus grunniens*	1	1	1
Total	20		

The fish fauna of the Mero site is distinctly lacustrine. The sturgeon, channel catfish, and smallmouth bass have a strong preference for cool, clear lake shallows. Although the white sucker, white bass, walleye, largemouth bass, and drum sometimes appear in more turbulent waters such as large rivers, they are more often found in the shallows of large clear lakes. With the exception of the largemouth bass, these fish do not prefer warm water or places with a great deal of rooted aquatic vegetation. Those fish which do prefer this type of habitat—the yellow perch and the "pan fish,"—are absent from the Mero faunal assemblage. Thus, the people of the Mero site seem to have been fishing along a shore of a large cool body of water characterized by a clean bottom and few aquatic plants—most probably Lake Michigan.

The absence of the fall spawning white fish and lake trout is negative evidence pointing to a spring and/or summer occupation of the site. On the other hand, the lack of great amounts of fish, which could be harvested during spring spawning runs, indicates that fish were not being exploited to greatest advantage. If the Mero site was occupied neither at the time of early spring nor late fall fish runs, then it was probably occupied only during the warmest summer months. However, the appearance of the whistling swan in the upper midden indicates that the seasonal occupations were extended into the fall at some time during this period. It should be noted that no bird or turtle bone was recovered from the intermediate midden. At this latitude turtles are good indicators of summer occupation; and if the intermediate midden was a summer occupation, the remains of turtles should appear. In this case their absence is thought to be the result of human selection or of sampling error.

TABLE 22

IDENTIFIED AND UNIDENTIFIABLE BONE FROM THE MERO SITE,
DOOR COUNTY, WISCONSIN

	Lower	Inter-mediate	Upper	Totals	Percent	Percent of Each Class
Mammal						
Identified	3	7	20	30	7.2	
Unidentified	84	118	183	385	92.8	
Total	87	125	203	415		50.5
Bird						
Identified	0	0	9	9	60.0	
Unidentified	1	0	5	6	30.0	
Total	1	0	14	15		1.8
Turtle						
Identified	0	0	0	0	0	
Unidentified	6	0	3	9	100.0	
Total	6	0	3	9	9	1.1
Fish						
Identified	17	29	22	68	17.8	
Unidentified	37	118	160	315	82.2	
Total	54	147	182	383		46.6
Combined Total				822		100.0

TABLE 23

A   POUNDS OF MEAT REPRESENTED BY VARIOUS CLASSES
OF ANIMALS AT THE MERO SITE, DOOR COUNTY, WISCONSIN

	Lower	Per-cent	Inter-mediate	Per-cent	Upper	Per-cent
Mammal	138	75.8	138	73.8	173.5	72.3
Bird	0	–	0	–	18.5	7.7
Fish	44	24.2	49	26.2	48.0	20.0
Total	182	100.0	187	100.0	240.0	100.0

B   NUMBER OF IDENTIFIED SPECIES OF EACH CLASS
OF ANIMALS AT THE MERO SITE

	Lower	Per-cent	Inter-mediate	Per-cent	Upper	Per-cent
Mammal	2	28.6	2	33.3	6	31.6
Bird	0	–	0	–	6	31.6
Fish	5	71.4	4	66.7	7	36.8
Total	7	100.0	6	100.0	19	100.0

C   NUMBER OF IDENTIFIED INDIVIDUALS OF VARIOUS SPECIES
OF EACH CLASS OF ANIMALS AT THE MERO SITE

	Lower	Per-cent	Inter-mediate	Per-cent	Upper	Per-cent
Mammal	2	28.6	2	22.2	6	30.0
Bird	0	–	0	–	7	35.0
Fish	5	71.4	7	77.8	7	35.0
Total	7	100.0	9	100.0	20	100.0

The number of identified and unidentifiable bones of each
class of animals is shown in Table 22. Although mammal and
fish bone each comprise about 50 percent of the total sample,
a computation of the amount of meat represented by these bones,
shown in Table 23, indicates that nearly 75 percent of the meat
consumed during the occupation of all three stratigraphic units
was mammal. Most of the remaining 25 percent of the meat is
fish. It is often useful to examine the number of species of
each class as a gauge of the intensity of exploitation. The under-
lying assumption is that increased exploitation of a class will
result in an increase in the number of species belonging to that
class. Even when there is specialization for one species of a
class there is generally increased exploitation of the class to
which that species belongs. The number of individuals of each
class is also shown in Table 23. Here we see that hunting seems
to have remained stable through time while there was some decrease in the number of fish species. In this respect we see a
quantitative as well as a qualitative difference between the fauna
of the Middle Woodland component in the lower and intermediate
levels and the Late Woodland component represented by the upper
level. This data seems to indicate a decrease in the importance
of fishing through time, perhaps as a result of more intense use
of agricultural resources in conjunction with hunting. As an analyti
device, however, more variables are eliminated in calculations base
on pounds of meat represented by the sample. This technique
shows little change in the frequency of meat obtained from mammal
birds or fish through time.

The Heins Creek Site

The Heins Creek site is located in Door County, Wisconsin
near the Mero site. The occupation at Heins Creek by early
Late Woodland peoples has been dated at A.D. 732±150. In the
archaeological sequence of Door County the Heins Creek occupation can be temporally palced between the intermediate and upper
level of the Mero site.

The animal species identified from Locality 1 at the Heins
Creek site are listed in Table 24, while Table 25 shows the frequency of identified and unidentified bone. With the exception of
the fisher, all the identified mammal species still occur, at least
nominally, in Wisconsin. The bear, beaver and mink are rare in
most parts of the state today but were once fairly abundant. The
fisher is now found only in the boreal forest of Canada but once
ranged farther south and was probably a common species to the

TABLE 24

ANIMAL SPECIES FROM THE HEINS CREEK SITE, DOOR COUNTY, WISCONSIN

Species	Number of Bones	Number of Individuals	Pounds of Meat
Deer *Odocoileus virginianus*	5	1	100
Beaver *Castor canadensis*	11	2	76
Bear *Ursus americanus*	4	1	210
Muskrat *Ondatra zibethicus*	1	1	2
Fisher *Martes pennanti*	1	1	7
Mink *Mustela vison*	1	1	0.5
Common loon *Gavia immer*	3	1	5
Red throated lool *Gavia stellata*	2	1	5
Holboell's grebe *Podiceps grisegena*	4	3	3
Horned grebe *Podiceps auritus*	1	1	1
Pintail duck *Anas acuta*	1	1	1.5
Duck *Aythya* sp.	1	1	1
Passenger pigeon *Ectopistes migratorius*	1	1	0.5
Crow *Corvus brachyrhynchos*	1	1	0.5
Sturgeon *Acipenser fulvescens*	12	1	36
Northern pike *Esox lucius*	2	1	3
Channel catfish *Ictalurus punctatus*	7	1	3
White sucker *Catostomus commersoni*	10	4	8
Smallmouth bass *Micropterus dolomieui*	15	5	10
Walleye *Stizostedion vitreum*	9	2	4
Total	92	31	477.0

TABLE 25

IDENTIFIED AND UNIDENTIFIED ANIMAL BONE FROM
THE HEINS CREEK SITE, DOOR COUNTY, WISCONSIN

	Number of Bones	Percent of Totals	Percent Each Class
Mammal			
Identified	23	7.8	
Unidentified	272	92.2	
Total	295		42.8
Bird			
Identified	14	38.9	
Unidentified	22	61.1	
Total	36		5.2
Turtle			
Identified	0	0	
Unidentified	34	100.0	
Total	34		4.9
Fish			
Identified	55	16.9	
Unidentified	270	83.1	
Total	325		47.1
Combined Total	690		100.0

southern limits of the mixed coniferous-deciduous forests of the Carolinian-Canadian transition zone of Minnesota, Wisconsin and Michigan.

Two very interesting birds appear in the Heins Creek faunal assemblage—the red throated loon and Holboell's grebe. Both birds nest in the Canadian arctic during the summer months but winter on the Gulf and Atlantic Coasts of the United States. Both birds are rare transients in Wisconsin, though the red throated loon occasionally winters on Lake Michigan. These birds are most numerous in Door County during October and November. The pintail duck, passenger pigeon and probably the crow are only summer visitants to this area and migrate southward for the winter. Only the common loon and horned grebe are permanent residents of Door County. Evidence from the presence of migratory birds in the Heins Creek midden indicates a summer and fall occupation of the site.

The fish fauna of the Heins Creek site is lacustrine and gives definite indication of the type of aquatic habitat that Heins Creek peoples were exploiting. The sturgeon, channel catfish, white sucker, smallmouth bass and walleye all prefer clean relatively cool water in places where there is a firm gravel or bedrock bottom with little or no rooted vegetation. The northern pike is the only representative of fishes such as the bowfin, bull heads, perch, largemouth bass and the "pan fish" which prefer shallow marshy conditions with a profusion of aquatic vegetation. Here, as at the Mero site, the people seem to have been fishing neither in streams nor marshes but along the beaches of Lake Michigan.

All in all, the Heins Creek fauna seems to be oriented toward the water. Fourteen of the twenty species identified live either in or near an aquatic environment. Only the deer, fisher, mink, bear, passenger pigeon and crow are at home away from water and even the crow and mink frequent the shores of lakes and streams. The fisher, bear and passenger pigeon are species typical of mature forest while the deer prefers forest edges.

A calculation of the amount of meat represented by the animal remains at Heins Creek (Table 26) shows that mammals were far more important than birds or fish as a source of meat. Whereas the number of species of each class of animals was nearly equal, the number of individuals of these classes is not equally represented. Section C of Table 26 shows that 42 percent of the identified individual animals were fish. If this table can be used as a gauge of exploitative intensity, then fishing was employed more frequently than fowling or hunting, though the latter produced a higher yield in terms of food resources.

TABLE 26

A　　POUNDS OF MEAT REPRESENTED BY VARIOUS CLASSES
OF ANIMALS AT THE HEINS CREEK SITE, DOOR COUNTY, WISCONSIN

	Pounds	Percent of Total
Mammal	395.5	82.9
Bird	17.5	3.7
Fish	64.0	13.4
Total	477.0	100.0

B　　NUMBER OF IDENTIFIED SPECIES OF EACH CLASS OF
ANIMALS AT THE HEINS CREEK SITE

	Number of Species	Percent of Total
Mammal	6	30.0
Bird	8	40.0
Fish	6	30.0
Total	20	100.0

C　　NUMBER OF IDENTIFIED INDIVIDUALS OF VARIOUS SPECIES
OF EACH CLASS OF ANIMALS AT THE HEINS CREEK SITE

	Number of Individuals	Percent of Total
Mammal	7	22.6
Bird	10	32.2
Fish	14	45.2
Total	31	100.0

Fauna Comparison of the
Mero and Heins Creek Sites

In view of the close areal and temporal distribution of these two sites, one would expect that their faunas would show a marked similarity. This is indeed the case. The faunal assemblages from both sites contain species which are more or less typical of Door County today. The habitat preference of these species is, moreover, strongly associated with the aquatic habitat. Both sites seem to have been occupied at approximately the same season, that is, through the summer probably into the early fall.

Although the faunal sample is very small, some observations can be made on the change of subsistence pattern through time. Looking first at the amount of meat provided by each class of animals (Table 27), we see little change in the quantity of mammal meat which varies between 72 percent and 82 percent. There is also little variation in the quantity of fish which provides 13 percent of the meat at Heins Creek to 26 percent at the intermediate midden at Mero. The meat provided by fowl shows a slight increase through time. Few, if any, fowl were exploited during the first two occupations at the Mero site — birds providing 3.7 percent of the meat at Heins Creek and 7.7 percent at the upper midden at Mero. Table 27 shows the number of individual animals identified from each occupation and the number of identified species. These two tabulations show similar trends; hunting seems fairly constant through time, fishing seems to decrease in the Heins Creek and Late Woodland occupation at Mero, and there is a corresponding increase in the number of fowl taken during these latter two occupations.

These three techniques of comparison, as well as the faunal list, show that the subsistence patterns of the two Middle Woodland occupation at the Mero site are very similar to each other, and at the same time different from the subsistence patterns of the Late Woodland occupations at Heins Creek and the upper midden at Mero. While the lower and intermediate occupations at Mero were probably of shorter term than the upper midden and the Heins Creek occupations, there seems to have been more emphasis on fishing during the earlier period. It is also evident that people of the later period exploited a greater number and wider range of animal species. Both sites seem to have been occupied during the summer months, but the two Late Woodland components were apparently of longer duration and extended into the fall season.

TABLE 27

QUANTITATIVE COMPARISON OF THE FAUNA OF THE
MERO AND HEINS CREEK SITE

Stratigraphic Units	Mammal	Per-cent	Bird	Per-cent	Fish	Per-cent
Number of Identified Species of Each Class						
Mero Upper Midden	6	31.6	6	31.6	7	36.8
Heins Creek	6	30.0	8	40.0	6	30.0
Mero Intermediate Midden	2	33.3	0	–	4	66.7
Mero Lower Midden	2	28.6	0	–	5	71.4
Number of Identified Individuals of Each Class						
Mero Upper Midden	6	30.0	7	35.0	7	35.0
Heins Creek	7	22.6	10	32.2	14	45.2
Mero Intermediate Midden	2	22.2	0	–	7	77.8
Mero Lower Midden	2	28.6	0	–	5	71.4
Pounds of Meat Represented by Various Classes of Animals						
Mero Upper Midden	173.5	72.3	18.5	7.7	48	20.0
Heins Creek	395.5	82.9	17.5	3.7	64	13.4
Mero Intermediate Midden	138	73.8	0	–	49	26.2
Mero Lower Midden	138	75.8	0	–	44	24.2

ANIMAL REMAINS FROM THE JUNTUNEN SITE,
MACKINAC COUNTY, MICHIGAN

The Juntunen site (20 MK 1) is located 17 feet above the present level of Lake Huron on the western tip of Bois Blanc Island which lies about two and one half miles north of Cheboygan in the Straits of Mackinac. Bois Blanc is separated from Round Island to the west by a shallow channel approximately one quarter mile in width. Through this channel passes the main current draining Lake Michigan into Lake Huron. To the northwest of Round Island, and separating it from Mackinac Island, is a wide deep channel of the drowned Mackinac River which connected Lakes Michigan and Huron during the Chippewa-Stanley low water stage. The water surrounding Bois Blanc Island is extremely clear with a transparency of fifteen meters. July surface temperature is approximately 18 degrees Centigrade (64.4F.) which is about the coldest surface reading in the Lake Huron basin. Although the dynamics of the water mass of Lake Huron is not well known, it appears to be subject to tremendous seasonal variation (Ayers, Anderson, et al. 1956). We can, however, for the purposes of this study, characterize the waters near Bois Blanc Island as being cold and extremely clear. The waters off the northeastern and western tip of Bois Blanc may well be classified as shoal areas. Waters less than 18 feet in depth extend more than a mile and one-quarter northwest of the site and there is an area of water less than 12 feet in depth extending southwestward more than one-half mile into the lake. Water exceeding no more than 6 feet in depth may be found as far as 500 to 900 feet from the shoreline of the western tip of the island. These shallow areas are, therefore, quite extensive and, as we shall see, very important in the subsistence economy of Juntunen site peoples.

The Juntunen site itself is situated on a low sand beach ridge approximatley 600 feet from the lake shore. This beach is undoubtedly an eroded remnant of a post-Algoma beach. To the east of the site there is a series of higher beaches of the earlier

Lake Nipissing stage. Beyond these beaches to the east, the island is quite low with lakes and extensive conifer swamps. The low sandy coastal area between the lake and the highest Nipissing beaches are covered with pines and swamp conifers but with local deciduous stands in the better drained areas. On the western end of the island in the area above the Nipissing beach the flora consists of sugar maple, beech, elm, yellow birch, hemlock, white pine and other conifers. The remaining low areas of the island, particularly behind the coastal strip and over all of the eastern end of the island, are forested with sugar maple, yellow birch, elm, basswood, white birch, beech, white pine, fir, spruce and cedar. These two zones may be readily observed as the dark coastal conifers contrast sharply with the light deciduous trees of the interior.

The western end of Bois Blanc Island enjoys slightly more than 140 frost-free days per year, while the eastern part of the island has less than 140 frost-free days. Though the difference seems slight, 140 frost-free days is critical for the cultivation of maize. The mean July temperature on most of the island is about 68 degrees Fahrenheit while the mean January temperature is 16 degrees to 20 degrees Fahrenheit. The mean annual precipitation is 28 to 30 inches. It is interesting to note that there is a decrease in both length of growing season and mean annual temperature both to the north of Bois Blanc in the Upper Peninsula and to the south in the northern part of the Lower Peninsula. Both of these areas are considered to be ones of floral and faunal transition between the more northern and southern biomes. For the purposes of this paper, the biotic provinces set up by Dice (1943) were used as a general classificatory device to show the floral and faunal affinities of each species recovered from the Juntunen site. According to Dice's scheme the Upper Great Lakes transition area is called the Canadian province. The southern boundary of this province is coterminous with the most northerly dominance of the oak-hickory community and the southern limit of the white and Norway pine community (Dice 1932). South of this line in northeastern United States is the Carolinian province characterized by the beech-maple climax association with oak-hickory representing an important successional stage. The northern limit of the Canadian province includes all important stands of sugar maple, white and Norway pine (Dice 1938). The province north of this line is called Hudsonian and is characterized by the typical boreal forest. We are thus, in effect, dealing with the flora and fauna of three provinces—the larger Hudsonian and Carolinian provinces with rather well defined assemblages, and

an area of transition, the Canadian biotic province. The latter
is characterized by the blending of the species of the two larger
provinces. In addition, we have a zone of transition between the
Carolinian and Canadian provinces which extends as far north
as the western end of Bois Blanc Island. The Juntunen site is
located in this zone.

The location of the Juntunen site in the geographical center
of the Canadian province, yet technically located in the Carolinian-Canadian transition zone, places it in an ideal position for
the study of ecological change since minor climatic fluctuations
should result in noticeable changes in the biotic assemblage.
Since there is an area of conifer dominance to the south of Bois
Blanc Island in the north-central area of the Lower Peninsula, a
cooling of the climate should result in the influx of northern
Canadian and Hudsonian species from the south as well as from
the north. The species typical of the Carolinian province would,
of course, also be derived from the Lower Peninsula and particularly from the western margin of the Lower Peninsula since the
Carolinian-Canadian transition zone extends farthest north in this
region (Figure 1, p. 6).

The Juntunen site on Bois Blanc Island is separated from the
Lower Peninsula of Michigan by two and one half miles of water.
The exact effect of the site's location in an isolated insular
situation will not be discussed in full since it is thought to have
had little effect on the large majority of species recovered from
the site, namely, fish, birds and large mammals. To be sure,
the small mammals and reptiles are probably affected to a
greater or lesser extent and there are indeed several small
species which seem to have become isolated on the island. Some
parts of Bois Blanc Island have probably been free for occupation
since the retreat of the high waters of Glacial Lake Algonquin
at about 9000 B.C. After about 8000 B.C., during the Chippewa-
Stanley low water stage, Bois Blanc was connected with the
Lower Peninsula and separated from the Upper Peninsula by
only the Mackinac River. During the Nipissing stage at approximately 2000 B.C. lake waters again covered most of Bois Blanc
Island, but since that time it has retained most of its present
area. Since the period 10,000 years ago, when the island was
connected to the mainland, the only passage to and from the
island for animal life would have been flying, swimming, rafting,
or more likely, passage across the winter ice.

A detailed report on the depositional history of the Juntunen
site was completed by Mr. Henry T. Wright when he was working for the Museum of Anthropology, University of Michigan. The

following account is a synopsis taken directly from his report. Mr. Wright (n.d.) divides the stratigraphic sequence into 26 discrete geological units. These are in turn grouped into 6 cultural units or levels of occupations. The earliest extensive level of the site is a humus zone of a forest podzol, and the first major occupation is found on this soil formation. Presumably, this level was occupied at about A.D. 825±75 (M-1142, Crane and Griffin 1961:110). The forest cover was apparently removed during this first occupation so that this occupation was followed by a period of rapid and intense sand deposition over all of the site. This is level B. Cultural material of this level is bedded within the sand deposit and there was apparently no stable surface or soil formation. The 1.5 feet of sand deposited in this level is thought to be a result of a five foot rise in lake level.

Level C is short period of soil stabilization which is evidenced by a weak meadow soil over most of the site. The cultural occupation of level C has been dated at A.D. 900±75 (M-1141, Crane and Griffin 1961:110), and is followed by a period of deposition which accumulates up to 0.3 feet of sand on the forefront of the site. A major period of meadow soil formation followed the accumulation of sand. This horizon, level D, has been dated at A.D. 1060±75 (M-1140, Crane and Griffin 1961:110). By this time the deposition of sand and continual clearing of undergrowth had led to a significant change in the morphology of the site. That is to say, the destruction of the podzol formation and its micro flora would greatly increase the amount of time required for replacement of the climax forest vegetation. Continued clearing during the occupation of level D again allowed wind action to denude the site and this led again to sand deposition in level E. During much of this time the site was deserted. The growth of vegetation permitted stabilization and building of a meadow soil under a thick grass cover during the last aboriginal occupation which perhaps took place as late as A.D. 1320±75 (M-1188, Crane and Griffin 1963:233). This has been designated as level F. Cultivation activities in the 19th and 20th centuries have obscured the nature of subsequent deposition. It is believed, however, that the site never regained its climatic forest cover.

In summary, Mr. Wright's reconstruction shows a long series of meadow soil formations separated by periods of sand deposition following the primary removal of the forest cover. The exact relationship between cultural occupations and meadow soil formation has not been evaluated but it seems apparent that there is some connection between the two. There is also reason to suppose that the periods of sand deposition may in fact be at least partially due to aboriginal clearing activities.

Besides affording an excellent opportunity for studying ecological and climatic change through time, the analysis of faunal remains from the Juntunen site is of equal importance as a study of the subsistence economy in the Upper Great Lakes area. This site seems, in fact, to be representative of a widespread and fairly specialized cultural adaptation around the margins of the Upper Great Lakes during the Late Woodland period. Sites of this type are distributed along the coast and on small coastal islands on the northern shore of the Lower Peninsual of Michigan, the northern and southern shore of Michigan's Upper Peninsula, the north shore of Lake Huron, in the Georgian Bay area and to some extent on the northern shore of Lake Superior; more simply stated on the lake shores of the Canadian province. These sites are rather large villages characterized by heavy accumulations of pot sherds, charcoal, and fish bone and, for the most part, seem to have been summer fishing stations. The importance of fishing in the subsistence of these people has long been recognized. Rostlund (1952) called this type of subsistence pattern the Inland Fishing Complex. Hickerson (1962) documents the importance of this pattern for the northern Ojibwa of Wisconsin. Jenness (1935) in his description of the Ojibwa of Parry Island gives a very excellent description of this type of economy and the seasonal activities involved. From December to March, families were scattered in their hunting grounds hunting large and small game. Families were generally camped several miles apart. The period between early February and mid March was the hardest for people utilizing this subsistence pattern. After March the Ojibwa often moved into maple groves to collect sap for sugar, during the same time fish were speared. In about mid April the Ojibwa hunted small game, as the larger game was in poor condition. Fish, however, were the staple dietary element from May throughout the summer. La Potherie in 1753 reports that the principal fish caught by the Ojibwa were whitefish and sturgeon and that the latter were speared in the vicinity of the islands of Lake Huron during the summer (Blair 1911). The abundance of fish and wild plant foods during the summer months made it economically possible for family groups to again meet and reside in villages. It was also during these summer encampments that gardens were planted, although garden products were, according to Perrot, of little importance in the economy of the Ojibwa (Blair 1911). From early November to early or mid December the village group was occupied with the spearing of whitefish and lake trout which spawn during these months. With the completion of fishing actvities the Ojibwa again broke up into family groups and dispersed for winter hunting. Alexander Henry spent the year of 1763 traveling with an Ojibwa family in the northern Lower Peninsula of Michigan. The journal of these wanderings has recently been published in an excellent article by George I. Quimby (1962). Even at this late date, this detailed account confirms in every respect the seasonal movements and activities reported by ethnographers and other early travelers.

Although we can neither prove that the peoples occupying the Juntunen site were proto-Ojibwa, nor that this site represents a seasonal stage in this type of subsistence pattern, we can say, on the basis of the seasonal character of the available and exploited resources, that the latter assumption is quite likely. This is especially probable since the Canadian province as a whole is climatically unsuited for large scale agriculture and as an ecologic zone probably never supported large big-game populations, such as the deer, which supplied a large part of the subsistence base farther south. Fish were, therefore, the only other abundant and reliable resource available. One of the major contentions of this study is that large aboriginal villages of the Upper Great Lakes were sustained and attained economic stability through an adaptation specialized in the exploitation of fish resources.

The analysis and interpretation of faunal material from archaeological sites involves several complex variables. These are in turn usually compounded by local problems at each site. There are two such problems at the Juntunen site (1) the great quantity of bone material and (2) the complexity of the stratigraphic sequence. Before dealing with general problems and procedures, it is best to discuss these specific problems of the Juntunen site.

Although bone remains are well preserved, as we shall later see, they are extremely fragmentary. This condition leads to a definite bias in the quantitative analysis, as quantitative reconstructions can be based only on the minimum number of known skeletal elements of each species. If the bone material is fragmentary, this sort of precise identification becomes nearly impossible. Very fragmentary remains can be identified no more precisely than mammal, bird, fish, etc. with identification based upon the structure of the bone itself. Thus, the actual number of identified species is small in relation to the total amount of bone present. The sample of identified remains is further reduced when a stratigraphic analysis is undertaken. Since the stratigraphic sequence at this site is so complex, less than one-fourth of the site's provenience units can accurately be assigned to any of the recognized occupation levels. Thus, the number of species assignable to any one of the levels is also reduced. Unfortunately, this reduction has made it necessary to group occupation levels in order to obtain samples of comparable size. For instance, levels B and C, as well as E and F had to be combined in the qualitative stratigraphic analysis although those levels could be considered separately in quantitative analysis.

One other general problem of faunal analysis needs special attention, namely, the effect of human selection on the faunal sample. Animal remains recovered from archaeological sites do not, in any sense, represent a random sample of the kinds of species or numbers of species found in the general area of the site when it was occupied. Instead, these remains represent those species which were selected from all the species available for exploitation. It would be foolish to assume that every species which was present in an immediate natural environment of the site is also present in the site deposit, or that the frequency of species in the site has any relationship to the frequency of the species in the natural environment. To be sure the frequency of the archaeological remains of a species may be, and often is, a reflection of the natural frequency of that species. It is, however, also a reflection of selection frequency. Judgments concerning a species' presence or absence from a site must, therefore, be made on the basis of a complete faunal assemblage which must be reconstructed from that part of that assemblage which happened to be selected.

MAMMALS

Black Bear *(Ursus americanus)*

The black bear once ranged over most of the North American continent and, thus, occurs in a wide range of habitats. It is known to occur on islands and has been reported from Mackinac Island just west of Bois Blanc (Burt 1954). The black bear hibernates from late January until early spring and though it was probably hunted the year around, it could seldom be found during hibernation (Jenness 1935).

Marten *(Martes americana)*

The present distribution of the marten is limited to the Hudsonian and northern Canadian provinces. This species inhabits large, dense coniferous forests. Its former range extended to the central part of Michigan's Lower Peninsula. Except for recent introductions into the Porcupine Mountains of the Upper Peninsula, it is absent from the state.

Mink *(Mustela vison)*

The mink originally ranged over most of North America. It is most frequently found near water during the summer months and in woods during the winter.

River otter *(Lutra canadensis)*

The otter is adapted to an aquatic existence and is found along lake, river and stream banks throughout its wide range.

Eastern chipmunk *(Tamias striatus)*

The eastern chipmunk ranges eastward from the Great Plains through the Canadian and Carolinian provinces. It inhabits hardwood forest and forest edges but is uncommon in swampy woodlands. This species burrows and is, no doubt, intrusive into many of the Juntunen site deposits.

Red squirrel *(Tamiasciurus hudsonicus)*

To a large extent the red squirrel inhabits evergreen forests, but also occurs in deciduous woodlands. Formerly, the red squirrel may have been more closely assoicated with coniferous forests than it is at present.

Beaver *(Castor canadensis)*

The beaver once ranged over most of North America where there were lakes and streams with wooded shores. On Bois Blanc Island the beaver inhabits both the lake shore proper and the inland swamps, although, it is undoubtedly more common in the swampy areas. Beaver was hunted in all seasons of the year but probably most frequently in the winter and early spring.

Woodland deer mouse *(Peromyscus maniculatus)*

The woodland deer mouse ranges over much of the northeastern and the western United States and throughout the boreal forest of Canada. This species is restircted to woodlands and seldom ventures into the open. Most of the Juntunen deer mice are probably intrusive.

Southern bog lemming *(Synaptomys cooperi)*

The range of the southern bog lemming covers the Canadian and Carolinian provinces. Its habitat includes bogs, meadows and swamps with thick ground vegetation. This species is one which burrows so that it may well be intrusive into the archaeological deposit.

Red-backed vole *(Clethrionomys gapperi)*

The range of this species extends from the Canadian tundra south through the Hudsonian and Canadian provinces. The red-backed vole may be found in northern deciduous and conifer swamps and other moist situations. This vole may also be intrusive.

Muskrat *(Ondatra zibethica)*

This aquatic species has a wide range covering almost all of North America and is always found in association with water courses and wet places with abundant marsh vegetation.

Porcupine *(Erethizon dorsatum)*

Although the porcupine is now almost exclusively a resident of the northern coniferous forests, there is some evidence that its range formerly extended farther south into the deciduous forests. These animals are slow, easy to capture and were available throughout the year.

Snowshoe hare *(Lepus americanus)*

The snowshoe hare extends southward to the southern limits of the Canadian province. Throughout its range this species prefers dense conifer swamps and thickets. Burt (1954) reports that the snowshoe presents an easy target to archers as the swish of passing arrows does not seem to alarm it, thus allowing several shots.

Whitetail deer *(Odocoileus virginianus)*

The whitetail deer occurs throughout the southern deciduous forests and reaches its northern limit at the northern margin of the Canadian province. It does, however, become increasingly scarce to the north with increasing dominance of climax coniferous forest. This species is typically associated with edge situations between forests and open areas. The deer takes readily to water and has been reported on several islands in Lakes Michigan and Huron.

Moose *(Alces alces)*

Although the moose is now absent from all of Michigan except Isle Royale in Lake Superior and an occasional stray in the Upper Peninsula, it formerly reached the southern margin of the Canadian province. The moose prefers forested regions where there are numerous swamps and shallow lakes.

Woodland caribou *(Rangifer caribou)*

This species is restricted to the coniferous forest of the Hudsonian and Canadian provinces. It is now absent from Michigan but once ranged over all of the northern part of the state including several of the larger islands of Lake Michigan. The woodland caribou prefers large bogs and swamps and moist coniferous woodlands.

Domestic dog *(Canis familiaris)*

The dog is, of course, a companion of man and is to be found in close assoication with him. The dogs of the Juntunen site appear to be of a rather homogeneous population. A more detailed description of these dogs is included in a later section of this report.

The mammalian fauna of the Juntunen site could be said to be typical of the Canadian biotic province in that this province itself is one of transition between the northern boreal Hudsonian province and the southern deciduous Carolinian province. The marten, red squirrel, red-backed vole, porcupine, snowshoe hare, moose and caribou are most typical of the Hudsonian province, while the eastern chipmunk, southern bog lemming and the whitetail deer are more often thought of as being representative of the deciduous Carolinian province. The other species present have ranges which encompass both larger natural areas as well as their transition zone. One striking feature is the homogeneity of the habitat preference of many of these species. We find that those species which prefer moist woodlands, bogs and conifer swamps dominate the faunal assemblage. These include the bog lemming, red-backed vole, snowshoe hare, the moose and caribou. In addition, the mink, otter, beaver and muskrat are found in or very near aquatic situations. We thus have a picture of the general terrain as being composed of lowlands, bogs and swamps dominated by a largely coniferous forest

Several mammal species which are typical of the Canadian transition zone do not appear in the Juntunen faunal assemblage.

Their absence is due either to sampling error, selective hunting
or the absence of the species from the area. Absent species include the raccoon, fisher, long-tailed and short-tailed weasel,
wolverine, skunk, red fox, timber wolf, lynx, cougar, bobcat, gray
squirrel, northern flying squirrel, the meadow vole, cotton-tail
rabbit and the elk. Many of these species reach their northern
limits near Bois Blanc Island and these may have been entirely
absent. These include the raccoon, long-tailed weasel, cougar,
gray squirrel, southern flying squirrel, the cottontail rabbit
and the elk. Other species such as the weasel, the flying squirrel
and many of the smaller mammals are rather secretive and probably were not collected by aboriginal hunters. There is, moreover,
no apparent reason why such species as the fisher, wolverine,
skunk, red fox, the wolf, lynx, cougar, and the bobcat would not
be killed and they most certainly were present. These species
are the medium to large carnivores and most or, at least, some
of these species usually appear in Late Woodland refuse deposits.
It is suggested that the absence of these species may be in part
due to religious practices or food taboos.

The mammals of the Juntunen site are not of much help in
determining the season of the site's occupations as all these
species were available and were hunted throughout the year. Since
historic records and ethnographies from this area tell us that
large mammals were hunted almost exclusively in the winter months
(Kinietz 1940; Jenness 1935), the problem of relating these remains
with seasonality is thus a quantitative problem.

BIRDS

Common golden-eye *(Bucephala clangula)*

The golden-eye is a summer and/or winter resident of the
Juntunen site area. This bird is one of the more common diving ducks.

Canada goose *(Branta canadensis)*

This goose is only a summer resident in the Bois Blanc
area.

Common loon *(Gavia immer)*

The common loon is a summer resident in this area. It
is also a rare winter resident. This big, fish-eating bird inhabits large, deep lakes. It is hard to approach on open water
as it dives and swims great distances under water. It is, how-

ever, virtually helpless on land. Nesting takes place in the vegetation on the edges of lakes.

Ring-billed gull *(Larus delawarensis)*

The ring-billed gull is a permanent resident of this area.

Caspian tern *(Hydroprogne caspia)*

This tern is a summer resident of the Upper Great Lakes. It is often found is association with the ring-billed gull.

Goshawk *(Accipiter gentilis)*

The goshawk is a permanent resident in this area. Its habitat is the forest and especially coniferous forest.

Red-shouldered hawk *(Buteo lineatus)*

This hawk is a summer resident of the Upper Great Lakes. It inhabits both wooded and open areas, but is most common in swampy, moist woodlands where it replaces the red-tailed hawk, which prefers dry woodlands.

Bald eagle *(Haliaeetus leucocephalus)*

This large bird is a summer resident of this area. It is always found near water where it feeds mainly upon fish refuse.

Barred owl *(Strix varia)*

This owl is both a summer and winter resident over all of its range. The barred owl is commonly found in wet or swampy woodlands where it is the nocturnal counterpart of the red-shoulder hawk.

Saw-whet owl *(Aegolius acadicus)*

This tiny owl is our smallest bird of prey. It is a permanent resident of the Great Lakes area and is extremely tame. Its habitat is chiefly coniferous forests and swamps.

Ruffed grouse *(Bonasa umbellus)*

The ruffed grouse is a permanent resident over all of its range. It frequents woodlands with openings and second growth.

Turkey *(Meleagris gallopavo)*

The turkey was a permanent resident within its former range. The turkey is an inhabitant of extensive deciduous woodlands. The northern limit of its original range was coterminous with the northern edge of the Carolinian province as it transects Michigan's Lower Peninsula. The occurrence of turkey remains at the Juntunen site exceeds by 200 miles its most northern historic range.

Blue jay *(Cyanocitta cristata)*

The blue jay is a permanent resident in the Upper Great Lakes area. It inhabits wooded areas and edges.

Common crow *(Corvus brachyrhynchos)*

This bird is probably a summer resident in the Bois Blanc area. Its habitat is variable and it often feeds on carrion.

Common raven *(Corvus corax)*

The raven's range extends southward to the southern edge of the Canadian province in the Eastern United States; it is a permanent resident over all of its range. The raven is a wary bird and frequents shorelines in this region where it feeds on dead fish and molluscs.

Passenger pigeon *(Ectopistes migratorius)*

Although this bird is now extinct, it was once extremely abundant. The passenger pigeon was a summer resident and nested in large colonies, mostly in the northern Lower Peninsula of Michigan. It is known to have nested in both Emmet and Cheboygan counties in mid March. This pigeon is thought to have begun its southward migration in early September. (Mershon 1907)

In a general summary of the avian fauna of the Juntunen site, we find several interesting things on which to elaborate. For a site located on the water and whose peoples relied heavily on aquatic resources there were surprisingly few ducks, especially in view of their usual abundance even in strongly agricultural sites. The only identifiable duck present was the golden-eye. On the other hand, the most abundant avian species was the common loon, an extremely wary aquatic bird. The loon may have been taken either in fish gill nets or perhaps along the shore while it was nesting. Perhaps the absence of the diving, fish-eating ducks, the mergansers, is negative evidence in support of the theory that they were captured while nesting.

Many of the other birds of this site are carrion eaters. These include the bald eagle, Caspian tern, ring-billed gull, the crow and the raven. There is little doubt that these birds would be enticed by fish-strewn Indian villages.

The passenger pigeon and Canada goose were probably extremely abundant during the spring and fall seasons. Absence of juvenile birds of these species indicate, however, that they were collected in the summer and/or fall seasons. The Canada goose, loon, red-shouldered hawk, Caspian tern, bald eagle, crow and passenger pigeon were available only from spring to fall, while the other species are permanent residents. Even though many summer resident ducks which would be available only during the warmer months are absent, so are many ducks which are winter visitants to the Great Lakes area. The avian fauna thus indicates that the Juntunen site was occupied at least during the ice-free months of the year.

The raptorial bird remains recovered give us a nice idea of the ecology of the island itself. The red-shouldered hawk, barred owl and the saw-whet owl are all inhabitants of coniferous swamp areas, while the goshawk prefers dryer coniferous forest. The red-shouldered hawk and its nocturnal counterpart, the barred owl, here replace the red-tailed hawk—great horned owl relationship of drier forests.

The occurrence of the wild turkey some 200 miles north of its historic range leads one to suspect that the range of this bird was at some periods extended northward. Perhaps this northward extension reflects a warm climatic period.

There is evidence for the use of at least two species, the loon and the bald eagle, in religious activities.

REPTILES

Snapping turtle *(Chelydra serpentina)*

The snapping turtle has, by and large, a southern distribution although it extends northward throughout the Canadian province. This species is an aquatic turtle which seldom basks.

Painted turtle *(Chrysemys picta)*

This turtle is confined in its distribution to the Carolinian and Canadian provinces. It prefers shallow marshes, ponds and

lake banks where there is a profusion of aquatic vegetation. It
is the most conspicuous turtle in most northern areas, often
basking for long periods (Conant 1958).

Blanding's turtle *(Emys blandingi)*

The range of the Blanding's turtle is largely confined to the
Canadian province though its spotty distribution to the south and
east may be relic populations of a wider distribution during
cooler periods. Although essentially aquatic, this turtle may
frequently be encountered on land in areas where marshes and
bogs are plentiful.

The occurrence of these three turtle species at the Juntunen
site is another strong indication of a summer occupation, as these
three species are available only during the warm parts of the year.
There is a great deal of evidence that turtles were collected in
order to use their hard bony carapaces for implements. Although
a more or less extensive modern survey of the amphibians and
reptiles of Bois Blanc has been made, none of these species
have been collected. They may be, however, still extant on the
island.

FISH

Lake sturgeon *(Acipenser fulvescens)*

The lake sturgeon is a bottom living fish of the shallow
waters of lakes and large rivers. It was formerly extremely
abundant in the Great Lakes and the large rivers of the Great
Lakes drainage. Maximum availability was reached in the spring
when the sturgeon ascended the large rivers or concentrated in
shallow lake waters for spawning. This species may attain
sizes up to 300 pounds in the Great Lakes, but the average size
is probably more on the order of 20 pounds. The sturgeon was
probably the most important single species in the subsistence
of the Indians of the Upper Great Lakes. Almost every historic
record of sturgeon fisheries in this area mentions that the fish
were taken with spears (Carver 1818; Jenness 1935; Schoolcraft
1820). According to Rostlund (1952), sturgeon were captured in
the Great Lakes region with both nets and spears, but spears and
sturgeon are mentioned together so frequently in the old sources
that the sturgeon fishery among some tribes of the region can
be considered a specialized or standardized spear fishery.
Technically speaking, these references to spearing are probably
inaccurate. Archaeological "spearheads" in the Great Lakes
area are usually harpoons, in that the head becomes detached

from the shaft, and the fish is held by a line which is attached to the butt of the harpoon point.

Longnosed gar *(Lepisosteus osseus)*

This species reaches its northern limit of distribution in the area of Bois Blanc Island. One of the common habits of the gar is to bask near the surface of the water on warm days at which time it can be easily approached. The gar is quite often taken in gill nets as its long, beak-like mandibles are readily entangled. Spawning takes place in shallow waters in the spring.

Lake trout *(Salvelinus namaycush)*

The lake trout is a large fish averaging from between 5 to 10 pounds in the Great Lakes, but reaching weights of 50 pounds. In the Great Lakes Basin this fish is confined mainly to the large lakes themselves because only these are deep enough to supply the cold, well oxygenated water to which the lake trout retires during the summer months. In late October or early November the lake trout becomes accessible when it moves into shallow water to spawn on rocky shoals. The same spawning areas are selected year after year (Scott 1954). After spawning, this species usually returns to deeper water.

Whitefish *(Coregonus* sp.)

The whitefish which occurs on the Juntunen site has not been identified to species, but the general size of the whitefish remains indicates that these are largely the remains of the lake whitefish *C. clupeiformis*. This fish originally attained weights of up to 20 pounds, but probably averaged between 5 and 10 pounds. All whitefish inhabit the deep, cool waters of lakes. It is a fall spawner and moves into shallow shoal areas near the end of November or the beginning of December for this purpose. Like the lake trout, whitefish are available in quantity only during the spawning period. Rostlund (1952) points out that two of the most famous whitefish spawning grounds were the Straits of Mackinac and Sault Sainte Marie. The most economical method of catching this species, and the one most frequently mentioned in historical records, is with nets. Gill nets as well as scoop nets were often employed in this respect (Rostlund 1952; Catlin 1926). However, the whitefish also was frequently taken with spears by the Ojibwa of Parry Island (Jenness 1935).

Northern redhorse sucker *(Moxostoma aureolum)*

This sucker seldom reaches a length of more than 20 inches. It is a bottom feeder which is available in tremendous quantity in the spring when it spawns on clean gravel bottoms of streams and lake edges.

Silver redhorse *(Moxostoma anisurum)*

This species is commonly found in the larger lakes and rivers and it may exceed the northern redhorse in size often reaching 2 feet in length. The silver redhorse also spawns in the spring in the shallow waters of lakes and streams at which time it can be easily taken with a spear.

White sucker *(Catostomus commersoni)*

The white sucker's average weight is about 2 pounds. This fish makes annual spawning runs in late May or early June at which time it ascends small streams or shallow shoal areas of lakes in great numbers. Modern fishermen catch large numbers of these suckers with dip nets during the spawning period. It is, however, available throughout the year in shallow lake waters.

Longnose sucker *(Catostomus catostomus)*

The longnose sucker is generally a little larger than the white sucker, sometimes attaining weights of over 5 pounds. This species frequently spawns at the same time and in the same place as the white sucker. It differs from the latter in that it frequents cooler and deeper water (Scott 1954).

Brown bullhead *(Ictalurus nebulosus)*

The brown bullhead averages about 1/2 pound in size. It prefers quiet, weedy, mud bottomed lakes. Spawning takes place in late spring, usually beneath an overhanging bank.

Channel catfish *(Ictalurus punctatus)*

The channel catfish is the largest catfish of the Great Lakes. It occasionally reaches a weight of 30 pounds, and 10 to 15 pound fish are common. This species prefers cooler and cleaner water than most other catfish. Spawning takes palce in shallow water during the spring.

Northern pike *(Esox lucius)*

Although the northern pike may reach 20 pounds, its average size is probably closer to 3 or 4 pounds. This fish frequents the shallow waters of lakes during the warm summer months where it floats just beneath the surface. The pike seeks deeper water in the fall and winter. After the ice breaks up in the spring, the pike again returns to shallow water to spawn.

Yellow perch *(Perca flavescens)*

The yellow perch is an extremely common fish in the Great Lakes, but seldom exceeds 1 pound in weight. The perch spawns in shallow waters, usually in late April or early May. Due to the general small size of this fish, it was probably taken in nets.

Yellow walleye *(Stizostedion vitreum)*

This fish is one of the most common of the Great Lakes drainage. The average weight of the walleye is probably between 3 and 5 pounds, but it sometimes reaches 20 pounds. Walleyes spawn in the spring shortly after the ice breaks up. Spawning takes place in 1 to 5 feet of water on shoals. This fish remains in shallow water during the early summer, but may seek deeper water in the late summer.

Sauger *(Stizostedion canadense)*

The average weight of this fish is less than a pound. Its life habits are similar to the walleye which it resembles except that the sauger will frequent more muddy bottoms and more turbid waters.

Largemouth bass *(Micropterus salmoides)*

This species prefers warm weedy waters. Spawning takes place in the spring and each fish has a nesting site which it vigorously defends. The average size of the largemouth is between 2 and 3 pounds.

Smallmouth bass *(Micropterus dolomieui)*

This species is somewhat smaller than the largemouth bass. The spawning habits of the two fish are similar, although the smallmouth prefers cooler and clearer waters than the largemouth (Scott 1954).

Rock bass *(Ambloplites rupestris)*

This fish is frequently found in the shallow waters of lakes. It is usually smaller in size than the smallmouth bass, weighing on the average about 1/2 pound. The habitat of the rock bass is similar to that of the smallmouth.

Freshwater drum *(Aplodinotus grunniens)*

The freshwater drum is a southern species which reaches its northern limit in the vicinity of Bois Blanc Island. It occurs in all of the Great Lakes except Lake Superior. The most northern record of the drum in Michigan, according to the files of the Fish Division of the University of Michigan Museums, is from Au Sable Point, although a fossil drum cranium has been reported from a Nipissing age marl deposit in Cheboygan County (Hubbs 1940). The drum is a bottom dwelling fish which has been known to attain weights up to 10 pounds. Fish weighing about 2 pounds are average. This species frequents shallow waters with muddy or sandy bottoms and is a spring spawner.

The fish fauna of the Juntunen site, even more than the avian fauna, gives us a clue to the season the site was occupied. The abundant occurrence of sturgeon indicates that the site must have been occupied at least by late spring and probably soon after the ice went out. We may also be quite sure from the abundant whitefish and lake trout that the site was occupied until late November or early December when these fish spawn. The fact that these latter species were only abundantly available in shallow waters at this season is excellent evidence for occupation at this season.

Most of the fish species at the Juntunen site are those which prefer cool clear waters with sand or gravel bottoms, the only exception is the brown bullhead.

It must be noted that essentially all the large fish of this region are represented in this sample. There are, in fact, only four notable exceptions—the burbot *(Lota lota)*, the bowfin *(Amia calva)*, the muskellunge *(Esox masquinongy)*, and the quillback carpsucker *(Carpiodes cyprinus)*. The quillback carpsucker and bowfin both reach the northern limit of their ranges in the region of Bois Blanc Island and perhaps were not present. The bowfin is, moreover, an extremely repugnant looking fish, at least by modern standards, and was perhaps avoided. The burbot is, like the whitefish and lake trout, a deep-water fish throughout most of the year. It becomes available only during spawning which takes place from January to March. The absence of the burbot may be taken as additional evidence in support of an April to December habitation period or at least fishing period. Burbot remains have been reported from the 1715-1761 French settlement at nearby Fort Michilimackinac (Cleland n.d.). The muskellunge was most certainly available in the Bois Blanc waters and no reasonable theory can be put forth to explain its absence. However, this species does appear to be very rare in the middens of prehistoric sites.

The total fish fauna of the Juntunen site, of course, represents only a small sample of the species actually present in the waters of the Mackinac Straits area. Those species whose remains are missing include the many smaller species of minnows, chubs, etc. The exploitation of larger fish to the exclusion of the smaller species is a clue to the fishing method. The use of non-selective fishing techniques such as the seine, pound net, trap, and weir generally produces a more representative sample of the total fish fauna. This is to say, small fish as well as large fish are taken. Although people living on the Juntunen site made cordage, as is evident from the cord impressed decorations of their pottery, there are several good reasons for arguing that these people did not fish with nets. These reasons are as follows: (1) The sheer work involved in making and repairing primitive nets, if these nets were used to catch such large and strong fish as lake trout or sturgeon, would make this type of fishing impractical. (2) As we have pointed out, remains of small and medium sized fish are very scarce on the site. (3) No fishnet sinkers have been reported from the Juntunen site. In the early historic period nets did not seem to be too popular in this immediate region. According to Smith and Snell (1891) seines were introduced to the Mackinac Island fishing community in 1840, but they were not a success; they also reportedly failed again at a later time. In the early history of Mackinac, the Indians were largely dependent upon their spears for their fish supply and that kind of apparatus was extensively used.

There are, however, two arguments for the possibility that nets were used by these people: (1) the frequent mention of gill nets in early historic accounts; and, (2) the tremendous quantity of whitefish remains at the Juntunen site, a fish not easily speared It, therefore, seems reasonable to reject the idea that small mesh nets or traps were used, but to consider the likelihood of the use of large mesh gill nets for whitefish.

Another fishing technique, the use of fishhooks is easily dismissed by the following arguments: (1) Fishing with hooks (angling) is not, under ordinary circumstances, a profitable way to exploit fish resources. (2) The two main species represented at this site, the sturgeon and whitefish, feed on small organisms and seldom take a hook. (3) The tremendous quantity of fish from the site infers a more profitable exploitative technique. (4) No fishhooks were recovered from the Juntunen site.

Harpoon fishing, on the other had, appears to have been an important exploitative technique at this site as evidenced by the four points below. (1) It is the larger fish of the large species which are represented at the site. (2) Harpoon fisheries are economically productive where fish are large and very abundant. (3) Almost all the historic accounts of Indian fisheries in the Upper Great Lakes mention "spear" fishing. (4) Harpoons were recovered from the site.

There, thus, seems to emerge a rather clear picture of the Juntunen site fishing which can, no doubt, be expanded as a representative of a highly developed Late Woodland inland shore fishery in the Upper Great Lakes region. This fishery complex exploited a variety of fish species as they became abundant during the early spring and late fall spawning periods. In addition, fish resources played an important part in the summer economy. It cannot be emphasized enough that the two major spawning periods were those which were critical in the fishing pattern. The spring spawning period was crucial in that it occurred just at the time when other animal and plant resources were most scarce. Thus, fishing in this area significantly raised the minimum quantity of food resources available, and, therefore, afforded a corresponding increase in the level of population density. The fall spawning period was likewise important as it supplied a fish store for the winter period.

All species whose remains were recovered from the Juntunen site are listed in Table 28. In order to proceed with a general habitat analysis, all of the terrestrial species are assigned to the biotic province and habitat with which they are most closely associated. In assigning species to these specific provinces and habitats, cognizance has been taken of the fact that their ranges are seldom restricted to these categories. For general purposes, however, it is within these geographical and ecological boundaries that they occur most frequently. A 2 is used to designate primary distribution within a particular category while a 1 denotes an area of secondary importance. Those species whose ranges are so wide as to include more than two of the categories are classed as cosmopolitan.

TABLE 28

ANALYSIS OF THE DISTRIBUTION AND HABITATS
OF THE JUNTUNEN SITE FAUNA

Species	Biotic Distribution					Habitat				
	Hudsonian	Canadian	Carolinian	Cosmopolitan	Aquatic	Swamp and Bog	Coniferous	Deciduous	Transition Community	Cosmopolitan
Black bear				2			2			2
Marten	2	1					2			
Mink				2		2				
Otter				2		2				
Eastern chipmunk		1	2					2	1	
Red squirrel	2	2	1				2	1		
Beaver				2		2				
Woodland deer mouse				2			1	1		
Southern bog lemming		1	2			2				
Boreal red-backed vole	2	1				2		1		
Muskrat				2		2				
Porcupine	2	1					2	1		
Snowshoe hare	2	1				2	1			
Whitetail deer		1	2					1	2	
Moose	2	1				2	1	1		
Woodland caribou	2	1				2	1			
Golden-eye				2	2					
Canada goose				2	2					
Common loon	2	1			2					
Ring-billed gull		1	2		2					
Caspian tern		2			2					
Goshawk				2			2	1		
Red-shouldered hawk		1	2			2				
Bald eagle				2	2	1				
Barred owl				2		2				
Saw-whet owl				2		2	1			
Ruffed grouse	2	1					1		2	
Turkey			2					2		
Blue jay		1	2					2	1	

TABLE 28--Continued

| Species | Biotic Distribution | | | | Habitats | | | | | |
	Boreal	Great Lakes Basin	Mississippi and Ohio Drainage	Cosmopolitan	Deep water	Shallow Water	Sand or Gravel Bottom	Mud Bottom	Spring Spawner	Fall Spawner
Sturgeon	2	1				2	2		2	
Longnose gar		1	2			2	2		2	
Lake trout	2	1			2		2			2
Whitefish	2	1	1		2		2			2
Northern redhorse sucker	2	1		2		2	2		2	
Silver redhorse sucker				2		2	2		2	
White sucker	2	1				2			2	
Longnose sucker	2	1			1	2			2	
Brown bullhead		1	2			2		2	2	
Channel catfish		1	2			2	2		2	
Northern pike	2	1	1			2	2		2	
Yellow perch	1	2	1			2	2		2	
Yellow walleye				2		2	2		2	
Sauger				2		2	2		2	
Largemouth bass		1	2			2	2	1	2	
Smallmouth bass		1	2			2	2		2	
Rock bass		1	2			2	2		2	
Freshwater drum		1	2			2	2		2	
Score	15	16	17	8	5	32	30	3	32	4

TABLE 28--Continued

Species	Biotic Distribution				Habitats					
	Hudsonian	Canadian	Carolinian	Cosmopolitan	Aquatic	Swamp and Bog	Coniferous	Deciduous	Transition Community	Cosmopolitan
Crow				2						2
Raven	2	1				2	1			
Passenger pigeon		1	2					2		
Blanding's turtle		2			2	1			1	
Midland painted turtle		1	2		2	1				
Snapping turtle		1	2		2	1				
Score	20	24	21	26	18	30	15	15	7	4

As may be seen in the totals for the distributional patterns of the land vertebrates, the Hudsonian province ranks 20, the Canadian province 24, and the Carolinian province 21 while Cosmopolitan ranks 26. This is exactly the expected situation, since the Canadian province falls both geographically and ecologically between the northern Hudsonian and the southern Carolinian provinces and, as previously mentioned, is defined as an area of transition or ecotone between these two.

The difference of habitat preference as shown by the scores of this part of Table 28 is more striking. While there is a balance between the deciduous and coniferous habitats, there is a strong predominance of species that inhabit swampy situtations. The relative number of species associated with aquatic environments is also quite high while very few species can be ranked as Cosmopolitan. This trend is also to be expected both from the present ecology of Bois Blanc Island, which is low and swampy over much of its area, and the apparent selection involved in the reliance of the Juntunen site peoples on the resources of the lake and swamp.

The distribution of the fish species recovered is tabulated by drainage pattern. Again, the species represented in the site were almost equally a mixture of fish typical of the Mississippi-Ohio drainage and those typical of the northern boreal area. Most of the Juntunen species were those which preferred shallow water with clean sand or gravel bottoms and most were spring spawners.

The habitat preference of the species within each of four major occupation zones is caluclated in order to determine if there has been any notable change in the fauna through time. Table 29 shows the percentage of species from four occupation levels of the site which occur in the three biotic provinces (see also Figure 4). The most significant change appears in the contrast between occupation A and occupation D. The fauna of occupation A (AD 835) is characterized by a greater percentage of northern Hudsonian species and at the same time a low percentage of species more typical of the southern Carolinian province. This was followed by a decrease in boreal species and an increase in Carolinian species in occupations B and C. This trend culminates in occupation D, somewhere between A.D. 910 and A.D. 1060, when the percentage of Carolinian species increased at the expense of Hudsonian species to a point where they were about equally balanced. During the succeeding E and F occupations, Hudsonian fauna again became established as the dominant type. It should be noted at once that these changes were not of great magnitude. They appear instead to be reflections of a minor period of increased warmth which was characterized by the northward movement of several Carolinian species. The chance that this change was due to a differential in hunting selection is minimized both by the gradual nature of the change and by the apparent similarity in the intensity, seasonality, and in the selective patterns of occupations A and D.

Examination of the percentages of species preferring different habitat types as shown in Figure 4 also reveals some interesting stratigraphic changes. In this sequence, the most noticeable change occurred in occuaptions B and C where there was an abrupt decline in the percentage of swamp and bog species associated with an increase in the percentage of those species favoring both deciduous and transitional type communities. This change is felt to be both the result of selection and a change in the physical environment of the site. It is, first of all, unlikely that there was any significant change in the amount of swampy habitat near the site since this type of habitat would have been isolated from any lake level rise by older and higher

Figure 4

Percentage of Species in Each Biotic
Province and Habitat Type by Occupation
Levels at the Juntunen Site

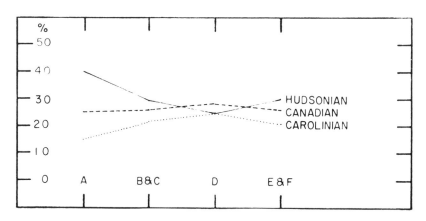

A. Biotic Provinces

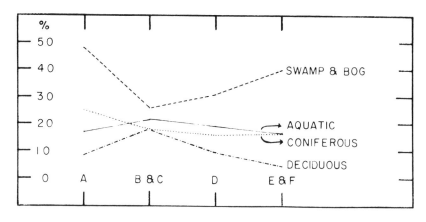

B. Habitats

TABLE 29

PERCENTAGE OF SPECIES OCCURRING IN EACH HABITAT TYPE
CALCULATED BY OCCUPATION LEVEL AT JUNTUNEN SITE, MACKINAC COUNTY, MICHIGAN

Occupations	A Biotic Province					B Habitat Type				
	Hudsonian	Canadian	Carolinian	Cosmopolitan	Aquatic	Swamp and Bog	Coniferous	Deciduous	Transitional	Cosmopolitan
Levels E and F	30	26	21	21	17	40	17	4.4	4.4	2
Level D	25	28	25	20	19	31	16	9.5	4.7	2
Levels B and C	29	26	22	22	22	26	18	18	14	--
Level A	40	25	15	20	17	48	25	8.5	--	--
All Levels	22	25	22	29	20	33	18	15	7.8	4

beach ridges. This then points to a decline in the selection of these species. Since, however, the increase in the percentage of deciduous and transition community type species occurs at the expense of swamp and bog species, these species may have been more locally abundant. The geomorphology of level B does tend to support the hypothesis since this level is characterized by a period of accumulation of windblown sands. Such conditions would, no doubt, result in a serial stage characterized by the dominance of grasses and shrubs. In addition, occupation B seems to have been a relatively short-term fishing station with a predominance of species taken directly from the lake or its immediate margins.

Table 30 is a list of the species recovered from the Juntunen site as they occurred in the six major occupation levels. Although the total biotic associations and habitat preferences of the species of the major occupation levels have already been discussed in some detail, it is necessary to note some of the more particular occurrences of species within this framework. Occupation A contains five species which do not recur in later levels—the channel catfish, saw-whet owl, ringbilled gull, the otter, and the red squirrel. Of these species, only the red squirrel is typically a northern species. The freshwater drum and the deer appeared for the first time in occupation level B. These were both more typically southern species. The deer reappears in occupation levels C and D while the drum reappears only in occupation D. Neither species occurs in the latest occupation levels of the site. The ruffed grouse and deer mouse both appeared in occupation level C and neither recurred in later times. The habitat preference of both of these species is quite nonrestrictive. The northern pike, chipmunk, Blanding's turtle, turkey, goshawk, bald eagle, and bear appeared for the first time in occupation level D. The pike, Blanding's turtle, turkey, goshawk, and bear do not appear again. The appearance of the turkey in this level is quite interesting since this bird is closely associated with the deciduous forest, and since historic times has been restricted to the Carolinian province whose northern border is about 200 miles to the south of the Juntunen site. The appearance of the turkey in this region seems to correspond with a general northward shift in fauna which was more typical of a southern climate during the period of about A.D. 1000. Only the snapping turtle appeared for the first time in occupation E and subsequently did not reappear. Occupation level F, the latest occupation level, excluding recent deposits, contained four new species. This level presumably includes occupation level F and more recent deposition. These species were the red-shouldered hawk, blue jay, crow, and the northern redhorse sucker. The habitat preference of these

TABLE 30

QUANTITATIVE ANALYSIS OF SPECIES BY LEVEL
FROM THE JUNTUNEN SITE, MACKINAC COUNTY, MICHIGAN

Species	A	A-B Transition	B	C	D	E	F
Sturgeon	119	2	45	55	17	15	11
Whitefish	64	45	5	11	31	14	16
Walleye	20	1	2	1	5	5	14
Passenger pigeon	2	0	2	1	2	9	11
Dog	15	0	6	19	6	6	14
Beaver	17	0	10	5	5	9	16
Lake trout	5	14	1	2	2	0	2
Loon	3	0	0	1	2	8	2
Snowshoe hare	5	0	1	1	2	0	3
Longnose sucker	1	8	1	0	9	0	1
Yellow perch	7	0	1	2	4	0	0
Smallmouth bass	3	0	1	0	2	0	2
Painted turtle	1	0	2	4	2	0	0
Caribou	2	0	0	1	1	0	2
White sucker	5	0	1	0	10	0	0
Raven	4	0	0	0	1	0	1
Canada goose	1	0	2	0	0	1	0
Moose	2	0	0	0	3	1	0
Longnose gar	14	0	0	0	1	0	0
Largemouth bass	1	0	0	0	1	0	0
Silver redhorse sucker	6	0	0	0	1	0	0
Porcupine	2	0	0	0	0	0	1
Red-backed vole	1	0	0	0	0	1	0
Channel catfish	1	0	0	0	0	0	0

TABLE 30--Continued

| Species | Levels | | | | | | |
	A	A-B Transition	B	C	D	E	F
Saw-whet owl	1	0	0	0	0	0	0
Ringbilled gull	1	0	0	0	0	0	0
Otter	1	0	0	0	0	0	0
Red squirrel	1	0	0	0	0	0	0
Whitetail deer	0	0	1	1	1	0	0
Freshwater drum	0	0	2	0	1	0	0
Brown bullhead	0	0	2	0	0	0	0
Ruffed grouse	0	0	0	1	0	0	0
Deer mouse	0	0	0	1	0	0	0
Bald eagle	0	0	0	0	2	1	3
Chipmunk	0	0	0	0	1	1	0
Pike	0	0	0	0	2	0	0
Blanding's turtle	0	0	0	0	3	0	0
Turkey	0	0	0	0	5	0	0
Goshawk	0	0	0	0	1	0	0
Bear	0	0	0	0	1	0	0
Snapping turtle	0	0	0	0	0	1	0
Northern redhorse	0	0	0	0	0	0	4
Crow	0	0	0	0	0	0	2
Blue jay	0	0	0	0	0	0	2
Red-shouldered hawk	0	0	0	0	0	0	1
Cow	0	0	0	0	0	0	x
Pig	0	0	0	0	0	0	x
Chicken	0	0	0	0	0	0	x

species and the other species of occupation level F most closely
resembles those of occupation A.

Apart from the species that were restricted to the afore-
mentioned levels, some species were more or less distributed
in the lower, middle, or upper levels of the site. The red
squirrel, otter, saw-whet owl, ring-billed gull, and channel catfish, the longnose gar, silver redhorse sucker, and the porcupine
were all largely restricted to the lower parts of the site. Species
which occurred predominantly in the middle levels of the site include the longnose sucker, drum, painted turtle, Blanding's turtle,
deer, ruffed grouse, deer mouse, turkey, bear, and goshawk.
Those few species which occurred predominantly in the upper
levels include the loon, bald eagle, northern redhorse sucker,
red-shouldered hawk, crow, and blue jay. The loon, raven, porcupine, and red-backed vole seem to have been more or less
related to the earliest and latest levels of the site, but were not
frequent in the middle levels. Most of the other species were
evenly distributed in all levels of the site. This distribution of
species within these wider stratigraphic categories again seems
to indicate that the middle occupations occurred in a warmer
period than either of the earliest or latest occupations.

Table 31 is a list of the animal remains from the Juntunen
site arranged in their relative order of abundance. Whenever
possible, an estimate is also given for the number of individuals
represented by this total. The estimates of numbers of fish
are usually very conservative. Although general conditions for
the preservation of bone material were quite good at the Juntunen
site, the actual number of identifiable specimens was quite
small relative to the total amount of bone. This condition is
thought to be a function of both the intensity of occupation and
the nature of the bone material. In areas of intense occupation,
the bone was apparently subjected to much trampling under foot.
The skull plates of sturgeon, for example, though fairly strong,
were fragmentary, and seldom recovered intact. Since most of
the bone from the site was fragile fish bone, much of it was fragmented beyond indentification. In addition, most mammal bone
was probably intentionally broken. The figures given in Table
31, therefore, represent only a small percentage of the actual
animal bone which was recovered from the Juntunen site.

Table 32 goes further to illustrate this situation. In the thirteen
excavation units considered each scrap of bone is counted including
bone fragements less than one square centimeter in size. It can be
seen quite clearly that fish remains comprise over 85 percent of all
of the bone material. Of the fish remains, 62 percent are vertebrae.

TABLE 31

THE RELATIVE FREQUENCY OF IDENTIFIED ANIMAL
SPECIES FROM THE JUNTUNEN SITE, MACKINAC COUNTY, MICHIGAN

Scientific Name	Common Name	Number of Bones	Percent of Total Identified Bones	Minimum Number of Individuals
Acipenser fulvescens	Sturgeon	888	36.0	350
Coregonus (clupeiformis)	Whitefish	262	11.0	119
Castor canadensis	Beaver	245	10.0	46
Haliaeetus leucocephalus	Bald eagle	240*	10.0	12
Canis familiaris	Dog	196	8.0	31
Gavia immer	Loon	75	3.0	20
Stizostedion vitreum	Walleye	61	2.4	14
Ectopistes migratorius	Passenger pigeon	57	2.2	17
Lepus americanus	Snowshoe hare	37	1.5	18
Salvelinus namaycush	Lake trout	36	1.5	24
Lepisosteus osseus	Longnose gar	29	1.1	7
Catostomus catostomus	Longnose sucker	28	1.1	7
Tamias striatus	Chipmunk	26*	1.1	8
Peromyscus maniculatus	Deer mouse	23*	.8	5
Catostomus commersoni	White sucker	18	.7	5
Perca flavescens	Yellow perch	16	.6	5
Chrysemys picta	Painted turtle	16	.6	6
Corvus corax	Raven	15	.6	10
Cervidae	. . .	13	.5	..
Micropterus salmoides	Largemouth bass	12	.5	4
Lutra canadensis	Otter	11	.4	7
Alces alces	Moose	10	.4	7
Erethizon dorsatum	Porcupine	10	.4	5
Meleagris gallopavo	Turkey	10	.4	6
Rangifer caribou	Caribou	8	.3	3
Ursus americanus	Black bear	7	.3	6
Aplodinotus grunniens	Drum	7	.3	4
Moxostoma	Sucker	7	.3	..
Micropterus dolomieui	Smallmouth bass	7	.3	3
Moxostoma anisurum	Silver redhorse	6	.2	1
Larus delawarensis	Ring-billed gull	6	.2	3
Branta canadensis	Canada goose	6	.2	4
Anas	Duck	6	.2	..
Clethrionomys gapperi	Red-backed vole	5	.2	5
Corvus brachyrhynchos	Crow	4	.2	2
Odocoileus virginianus	Deer	4	.2	4

TABLE 31--Continued

Scientific Name	Common Name	Number of Bones	Percent of Total Identified Bones	Minimum Number of Individuals
Synaptomys cooperi	Bog lemming	4	.2	2
Moxostoma aureolum	Northern redhorse	4	.2	1
Emys blandingi	Blanding's turtle	3	.1	3
Ictalurus punctatus	Channel catfish	3	.1	2
Esox lucius	Northern pike	3	.1	2
Cyanocitta cristata	Blue jay	2	.1	1
Bucephala clangula	Golden eye	2	.1	1
Passiformes	Song bird	2	.1	2
Bonasa umbellus	Ruffed grouse	2	.1	2
Tamiasciurus hudsonicus	Red squirrel	2	.1	1
Chelydra serpentina	Snapping turtle	2	.1	1
Ictalurus nebulosus	Brown bullhead	2	.1	1
Salmo	Trout	2	.1	2
Hydroprogne caspia	Caspian tern	2	.1	1
Strix varia	Barred owl	1	. .	1
Accipiter gentilis	Goshawk	1	. .	1
Aegolius acadicus	Saw-whet owl	1	. .	1
Buteo lineatus	Red-shouldered hawk	1	. .	1
Martes americana	Marten	1	. .	1
Ondatra zibethicus	Muskrat	1	. .	1
Mustela vison	Mink	1	. .	1
Ambloplites rupestris	Rock bass	1	. .	1
Cyprinidae	Minnow family	1	. .	1
Stizostedion canadense	Sauger	1	. .	.
Gallus gallus	Chicken	9	.4	3
Bos taurus	Cow	8	.3	4
	Total	2,469	100.0	

*High total bone count due to articulated skeletons of buried or intrusive remains.

TABLE 32

QUANTITATIVE ANALYSIS OF THE BONES FROM EXCAVATION UNITS*
FROM THE JUNTUNEN SITE, MACKINAC COUNTY, MICHIGAN

	Fish Vertebrae	Fish Bone Unidentifiable	Turtle Bone Unidentifiable	Bird Bone Unidentifiable	Mammal Bone Unidentifiable	Fish Bone Identified	Turtle Bone Identified	Bird Bone Identified	Mammal Bone Identified	Total
Number of Bones	23,371	8,332	619	475	2,822	1,160	16	245	462	37,502
Percent of Total	62.31	22.21	1.65	1.27	7.55	3.09	.04	.65	1.23	100.0

*
1600–1070	1490–1010
1680–1240	1680–1255
1680–1245	1720–1210
1700–1140	1970–1185
1700–1160	1890–1125
1700–1190	1880–1130
1710–1180	

To these is added the large amount of extremely fragmentary fish bone so that the actual percentage of identifiable bone is very small.

Table 33 shows the quantitative analysis of bone from the various occupation levels of the Juntunen site. Occupation levels A and D contain the largest bone samples. When the actual density of bone per cubic foot of matrix is computed, there is a gradual diminuation of material between occupation levels F and A-B transition with a sharp increase again in occupation level A. Since neither the rates of cultural nor natural deposition were controlled, it is apparent that neither the total bone sample per level nor the amount of bone per cubic foot of matrix per level is an accurate indication of occupation density. However, these two scales will be of value in the comparison of bone concentration to concentrations of pottery, flint, and various artifact types.

Two interesting deviations appear in the gross quantitative analysis of bone type by occupation levels. Table 33 shows that 90.58 percent and 6.06 percent of the bone in all levels are fish and mammal respectively. In occupation level C, however, this ratio changes to 78.83 percent fish and 16.73 percent mammal bone. If it is assumed that winter ice would decrease the total fish harvest and therefore either absolutely or relatively increase the number of mammals taken during the winter period, it could quite safely be predicted that occupation level C was at least at one period occupied during the winter months. Applying the same rationale to the occupation(s) of level A-B transition where there is a very high percentage of fish bone, it seems to lend additional support to the hypothesis that this occupation was, indeed, a highly specific fishing station. The relative percentage of fish, mammal, bird, and turtle bone was fairly constant in other levels of the site. Referring again to Table 30, we are able to see some interesting differences in the nature of some of the Juntunen occupations as these are reflected in the occurrence of animal species in various occupation levels. Level A contained large numbers of bones of spring and fall spawning fish, summer birds, and a relatively high frequency of large mammal bones. It, thus, appears that the occupation(s) of this level took place from early spring until late fall and, in fact, some winter big game hunting may have taken place.

The occupation of level A-B transition was of a much different kind. Here we find that 99 percent of the bone is fish and that most of this represents fall spawning species such as the whitefish and lake trout. Spring spawners such as the

TABLE 33

QUANTITATIVE ANALYSIS OF BONE BY LEVEL FROM JUNTUNEN SITE, MACKINAC COUNTY, MICHIGAN

Levels	Fish Bone	Percent of Fish Bone	Mammal Bone	Percent of Mammal Bone	Bird Bone	Percent of Bird Bone	Turtle Bone	Percent of Turtle Bone	Total Bone	Percent of Total Bone	Cubic Feet of Matrix	Bones per Cubic Feet
F	1,043	95.43	41	3.75	7	.64	2	.18	1,093	8.05	33	33,12
E	1,769	91.47	100	5.17	39	2.02	26	1.34	1,934	14.25	68	28,44
D	2,218	91.46	152	6.27	21	.87	34	1.40	2,425	17.86	126	19,25
C	1,672	78.83	355	16.74	16	.75	78	3.68	2,121	15.62	162	13,09
B	1,641	91.93	55	3.08	22	1.23	67	3.75	1,785	13.15	161	11,09
A-B Transition	671	99.26	1	.15	2	.30	2	.30	676	4.98	174	3,89
A	3,284	92.71	119	3.36	82	2.32	57	1.61	3,542	26.09	114	31,07
Totals	12,298	90.59	823	6.06	189	1.39	266	1.96	13,576	100.00	838	16,20

sturgeon and walleye, so common in some levels, were represented by only a few bones. The high frequency of bones of one spring spawning fish, the longnose sucker, is not difficult to explain since this species moves into shallow water in the late fall, a habit which parallels the spawning movement of both the whitefish and lake trout. In view of this faunal assemblage, it is evident that the occupation of A-B transition represents a short term fall fishing station.

Occupation B is thought to represent still another type of seasonal variation of occupation of the site. Here we see a fauna characterized by a high frequency of spring spawning fish, particularly sturgeon, and a relatively small number of bones of fall spawning fish. It is, therefore, assumed that the occupation(s) of this level took place primarily during the spring and perhaps mid-summer. Although the occupation of level C seems to be very similar to the occupation which was just described for level B, the appearance of greater numbers of bones of fall spawning fish may indicate a slight extension of the season of occupation into the early autumn. In addition, it has already been suggested that the high frequency of mammal bones in this level may indicate winter hunting activity.

The three remaining occupation levels, D, E, and F are very similar to occupation A. All contained the bones of species which were available from early spring until the late fall and all had relatively low frequencies of large mammal bones. It would, thus, appear that these levels represent occupations which were continuous from early spring through the late fall season.

In summary, we are able to describe three primary occupation patterns from the habits of the species which occur in the Juntunen site deposits. The occupation of level A-B transition was apparently a short fall occupation for the specific purpose of exploiting the abundant fall spawning whitefish and lake trout. This occupation probably occurred during the month of November and early December. People who deposited the faunal refuse of level B, and perhaps level C, were concentrating their subsistence efforts upon catching spring spawning fish and although they may have continued to occupy the site during the summer, the faunal remains indicate that the main occupation took place during April and May. The third pattern is illustrated by the occupations of levels A, D, E, and F. Here the faunal record indicates long term occupations which began in the early spring, lasted through the summer, and terminated in the early winter or late fall. It is interesting to note, in view of the fact that agricultural activities were in evidence on the site by the time of the occupation of levels E and F, that the advent of food production did not change the character of the seasonal movements of people, nor the kinds of natural resources that they were exploiting. This fact certainly supports the theory that food production played only a minor supplementary role in the total subsistence of the people who occupied the Juntunen site.

It is evident that fish were the staple food element in the diet of Juntunen site peoples and that the very location and existence of the site was a function of available fish resources in that locality. In order to say this, one must think in terms of total food poundage rather than in terms of the number of fish bones recovered from the site. Table 34 is prepared to illustrate the amount of food provided by each of the most important meat species; all species which did not supply at least 100 pounds of meat were not included. Actually, the amount of meat shown in Table 34 represents less than one-tenth of the site deposit, a deposit which was accumulated during an unknown number of occupations by an unknown number of people over a period of 300 or 400 years. Yet, despite these uncontrolled variables, the data presented in Table 34 yields some significant information about the Juntunen site economy. We can readily see that sturgeon was by far the principal source of food for these people. When, however, we consider the total meat, fish, including sturgeon, supplied about two-thirds of the total meat while mammals supplied a little less than the remaining on-third. It will be noted that these estimates were made for the total meat, not the total diet. Although meat was most important in this economy, plant foods were also utilized during the summer months. If estimates were to be made of the percentages of various food elements in the total summer diet, plant foods would probably contribute about 15 percent of the total; fish about 60 percent; mammal about 20 percent; and bird, turtle, shellfish, etc., about 5 percent. It must be remembered, however, that by the very nature of hunting and gathering groups, these percentages would fluctuate greatly as dependency shifted from one resource to another as these became seasonally and geographically available. The Juntunen people, for instance, probably subsisted on 80 to 90 percent mammal foods during the winter hunting period.

One other interesting point is illustrated in Table 34, the relative efficiency of hunting as opposed to fishing as a subsistence activity. Here we see that the average weight of each fish caught was much less than the average weight of each mammal killed. Does this mean that fishing was a less efficient way of obtaining food? The answer is not simple and involves other

APPENDIX E

TABLE 34

APPROXIMATE AMOUNT OF MEAT SUPPLIED BY THE MOST
IMPORTANT GAME SPECIES OF THE JUNTUNEN SITE
MACKINAC COUTNY, MIGHIGAN (AFTER WHITE 1953)

Species	Approximate Number of Individuals Represented	Live Weight of Species in Pounds	Percent of Usable Meat	Pounds of Usable Meat Per Individual	Total Pounds of Usable Meat Per Species
Sturgeon	350	45	80	36	12,600
Moose	7	800	50	400	2,800
Beaver	46	55	70	38.5	1,771
Black bear	6	300	70	210	1,260
Whitefish	119	13	80	10.4	1,237
Dog	30	40	50	20	600
Lake trout	36	18	80	14.4	518
Caribou	3	200	50	100	300
Deer	4	150	50	75	300
Porcupine	10	15	70	10.5	105
Loon	20	7	70	4.9	98
Totals	631	1,643			21,589

		Percent of Total
Total Pounds of Usable Fish	14,355	66.49
Total Pounds of Usable Mammal	7,136	33.05
Total Pounds of Usable Bird	98	.46
Total	21,589	100.00

	Number of Individuals	Total Pounds of Usable Meat	Pounds of Usable Meat Per Individual
Fish	505	14,355	28.43
Mammals	106	7,136	67.32

variables such as the sizes of the fish and mammals available and, most important, their abundance. If mammals were as abundant as fish, it would have been more economical in terms of human energy expended to exploit mammals since each mammal killed yielded more food than each fish which was caught. If we can assume, however, that people who have adapted to the natural environment in which they live characteristically achieve an efficient means of exploiting that environment, then mammal hunting was not the most efficient subsistence activity for Juntunen site peoples. The efficiency of fishing is, therefore, not a function of size but of abundance. It was evidently more efficient to catch may relatively small fish than to kill few relatively large mammals. Aside from the efficiency involved in this subsistence pattern, we must also consider stability, a factor of equal importance. This is to say that fish provided a reliable resource and could be counted on as a food source day in and day out. On the other hand, mammals of this region were not reliable, and dependence upon them would have resulted in an alternation of periods of scarcity and plenty. Thus, in this region of fish-rich resources, it was profitable to exploit fish from the standpoint of both efficiency and reliability.

In addition to these advantages, the fish of the Upper Great Lakes were a nutritious food source. Fish, in general, contain adequate amounts of vitamins of the A and D groups and are a good source of thiamine (B_1) and riboflavin (B_2). Minerals such as calcium, phosphorus, and potassium constitute from 1 to 2 percent of the edible portion of fish. Fat content varies widely, but is generally between 20 and 25 percent while the protein content of all fish is fairly constant, ranging from between 15 to 20 percent of the edible portion. The real weakness of fish as a food source is the absence of any substantial amount of carbohydrate (Rostlund 1952). The energy value of food fish as expressed in calories per pound of the edible portion varies between 350 and 1,000 per pound. Sturgeon provides 415 calories per pound, while whitefish and lake trout both yield about 700 calories per pound (Atwater and Bryant 1899). Generally, the caloric value of the fish from the Juntunen site would have ranked quite high.

Considering the number of pounds of meat of the species listed in Table 34, this weight of fish would have provided about 40,000,000 calories. Calculating on an average of 1,000 calories per pound, mammals would have provided about 7,000,000 calories and, at 500 calories per pound, birds would have supplied about 100,000 calories. With the addition of the numerous food species which do not appear in Table 34, the total number of calories provided by the food materials which were analyzed probably amounted to at least 50,000,000. We may also suppose that the minimum daily nutritional requirement for maintaining these people in a healthy condition was about 1,500 calories per person per day. This means that the amount of food remains represented by the animal bones recovered from the Juntunen site supplied enough calories to support one person for a period of approximately 33,333 days, or, conversely, 33,333 people for one day.

In order to make a meaningful evaluation of the Juntunen subsistence potential, it is necessary to make some appraisal of the actual number of people who would have inhabited a site of this type in the Straits of Mackinac area. The population estimates of early travellers may not reflect aboriginal population densities because of European diseases, etc. Villages of 30 to 50 people along the south shore of Lake Superior may be an accurate estimate for this type of site (Schoolcraft, 1820). Thus 30 people could have subsisted for some 1,111 days on the food present. Since the site was apparently only occupied for about 200 days a year, this same amount of food would have supported 30 people for about five yearly occupations. Since only about one-tenth of the site was excavated, since only a small percentage of the animal bone could be identified as to species, and since plant remains were not considered in these calculations, these figures represent an extremely conservative estimate. If we expand the original estimate to include only the unexcavated part of the site, perhaps 30 people could have lived on the site for 50 seasons or 50 people for 30 seasons.

Calculations of this type are, of course, highly speculative since they hold constant the rate of deposition, area of deposition, population level, and diet—all factors which are never constant. These figures are presented, however, not as accurate ones, but only as rough estimates. Their true value will be in comparing the economy of the Juntunen site with that of other sites in the area when data on the latter become available. Data on nutrition will also be useful in this respect and may, in addition, be used in the study of the stature, weight, and pathology of the human population.

An analysis of the prehistoric fauna of the Juntunen site would not be complete without comparing its faunal assemblage with the species which now inhabit Bois Blanc Island. This comparison is hampered by our lack of knowledge of the present fauna of Bois Blanc Island. The amphibians and reptiles of the island are probably best known, but unfortunately few of these appeared in the site deposits. A survey of Bois Blanc mammals has been undertaken in the last few years by Dr. William H. Burt of the University of Michigan Museum of Zoology so that a good deal of information is available on the present mammalian fauna. It is unfortunate, however, that so little work has been done on the distribution of lake fishes in Bois Blanc waters. Knowledge of the avian fauna of the area is limited to a published check list of the birds of the Douglas Lake region of the northern Lower Peninsula (Nelson 1956).

It is surprising to find that the archaeological and modern faunal lists compare rather closely. Those differences which do arise seem to be the direct result of the impact of modern technology on the natural environment of the Upper Great Lakes area as a whole. Sturgeon have been nearly exterminated by commercial fishing, and the numbers of lake trout and white-fish have been greatly depleted by the introduction of the lam-rey eel. These have been largely replaced by the more prolific suckers and the introduced carp. The passenger pigeon was exterminated by 1900, and the wild turkey and many of the larger birds of prey disappeared or were drastically reduced. Excessive hunting and trapping caused the disappearance of the caribou, moose, otter, and marten and a reduction in the numbers of almost all mammal species. Later, the lumbering activities which cleared the land during the latter part of the 19th century wrought extensive changes in the ecology of the Upper Great Lakes area. The low secondary growth which replaced the virgin forests offered an excellent habitat for deer and other edge species such as the coyote, grouse, cottontail rabbit, and fox squirrel.

As an isolated island, Bois Blanc may not have felt the power of modern technology as much as most of the area, but its fauna and flora have, nonetheless, been irrevocably altered. Table 35 is a list of the mammalian fauna of Bois Blanc Island supplied by Dr. Burt. This table includes those species which had been observed up until October, 1962. All but six of these species were also recovered from the Juntunen site. The absence of the meadow vole and masked shrew in the archaeological deposit probably does not reflect ecological change, but probably these species were not collected by Juntunen site peoples because of their small sizes. It is also possible that these species did not frequent the site area, which was apparently rather dry and sandy with sparse vegetation, whereas both now

TABLE 35

PRESENT MAMMALIAN FAUNA OF BOIS BLANC

Burt, 1962	Juntunen Site
Sorex cinereus - Maksed shrew	
Procyon lotor - Raccoon	
Lutra canadensis - Otter	X
Mustela vison - Mink	X
Vulpes fulva - Red fox	
Canis latrans - Coyote	
Lynx canadensis - Lynx	
Tamiasciurus hudsonicus - Red squirrel	X
Castor canadensis - Beaver	X
Peromyscus maniculatus - Deer mouse	X
Clethrionomys gapperi - Boreal red-backed vole	X
Microtus - Meadow vole	
Ondatra zibethicus - Muskrat	X
Lepus americanus - Snowshoe hare	X
Odocoileus virginianus - Deer	X

prefer damp shaded conditions with thick grass cover. The raccoon and the coyote have both apparently extended their range to Bois Blanc since the site was occupied. This extension, at least in regard to the coyote, was probably due, in part, to the lumbering activities.

The appearance of the red fox in many areas of the Eastern United States since white contact has been a subject of much confusion and controversy. Although there was a native American red fox *(Vulpes fulva)* whose range seems to have been limited to the Hudsonian and perhaps Canadian provinces, the European red fox *(Vulpes vulpes)* was introduced in early colonial days for fox hunting. The latter "species" seems to have spread rapidly throughout the Carolinian province and to have crossed with the native red fox in the more northern areas. There is, therefore, some reason to question whether or not the red fox occurred on Bois Blanc before white contact.

The Canadian lynx is another mammal which has been reported from Bois Blanc Island in recent times but does not appear in archaeological deposits. Although Bois Blanc was certainly within the range of this species, it was probably absent from the Juntunen site because it was not killed by the Juntunen peoples. It has already been mentioned that some of the other large carnivores are strangely absent including the wolf, puma, bobcat, and wolverine.

One of the most notable features of Bois Blanc Island today is its tremendous deer herd. The annual hunters' deer kill per square mile on Bois Blanc is exceeded by few other areas in the Eastern United States. Yet, despite the present super-abundance of deer, only four deer bones were recovered from the Juntunen site. One must conclude that Bois Blanc supported few deer before the island was lumbered, and that the present abundance of deer is a function of the new ecological situation.

Two of the reptilian species are of particular interest in light of their present distribution. The eastern massasauga *(Sistrurus catenatus cantenatus)* a small rattlesnake, reaches the most northerly point of its range in Michigan on Bois Blanc. Since this snake formerly occurred locally throughout the Lower Peninsula, its presence here seems to strengthen the theory that the faunal affiliations of Bois Blanc are most closely linked with that peninsula. The queen snake *(Natrix septemvittata)* also occurs on Bois Blanc. This is of great interest since it is not only the most northern point of the queen snake's range, but it is also some 125 miles north of other known records in Michigan. Except for its presence on Bois Blanc, the northern limit of the queen snake's range is coterminous with the northern edge of the Carolinian province in the central part of the Lower Peninsula. This isolated occurrence suggests that the queen snake once had a wider range during more favorable (warmer) times and that a subsequent less advantageous (cold) period caused a retraction in its range, leaving the Bois Blanc population stranded. This inferred warm period may have been during the Altithermal or it may have been the warmer period of the Juntunen sequence which dates about A.D. 1000 and which is characterized by the introduction of other typically Carolinian species such as the deer and turkey. The latter explanation may be more likely since the Altithermal precedes and also corresponds with the Nipissing high lake level which would have made Bois Blanc even more inaccessible because of the presence of a second wide land channel through southern Cheboygan County in addition to increased width of the present channel.

There is also evidence of a northward movement of the prairie vole *(Microtus ochrogaster)* during this later period. The prairie vole is now limited to Berrien and Cass Counties, the two most southwestern counties in Michigan (Burt 1954). The remains of a prairie vole were recently recovered by W. O. Pruitt in Leelanaw County on Michigan's northwestern Lower Peninsula. These remains were dated at A.D. 1220±250 (M-208; Crane 1956).

It thus seems possible that there was general northward movement of southern species at about A.D. 1000, accompanying a minor warming period, and that this was represented in the Juntunen faunal profile. And, in contrast, there are several species in the archaeological fauna whose ranges have retracted toward the north. In the cases of the black bear, otter, beaver, and mink, this "retraction" was simply the result of the survival of these species in less densely populated peripheral areas. The northward movement of the marten, moose, and certainly the woodland caribou, however, reflected climatic and ecological changes as well as a retreat before civilization. Most notable in this respect is the moose which normally does not thrive in the same habitat as the deer. The changes which produced the northward encroachment of the deer and other southern species were, no doubt, the same changes which caused the northward retreat of the moose and other now typically northern species.

Table 36 is a list of the Mollusca from the Juntunen site. These species were identified by Barry Miller of the Museum of Paleontology, University of Michigan. As a whole, molluscs

TABLE 36

MOLLUSCA OF THE JUNTUNEN SITE, MACKINAC COUNTY, MICHIGAN

Species	Number of Individuals	Percent of Total
Terestrial gastropods		
Helicodiscus parallelus	79	32.8
Anguispira alternata	32	13.3
Zonitoides arborea	25	10.4
Triodopsis albolabris	19	7.8
Polygyra	7	2.9
Stenotrema fraterna	3	1.2
Polygyra albolabris	2	.8
Retinella electrina	1	.4
Zonitoides nitida	1	.4
Discus cronkhitel	1	.4
Aquatic gastropods and pelecypods		
Unionidae	15	6.2
Pleurocera acuta	14	5.8
Goniobasis livescens	13	5.4
Elliptio dilatatus	11	4.6
Pleurocera spp.	10	4.1
Ligumia recta	3	1.2
Ligumia nasuta	2	.8
Ligumia	2	.8
Strophitus spp.	1	.4
	241	99.8
Exotic species		
Anculosa	2	
Prunum apicinum (formerly Marginella)	762	

were quite rare on the Juntunen site and of slight importance in the subsistence economy. A great many of the terrestrial gastropods were recovered in the proximity of the ossuary where they were apparently drawn by decaying organic material. A few other molluscs were scattered throughout the refuse deposit. Nevertheless, some effort must have been made to collect the aquatic species and possibly the larger terrestrial species.

Most of the molluscs of the Juntunen site were rather common species which thrived under a wide variety of habitats. Yet, even though some of these species were collected, a habitat analysis of this list would probably be meaningless. There are, however, two interesting species, both of which are extensively southern. The pelecypod *(Elliptio dilatatus)* is not common in the northern Lower Peninsula of Michigan, and the most northern record of this species in the extensive files of the Mullusc Division of the University of Michigan Museum is from Alpena, at least 50 miles southeast of Bois Blanc Island. The same situation is true of *Pleurocera acuta*, the appearance of these species on Bois Blanc seeming to constitute or approximate the northern limits of their range. Perhaps, at least in the case of *E. dilatatus*, the Juntunen samples may have represented a northward extension during warmer times or relic populations from previous warmer periods.

Two interesting exotic species were also recovered—a freshwater gastropod *(Anculosa)* which commonly occurs throughout Tennessee and Alabama, but not much north of the Ohio River, and a marine gastropod *(Prunum apicinum)*, which occurs along the Eastern and Gulf coasts of the United States from the Carolinas to Texas. Both species were used as beads and those made from *P. apicinum* were much more abundant. Burial #19 of feature #11 apparently was interred wearing a shirt or vest to which seven hundred *Prunum* shells were attached. These shells are one of the few indications of trade contact between Juntunen peoples and people of other areas.

Domestic dog remains were very common at the Juntunen site. One hundred ninety-six dog bones were recovered and these are thought to represent about 31 individuals. Dog bones were encoutnered in all levels of the site. In only one instance, feature #5, square 1970-1185, was there enough bone from one individual to reconstruct a complete skull. This was a young animal which was intentionally buried. Seven other mandibles or maxilla are complete enough for metric analysis and these data are given in Table 37. The measurements presented here follow Haag (1948). After compiling a great many measurements

TABLE 37

THE MEAN VALUES OF EACH MEASUREMENT OF THE JUNTUNEN SITE DOGS

Occipital length	181 cm.	Alveolus P^2-M^2	55 cm.
Basal length	159.5 cm.	Alveolus M^1-M^2	17.75 cm.
Condylo-basal length	165 cm.	Length carnassial P_4	16.6 cm.
Palatal length	88 cm.	Alveolus I_1-M_3	84.5 cm.
Width at M^1	59.5 cm.	Alveolus $C-M_3$	85 cm.
Width a canines	32.25 cm.	Alveolus P_1-M_3	69.25
Width at mastoids	72 cm.?	Alveolus P_2-M_3	66.25
Width at occipital condyles	34 cm.	Alveolus P_3-M_3	56.5 cm.
Width at zygomatic arch	100 cm.	Alveolus P_4-M_3	44.9 cm.
Nasal length	57.5 cm.	Alveolus M_1-M_3	33.2 cm.
Occiput-nasion	102 cm.	Length carnassial M_1	20.4 cm.
Orbit-alveolus I^1	76 cm.	Condylo-symphysis length	125.6 cm.
Supraorbital width	50 cm.	Bicondylar width	88 cm.
Interorbital width	. . .	Humerus	136.25
Cranial height	62 cm.	Diameter humerus head	35 cm.
Least cranial width	35 cm.	Traverse head	22.25 cm.
Maximum cranial width	55 cm.	Radius	149 cm.
Meatus-alveolus I^1	143 cm.	Ulna	180 cm.
Alveolus I^1-M^2	89 cm.	Ulna notch	149.5 cm.
Alveolus $C-M^2$	73 cm.	Femur	164.5 cm.
Alveolus $P1-M^2$	61 cm.	Tibia	161.5 cm.

of North American dogs, Haag concludes that there are eight statistically significant populations of dogs in America north of Mexico. These categories listed in increasing order of size are as follows:

1)   Kentucky shell-heap dogs

2)   Alabama shell-heap dogs

3)   Small Kodiac Island dogs

4)   Woodland-Mississippi dogs

5)   Northwest coast shell-heap dogs

6)   Large Kodiak Island dogs

7)   Siberian dogs

8)   Eskimo dogs

There, thus, appears to be both a north to south gradient in size with the largest dogs in the north, and a temporal gradient, in that Archaic dogs are smaller than Woodland and Mississippian dogs.

The dogs of the Juntunen site were larger than either their temporal or geographic position would indicate. Compared with Haag's size range, the Juntunen dogs consistently fell between the Northwest coast shell-heap dogs and the large Kodiak dogs. The Juntunen dogs, on the whole, were also slightly larger than both the dogs of the late prehistoric Moccasin Bluff site in southwestern Michigan and the dogs from the West Twin Lakes mound in the Lower Peninsula of Michigan, a site dating about A.D. 900. Morphologically, the Juntunen dogs closely resemble Haag's Woodland-Mississippi population. The muzzle is narrow and high, and there was only a slight degree of inflation behind the supraorbital process. The brain case was well rounded and the sagittal crest was weak (perhaps because this specimen represents a rather young individual). In a lateral view, the sagittal profile is quite convex and in this point differs from the generalized Woodland-Mississippian dog which has a horizontal sagittal profile. However, the most significant difference between these two populations lies in the size. The Juntunen dogs appear to be a very large variety of the Woodland-Mississippian dog. Haag (1948) tells us that the size of dogs is affected to some degree by the amount of vitamin D which they recieve. Fish is, of course, an abundant source of vitamin D, and the Juntunen dogs probably ate a large amount of fish offal which may account to some degree for their larger size. Another possibility was the presence of a larger type of dog in the boreal region of Canada which was intermediate in size between the southern Woodland-Mississippi dogs and the northern Eskimo and Kodiak dogs. In view of Haag's north to south size continuum and the geographic position of the Juntunen dogs in the continuum, this possibility seems quite likely.

Allen (1920), who preceded Haag in the study of native American dogs, originally called Haag's Woodland-Mississippian dog the "larger or common Indian dog" and remarked that the northern variety of this type seemed to attain a larger size than its southern relatives. The skull Allen illustrated from the Peel River district of the Yukon Territory and the measurements given for this skull seem to correspond rather well to those from the Juntunen site. Ritchie (1945) remarked that the larger variety of dog he recovered at Frontenac Island resembled Allen's common Indian dog but that it was somewhat larger. The new measurements of this dog given by Ritchie are quite close to those of the Juntunen dogs.

It is apparent from the dog remains at the Juntunen site that, besides the possible use of the dogs as pets or in hunting, that they were also used as food. First, the dog remains were quite fragmentary and scattered, showing that they were treated in quite the same manner as the bones of game animals. In addition, there is good evidence of butchering. In feature #39, square 1700-1160, which was a large refuse pit of either the C or D level, there were four cervical vertebrae and a femur of a young dog, all of which show knife marks. The vertebrae were cut longitudinally along the mid-line of the centrum from the ventral surface. The rib cage was then evidently forced outward on each side so that the vertebrae were broken along the mid-line of their dorsal surface. The femur showed a few superficial knife marks on the bone's neck just below the head and was severed from the shaft slightly below these marks by one clean cut. This latter process would have removed the hind leg.

Dogs also seemed to have held some ceremonial significance. It has been mentioned that feature #5 was an articulated burial of a young dog. This animal was interred in a small round pit at one corner of what appeared to be a triangular fired area measuring about 10 feet across. In the other two corners, similar pits contained the articulated skeletons of a snowshoe hare and bald eagle. This feature was most surely some sort of ceremonia structure. Another instance of the use of the dog in ceremonial

activity was the inclusion of the right and left legs minus feet of a
dog in the medicine bundle associated with Burial 3 or feature #11.
Judging from both the quantity of dog bones and the apparent role of
dogs in subsistence and ceremonial activities, these animals were
of considerable importance to Juntunen site people.

Other than the dog and snowshoe hare burial in feature #5, the
only species which was deliberately interred was the bald eagle.
One burial occurred in feature #5 of square 1970-1185, which has
already been described in connection with the dog burial. This feature contained 133 eagle bone fragments from one individual. A
nearby square, 1970-1200, sheet 2-3, contained a burial of 24 eagle
bones. Square 1700-1200, feature #28, contained a burial of over 100
eagle bone fragments. The same square, feature #13 contained a
few eagle remains. And, square 1870-1100, feature #16, also
contained an eagle burial which was not recognized as such during excavation. All of these features seem to be associated with
cultural material dating no earlier than occupation level C, but
most of them seem to be associated with occupation levels E and
F. A few eagle bones were apparently not given this special
treatment since they appeared in the village refuse.

The bald eagle did not occur in occupations earlier than
level D indicating that peoples of the late occupations made a
conscious effort to take eagles and that these birds received
preferential burial no doubt in connection with some yet un-
recognized ideological concept. The above-mentioned burial
of feature #28 was that of an adult. The skeletal elements recovered included all the bones of both legs and the right side,
the vertebrae of the cervical region and a few of the distal
lumbar vertebrae. The pelvis, rib cage, almost all of the ster-
num, and the cranium were absent. This differential inclusion
of various elements is quite puzzling. The most likely explanation seems to be that and entire eagle was not buried but only
the skin containing the more distal elements of the skeleton.
This seems to be confirmed by the eagle remains of feature #5
which again contained only fragments of limb elements. All
of the limb bones of the eagle of feature #28 were broken and
in such a regular manner that it seemed purposeful. These
breaks may have been the result of the manipulation of the
skin. Another interesting aspect of this skeleton is a partially
healed fracture of the distal end of the right radius. This
bone was either purposely broken to keep the bird a captive or
it was in the process of healing when the bird was captured.
Both explanations seem equally plausible. The other eagle

burials contained a few assorted skeletal elements but most of these were far from complete.

The burial of eagle remains at the Juntunen site appears to have been common practice yet the deliberate burial of animals other than dogs is a rare cultural trait in the northeastern United States. The only other occurrence of an eagle burial in this area was reported by Ritchie (1945) from the Late Archaic Frontenac Island site. This burial (Trench 3, Section 1) appeared to represent an entire eagle with the exception of the skull. The absence of the skull was perhaps the result of later disturbances.

In square 1700-1200, the site of the eagle burials of features #28 and #13, there was a small pit at the level of square sheet #10 which contained the proximal end of an eagle humerus which had been neatly cut from the shaft 80 mm. below the head. The object of this cut was probably to obtain the shaft as a bone tube, and the left over end was simply buried. Numerous bone tubes from the site were made of bird bones.

It is interesting to note that there seems to have been a special clustering of eagle burials. At least two were recovered in the vicinity of square 1970-1185 and at least three from square 1700-1200. The significance of this pattern is open to speculation, but it appears that specific areas were designated for the burial of eagle bones.

The remains of 53 vertebrate species were identified from the Juntunen site on Bois Blanc Island in the Straits of Mackinac. A study of the habitat preferences of these species showed that they were fairly equally balanced between those which preferred the conifer forest to the north and those which favored the southern deciduous forest. Significantly, a stratigraphic analysis of these species by occupation level revealed that this balance was not maintained during the entire history of the site. The earliest occupation level A (A.D. 835) and the latest occupation levels E and F (A.D. 1200-1300) were very similar in that they both contained a high percentage of species which were most typically associated with the Hudsonian province to the north. The middle occupation levels B and C (A.D. 900-1000) were, however, characterized by a high percentage of species which occurred most frequently in the deciduous forest of the Carolinian biotic province to the south. The habitat preference analysis thus indicates a minor warm climatic episode at about A.D. 1000, and that during this time there was a general northward movement of southern animal species.

The presence of many species that were available only at
various seasons of the year indicates that almost all of the occupations of the site took place between April and late November. One exception was the occupation between levels A and B
which seems to have been a short, late fall occupation. Another
occupation level B, probably represented a short, early spring
occupation. There is no evidence of any extensive winter occupancy.

Ninety percent of the 13,500 bones recovered in the Juntunen
site excavations were fish bones. Although this figure empha-
sizes the importance of fish in the economic activities of the
Juntunen site only a little over 65 percent of the 22,000 pounds
of meat represented by this number of bones was from fish.
Mammals comprised most of the remaining meat. Although the
exact amount of plants and plant products utilized as food can
not be accurately assessed, they are thought to have constituted
less than 15 percent of the summer and fall diet. Finally, it
is interesting to note that there was no fluctuation in either
the variety of species or the quantity of species used as food
after the advent of corn at about A.D. 1000. This indicates
that agricultural products were actually of very limited importance in the total diet of these people. Fish, the staple element
of the diet, were a very reliable and nutritious source of food.
Except for a possible deficiency of carbohydrates, which are
absent in fish but easily supplemented from other sources, the
Juntunen site people seem to have had an excellent diet.

A yearly subsistence pattern, of which we have ample
ethnographic evidence, seems to have been praticed over a wide
area of the northern Upper Great Lakes region during Late Woodland times. This pattern which has been called the inland shore
fishing complex involves the formation of large, fairly permanent
summer villages of 30 to 50 people. During the early spring
when other food was scarce the fish spawning runs concentrated
large numbers of fish in shallow water areas where they
could be exploited for human consumption. Chief among these
spring spawning species was the sturgeon which was taken in
great numbers by harpoons. During mid and late summer,
fishing continued to be important but more time was spent
hunting mammals and birds and gathering plant foods. When
the lake waters began to cool in late November large numbers
of lake trout and whitefish moved into shallow water areas to
spawn. These species were taken with harpoon and gill nets
and then stored for winter use. The completion of this fish
harvest coincided with the advent of winter and the season
of hunting. The people left the villages in small family

groups to hunt moose, caribou, and beaver on their scattered inland hunting territories. In spring the fish runs again provided food and people returned to places where they were abundant.

APPENDIX F

ANALYSIS OF THE FAUNA OF THE MOCCASIN BLUFF SITE, BERRIEN COUNTY, MICHIGAN

The Moccasin Bluff site (20-BE-B8) is a large Woodland site located in Section 22, Township 7 south, Range 18 west of Buchanan Township, Berrien County, Michigan. This site produced cultural material from nearly every archaeological horizon from the Paleo-Indian to the historic period. The main occupations, however, date from the Woodland period and the greatest amount of this material seems to have post-dated A.D. 1200. The ceramic styles and techniques of this period indicate strong Upper Mississippian influence on a basic Woodland pattern. These occupations have been attributed to either the Potawatomi or Miami by Quimby (1952) since both groups were in the Berrien County area at contact times. Perhaps the material from the latest occupations of Moccasin Bluff can be most closely equated with the late Fisher focus and Huber focus material from northeastern Illinois.

Between 1940 and 1948, John C. Birdsell, of South Bend, excavated a series of refuse pits which contained large quantities of animal bone and potsherds and a few bone and stone tools. In 1948, Birdsell donated his collection to the University of Michigan Museum of Anthropology. Later in the same year, Lynn Howard wrote a short paper on the ceramics from this collection. He found that approximately 86 percent of the sherds were either Late Woodland or Upper Mississippian and that the remaining 14 percent were Hopewellian and could be equated with the Goodall focus of southern Michigan and northern Indiana.

Unfortunately, there is little data on the areal or stratigraphic location of these pits. Birdsell's catalogue numbers for the eight refuse pits are listed as follows: 29146 pit 2N, 29147 pit 1N, 29148, 29150, 29151, 29151 refuse pit in woods, 29343 and 29343 lot #2. Yet, despite some lack of control of the field data, this material provides a good faunal sample of a culture which, unlike that of its northern neighbors, was heavily dependent upon the cultivation of maize.

The remains of 32 animal species were identified from the refuse pits (see Table 38). The habitat preferences of these species indicated that in precontact times this region of Michigan was forested, although some forest openings seem to have been present. There are, of course, quite a few species which are closely associated with water; these include the fish, turtles, all the birds except the turkey, and the beaver, otter and muskrat. The appearance of the mandible of a domestic cat in pit #29343 is thought to have been due to recent disturbances since the mandible was obviously "fresh" in comparison to the other bones in the pit. Many of the bones of pit 29343 lot #2 were bleached and eroded and clearly from the surface. Such bones included the cottontail rabbit, red fox, *Bos* or *Bison* (probably the former), swan, duck, herring gull and wood duck. These were all species which did not appear in the other pits. In addition, several species commonly found in the other pits including the dog, turkey, and sturgeon did not appear in 29343 lot #2. It thus seems that this pit was anomalous in many respects and should perhaps be eliminated from consideration except for the fact that most of the other bones in this lot appeared to have been aboriginal. Howard (1948) also noticed that there was some recent surface material in some of the pits he used for his ceramic analysis. The pig maxilla, which was recovered from pit 29151, did not appear to be "fresh" and perhaps dates from the period of early French contact in the late 17th and early 18th century.

Referring to Table 38, we can see that sturgeon, deer, beaver, turkey, and dog bones were most numerous. When, however, the total amount of meat supplied by each of these species is examined (Table 39), the order of importance is rearranged. Deer supplied about 45 percent of the meat, elk 27 percent, sturgeon 9 percent, beaver 6 percent, and bear 5 percent. These totals do not represent percentages of the total diet because, as previously mentioned, these people were primarily dependent upon agricultural products. In as much as maize was the staple food element, products of the hunt were only a dietary supplement. Hunting was important, however, since game was the only source of protein, a vital dietary element.

The fact that game was not the dietary staple becomes apparent when examining the kinds and numbers of food species which were present. Instead of utilizing many different food resources as hunters and gathers do, these people were strongly selective in their hunting activities. For instance, fishing was apparently not practiced at all except for sturgeon which were

TABLE 38

FAUNAL REMAINS FROM THE MOCCASIN BLUFF REFUSE PITS

Species	Number of Bones								Totals	Percent of total Identified Bone
	29146 2N	29147 IN	29148	29150	29151	29151 Pit in Woods	29343	29343 Lot #2		
Deer Odocoileus virginianus	24	51	48	195	226	33	214	143	934	35.2
Beaver Castor canadensis	5	8	9	88	36	1	29	2	178	6.8
Dog Canis familiaris	4	3	3	12	19		17		58	2.2
Elk Cervus canadensis		2	1	15	1	4	14	2	39	1.5
Porcupine Erethizon dorsatum	2	3		2	14	1	8	1	31	1.2
Raccoon Procyon lotor	2	1		4	4		6	1	18	.7
Woodchuck Marmota monax	5			1			4	5	15	.6
Bear Ursus americanus		1		1	1		1		4	.2
Muskrat Ondatra zibethicus			1	1				2	4	.2
Wolf Canis lupus		1	1		1				3	.1
Cottontail Rabbit* Sylvilagus floridanus								3	3	.1
Otter Lutra canadensis	1	1							2	.1
Red Fox* Vulpes fulva								2	2	.1
Striped skunk Mephitis mephitis					2				2	.1
Gray squirrel Sciurus carolinensis				1					1	
Bobcat Lynx rufus					1				1	
Mole Talpidae		1							1	
Bison or Bos?*								1	1	

TABLE 38—Continued

Species	Number of Bones								Totals	Percent of Total Identified Bone
	29146 2N	29147 1N	29148	29150	29151	29151 Pit in Woods	29343	29343 Lot #2		
Pig *Sus scrofa*					1				1	—
Cat *Felis domestica*							1		1	—
Turkey *Meleagris gallopavo*	7		3	12	24		22		68	2.6
Canada goose *Branta canadensis*				1					1	—
Herring gull *Larus argentatus*								1	1	—
Wood duck *Aix sponsa*								1	1	—
Swan *Cygnus*								1	1	—
Duck *Anas*								1	1	—
Snapping turtle *Chelydra serpentina*	2			4			8		14	.5
Softshell turtle *Trionyx*	1		1	1	4		6		13	.5
Blanding's turtle *Emys blandingi*				3			4		7	.3
Map turtle *Graptemys*		2			1				3	.1
Painted Turtle *Chrysemys*				1					1	—
Sturgeon *Acipenser fulvescens*	129	136	170	316	300	32	156		1,239	46.7
Channel catfish *Ictalurus punctatus*							2		2	.1
Walleye *Stizostedion vitreum*							2		2	.1
Total Identified Bone	182	210	237	658	635	71	494	166	2,653	100.0

TABLE 38--Continued

Species	Number of Bones								Totals	Percent of Total Bone
	29146 2N	29147 1N	29148	29150	29151	29151 Pit in Woods	29343	29343 Lot #2		
Unidentifiable Bone										
Mammal	230	340	200	723	1,201	180	657	300	3,831	57.1
Bird	8	2	3	19	30	3	27		92	1.4
Turtle			12	22	41	2	50		127	1.9
Fish							2		2	–
Combined Total of Identified and Unidentifiable Bone	420	552	452	1,422	1,907	256	1,230	466	6,705	
Percentage of Total Bone in Each Pit	6.3	8.2	7.0	21.3	28.4	3.8	18.3	7.0		

TABLE 39

THE AMOUNT OF MEAT PROVIDED BY EACH IMPORTANT
FOOD SPECIES FROM MOCCASIN BLUFF

Species	Number of Indi- viduals	Average Live Weight	Percent of Live Weight that is Usable Meat	Pounds of Usable Meat /Individual	Pounds of Usable Meat of Species	Percent of Total Usable Meat
Deer	53	200	50	100	5,300	45,6
Elk	9	700	50	350	3,150	27,1
Sturgeon	30	45	80	36	1,080	9,3
Beaver	20	55	70	38.5	770	6.6
Bear	3	300	70	210	630	5.4
Dog	12	40	50	20	240	2.1
Porcupine	16	15	70	10	160	1.4
Raccoon	9	25	70	17.5	158	1.4
Turkey	15	12	70	8.5	128	1.1
Total	167				11,616	100.0

Average Weight per Individual equals 69.6 pounds

probably taken only when they became very abundant during the spring spawning runs. Neither were birds important except for the turkey which must have been actively hunted. Even the mammal remains showed strong hunting selection. Of the 131 individual mammals whose remains could be identified, 4 out of 10 were deer, 5 out of 10 were either deer or elk and 6 out of every 10 mammals killed were either deer, elk or beaver. When we consider that the remaining mammal species were certainly much more abundant in the natural environment than these three species we then see the manifestations of strong preference in hunting.

As expected, Moccasin Bluff, as an agricultural village, seems to have been occupied throughout the year. Deer skulls were recovered from which the antlers had been both removed and naturally dropped from the antler pedestal of the frontal bones. This, of course, tells us that these deer were killed during both the summer season when deer have antlers and during the winter when they do not.

Perhaps one of the most interesting and puzzling aspects of this study was the frequency of occurrence of deer mandibles in the refuse pits. These mandibles were first separated as being either right or left and then they were aged according to the degree of tooth wear. As this data was being recorded, it became increasingly clear that there were fewer left mandibles than right. We would, of course expect that these would be present in about equal numbers and that this ratio would be maintained in each pit. There were, however, a total of 18 left mandibles and 38 right ones and in 7 out of the 8 pits the number of right mandibles exceeded the number of left ones. If this condition was due to chance alone, we would expect only 1 or fewer pits to contain more left mandibles only 3.51 percent of the time. This is significant at the 5 percent level and indicates that some factor other than chance was responsible for producing this sample. In other words, left mandibles were not thrown into the refuse pits as often as right ones. There was also an interesting distribution in the ages of these mandibles. While the mean age of the right mandibles was about 2.7 years or about the mean age of a normal deer population, the mean age of the left mandibles was 5.0 years and the latter average age is quite old for deer (see Figure 5). We would, of course, normally assume that the average age of the right and left mandibles would be approximately equal and that this condition would be maintained in each separate pit. When the mean age of the right and left deer mandibles from five of the pits which

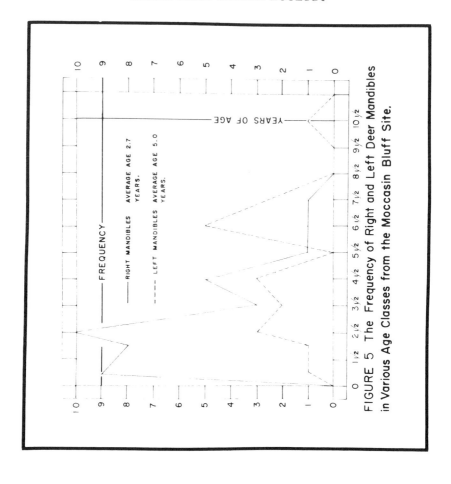

FIGURE 5 The Frequency of Right and Left Deer Mandibles
in Various Age Classes from the Moccasin Bluff Site.

contained the largest samples, were compared, it was discovered that this difference from the expected age could be due to chance alone about 18 percent of the time. Although this figure is not statistically significant at the 5 percent level, it does indicate that there was a strong tendency for left mandibles to be older than the right ones.

To phrase this in terms of the selection which must have been operating, we can say that the left mandibles of young deer were not thrown into the refuse pits as often as the left mandibles of older deer or as often as right mandibles of all ages. Stated as a positive proposition, we can say that the left mandibles of young deer were saved.

This leaves the problem of explaining why this condition arose. Certainly young mandibles have a feature which old ones do not, the inside or the lingual edge of the teeth has sharp cutting edges. If the mandibles were saved to obtain this cutting edge we must then explain why left mandibles were chosen over right ones. Although no deer mandible artifacts which employ the teeth as a cutting edge were recovered from this site, they have been reported from other sites. In the Ozark Bluff Shelter sites of Northwest Arkansas three right mandibles of young deer were recovered. These had handles hafted to the vertical ramus and showed a silica polish on the distal end of the horizontal ramus. They had obviously been used as sickles (Cleland 1965). Mandibles with similar silica polish on the distal end have also been recovered from Mississippian sites in southern Illinois (Brown 1964). Right deer mandibles were also used by the historic Iroquois for scraping green corn from the cob (Parker 1910 and Waugh 1916). When used for this purpose the mandible was held by the distal end of the horizontal ramus so that the lingual edge was applied in a downward stroke with the right hand. Since right mandibles were used for both sickles and scrapers in the above cases, the absence of left mandibles in the refuse pits at the Moccasin Bluff site cannot be explained in this manner. Perhaps these were used as some other type of tool or their absence may have had some ceremonial significance.

If the deer hunting pattern practiced by Moccasin Bluff hunters was based on stalking, we would expect that the mandibles of the deer they killed would show a bimodal age curve. That is to say we would get a "predator curve" with the great majority of deer being either very young or very old, assuming, of course, that the most vigorous deer (those between about 2 and 4 years old) would have the best chance of eluding the

hunter while very young and very old deer would be most easily
taken. Since the age distribution of the right mandibles at
Moccasin Bluff conforms with the age distribution of an average
deer population we can make some observations on hunting
technique. We can assume that deer were taken in the same
ratio as they occurred within various age classes of the
natural population. This infers some non-selective hunting
techniques such as traps, drives or perhaps surrounds. Trapping can probably be ruled out since it could not account for so
many deer, surrounds do not seem to warrant much consideration since this technique of hunting did not seem to be popular
in this area at contact time, although it has been reported among
the Miami (Kinietz 1940). Most probably these people practiced
some type of drive hunting which was the most common and
profitable hunting method practiced in this area.

Among the faunal remains of Moccasin Bluff were the remains of twelve dogs. Although mandible, maxillary fragments,
and teeth were plentiful, no crania was well enough preserved to
permit reconstruction. Metric observations were made on the
mandibles and this data is shown in Table 40. These measurements follow Hagg (1948). Comparing these measurements with
those given by Haag for Mississippian dogs are larger although
they fall well within the range given by Haag for the population.
If we look at the mean sizes given for dogs from the Fisher
site (which has strong cultural affinities with Moccasin Bluff)
we see that these are also somewhat larger than the generalized
Mississippian dog and that they compare quite closely in size
with the Moccasin Bluff dogs. Thus, these dogs appear to be
typical of the Mississippian period and compare well in size
to at least one other dog population located on the northern
margin of Mississippian influence in the Upper Great Lakes area.

In summary, the faunal remains of the Moccasin Bluff site
are representative of those accumulated by people who were not
dependent upon animal food but upon agriculture. Hunting seems
to have been concentrated on a few species particularly deer,
elk and beaver. Turkeys were also hunted and sturgeon were
caught when they became seasonally abundant. The Moccasin
Bluff area seems to have been heavily forested although some
clearings are indicated, perhaps the result of agricultural activities. Typical prairie species do not appear in the refuse deposits. An analysis of the occurrence of right and left deer
mandibles from various aged deer shows that the left mandibles
of young deer were not discarded with the same regularity as
left mandibles from older deer or as often as right mandibles

TABLE 40

METRIC ANALYSIS OF THE DOG MANDIBLES FROM MOCCASIN BLUFF

	Alveolus I_1-M_3	Alveolus C-M_3	Alveolus P_1-M_3	Alveolus P_2-M_3	Alveolus P_3-M_3	Alveolus P_4-M_3	Alveolus M_1-M_3	Carnassial Length M_1
Moccasin Bluff 29146	87	80.5	68.5	65	55.5	45	34	22
Moccasin Bluff 29146		84.5		73	61	49.5	32	22
Moccasin Bluff 29146	88	81	68.5	65	55.5	45	34	21.5
Moccasin Bluff 29343	83	76.5	64	60.5	52.5	43.5	34	21.5
Moccasin Bluff 29343	81	80		64.5	55.5	45	33.5	20
Moccasin Bluff 29150		80	69.5	65	55	44.5	33.5	22
Moccasin Bluff 29151								21
Moccasin Bluff 29343						44	32.5	20
Moccasin Bluff 29343								22.5
Moccasin Bluff								20
Moccasin Bluff								21
Sample Size	4	6	4	6	6	7	7	11

TABLE 40--Continued

	Alveolus I$_1$-M$_3$	Alveolus C-M$_3$	Alveolus P$_1$-M$_3$	Alveolus P$_2$-M$_3$	Alveolus P$_3$-M$_3$	Alveolus P$_4$-M$_3$	Alveolus M$_1$-M$_3$	Carnassial M$_1$ Length
Range	81 88	76.5 84.5	64 69.5	60.5 73	52.5 61	43.5 49.5	32 34	20 22.5
Mean	84.75	80.16	67.25	65.33	55.5	45	33.35	21.22
Mississippian dog mean	87	81.4	67.6	63.8	54.1	43.5	32.6	19.8
Fisher site mean	--	81.0	71.5	65.0	55.0	44.2	33.2	20.0

from all ages. The reason for this selection is not immediately apparent. The normal frequency of right mandibles in various age classes also suggests that a non-selective hunting technique such as the drive was used in hunting.

APPENDIX G

DISTRIBUTION OF VARIOUS ANIMAL SPECIES ACCORDING TO BIOTIC PROVINCE

Species	Eskimoan	Hudsonian	Canadian	Illinoian	Carolinian	Austro-riparian
Masked shrew	X	X	X		X	
Pygmy shrew	X	X				
Snowshoe hare	X	X	X			
Arctic hare	X					
Arctic ground squirrel	X					
Red squirrel	X	X	X			
Northern flying squirrel	X	X	X			
Beaver	X	X	X	X	X	X
Labrador collared lemming	X					
Greenland collared lemming	X					
Brown lemming	X					
Northern bog lemming		X				
Heather vole	X	X				
Meadow vole	X	X	X		X	
Tundra vole	X					

	Eskimoan	Hudsonian	Canadian	Illinoian	Carolinian	Austro-riparian
Muskrat	—————	—————	—————	—————	—————	—————
Meadow jumping mouse	—————	—————	—————	—————	—————	
Porcupine	—————	—————	—————			
Gray wolf	—————	—————	—————	—————	—————	—————
Arctic fox	—————					
Red fox	—————	—————	————— ?			
Black bear	—————	—————	—————	—————	—————	—————
Polar bear	———					
Marten	—————	—————	————— ?			
Ermine	—————	—————	—————			
Wolverine	—————	—————	———			
Mink	—————	—————	—————	—————	—————	—————
Otter	—————	—————	—————	—————	—————	—————
Lynx	—————	—————				
Moose	—————	—————				
Barren ground caribou	———					
Musk-ox	———					
Common loon	—————	—————				
Red-throated loon	———					
Arctic loon	——					
Whistling swan	———					
Canada goose	—————	—————	—————			
Common goldeneye	—————	—————	———			
Oldsquaw	———					
Harlequin duck	———					
Surf scoter	———					

	Eskimoan	Hudsonian	Canadian	Illinoian	Carolinian	Austro-riparian
Common scoter	——					
Ruddy duck	———	———	———			
Red-breasted merganser	———	———				
Goshawk	———	———				
Sharp shinned hawk	———	———	———	———	———	———
Rough-legged hawk	———		———		———	
Golden eagle	———	———				
Bald eagle	———	———	———	———	———	———
Marsh hawk	———	———	———	———	———	———
Osprey	———	———	———	———	———	———
Peregrine falcon	———	———	———	———	———	———
Pigeon hawk	———	———	———			
Spruce grouse	———	———				
Willow ptarmigan	———					
Rock ptarmigan	———					
Semipalmated plover	———					
Common snipe	———	———	———			
Spotted sandpiper	———	———	———	———		
Solitary sandpiper	———	———	———			
Lesser yellowlegs	———	———				
Least sandpiper	———					
Great black-back gull	———	———	———			
Herring gull	———	———	———			
Great horned owl	———	———	———	———	———	———

	Eskimoan	Hudsonian	Canadian	Illinoian	Carolinian	Austro-riparian
Hawk owl	—	—				
Short eared owl	—	—	—	—	—	—
Northern threetoed woodpecker	—	—				
Horned lark	—	—	—	—	—	—
Gray jay	—	—				
Boreal chickadee	—	—				
Robin	—	—	—	—	—	—
Gray cheeked thrush	—	—				
Water pipit	—					
Northern shrike	—	—	—	—	—	
Yellow warbler	—	—	—	—	—	
Pied-billed grebe		—	—	—	—	—
Double-crested cormorant		—			—	
American bittern		—			—	
Mallard		—	—	—	—	
Black duck		—	—		—	
Gadwall		—	—	—		
Pintail		—	—	—	—	—
Greenwing teal		—	—	—		
Bluewing teal		—	—	—		
Shoveller duck		—	—	—		
Ringneck		—	—	—		
Greater scaup		—				
Hooded merganser		—				
Common merganser		—				

	Eskimoan	Hudsonian	Canadian	Illinoian	Carolinian	Austro-riparian
Sparrow hawk		——————————————————————————————				
Ruffed grouse		———————————			——————	
Greater yellowlegs		—————————				
Ring bill gull		————————				
Common tern		———————————				
Black tern		———————————			——	
Boreal owl		———————————				
Saw-whet owl			————————————————————————————			
Common night hawk			————————————————————————————			
Belted kingfisher			————————————————————————————			
Yellow-shafted flicker			————————————————————————————			
Pileated woodpecker			———————————————————————			
Yellow-bellied sapsucker		————————————————————————————————				
Hairy woodpecker			————————————————————————————			
Purple finch			———————————————————————			
Pine siskin			————————————————————————————			
Red crossbill		———————————			——————	
Myrtle warbler	—————————————————————					
Black poll warbler	———————————					
Northern water thrush	————————————————————					
Rusty blackbird	———————————					
Pine grosbeak	————————————————————					
Hoary redpoll	————————————————————					
Common redpoll	————————————————————			——————	
White-winged crossbill	————————————————————			——	

	Eskimoan	Hudsonian	Canadian	Illinoian	Carolinian	Austro-riparian
Savannah sparrow						
Slate-colored junco						
Tree sparrow						
White-crowned sparrow						
Fox sparrow						
Lincoln's sparrow						
Lapland longspur						
Snow bunting						
Common American toad						
Wood frog						
Arctic shrew						
Water shrew						
Little brown myotis						
Silver haired bat						
Eastern chipmunk						
Deer mouse						
Red-backed vole						
Fisher						
Least weasel						
Striped skunk						
Woodland caribou						
Horned grebe						
Chipping sparrow						
White-throated sparrow						
Swamp sparrow						

	Eskimoan	Hudsonian	Canadian	Illinoian	Carolinian	Austro-riparian
Song sparrow		X	X	X	X	X
Common garter snake		X	X	X	X	X
Two-lined salamander		X	X			
Chorus frog		X	X	X	X	
Mink frog		X	X			
Leopard frog		X	X	X	X	X
Smoky shrew		X	X	X		
Long-tailed shrew			X			
Short-tailed shrew		X	X	X	X	X
Hairy-tailed mole			X		X	
Star-nosed mole			X		X	
Woodchuck		X	X		X	X
Eastern cottontail			X	X	X	X
Keen's myotis			X		X	
Big brown bat			X	X	X	X
Red bat			X	X	X	X
Hoary bat			X	X	X	X
Least chipmunk		X	X			
Franklin's ground squirrel		X	X			
Gray squirrel			X	X	X	X
Fox squirrel		X	X	X	X	X
Southern flying squirrel			X	X	X	X
Southern bog lemming			X		X	
Whitefooted mouse			X		X	
Pine vole			X	X	X	X

	Eskimoan	Hudsonian	Canadian	Illinoian	Carolinian	Austro-riparian
Coyote			───	───		
Gray fox		?	────────────────────────────			
Raccoon			────────────────────────────			
Long-tailed weasel			────────────────────────────			
Badger			───	───		
Bobcat			────────────────────────────			
Elk			───		───	
Whitetailed deer			────────────────────────────			
Black-backed three toed woodpecker		───				
Eastern phoebe			────────────────────────────			
Yellow-bellied flycatcher			────────────────────────────			
Least flycatcher		────────			───	
Olive-sided flycatcher		────────			───	
Tree swallow		────────			───	
Bank swallow		────────			───	
Barn swallow			────────────────────────────			
Cliff swallow		────────			───	
Common raven		────────				
Common crow			────────────────────────────			
Black-capped chicadee		────────			───	
Redbreasted nuthatch			────────────────────────────			
Brown creeper			────────────────────────────			
Winter wren			────────────────────────────			
Hermit thrush		────────────────────────────────				
Swainson's thrush		────────				

	Eskimoan	Hudsonian	Canadian	Illinoian	Carolinian	Austro-riparian
Golden-crowned kinglet		———	———	———	———	———
Cedar waxwing		———	———	———	———	———
Starling		———	———	———	———	———
Redeyed vireo		———	———	———	———	———
Solitary vireo		———	———	———	———	———
Philadelphia vireo		———				
Ruby-crowned kinglet		———				
Tennessee warbler		———				
Magnolia warbler		———	———			
Cape May warbler		———				
Black throated green warbler		———	———		———	
Black barnian warbler		———	———		—	
Palm warbler		———				
Oven bird		———	———		———	———
Connecticut warbler		———				
Mourning warbler		———	———		—	
Yellow throat warbler			———	———	———	———
Wilson's warbler		———				
Canada warbler		———	———		———	
American redstart		———	———		———	———
House sparrow			———	———	———	———
Redwinged blackbird			———	———	———	———
Common grackle			———	———	———	———
Brown-headed cowbird		———	———	———	———	———
Red-necked grebe			———			

	Eskimoan	Hudsonian	Canadian	Illinoian	Carolinian	Austro-riparian
Great blue heron			—		—	
Green heron			—	—	—	—
Black-crowned night heron			—		—	
Least bittern			—	—	—	—
American widgeon			—			
Wood duck			—		—	
Bufflehead duck			—	—	—	—
White wing scoter			—			
Turkey vulture			—	—	—	—
Cooper's hawk			—		—	—
Red-shouldered hawk			—	—	—	—
Broad-winged hawk			—	—	—	—
Rough-legged hawk			—	—		
Red-tailed hawk			—	—	—	—
Sharp tailed grouse			—			
Sandhill crane			—	—		
King rail			—	—	—	—
Common gallinule			—	—	—	—
American coot			—	—	—	—
Piping plover			—			
American woodcock			—	—	—	—
Upland plover			—		—	
Wilson's phalarope			—			
Caspian tern			—			
Mourning dove			—	—	—	—

	Eskimoan	Hudsonian	Canadian	Illinoian	Carolinian	Austro-riparian
Yellow-billed cuckoo			————	————	————	————
Black-billed cuckoo			———		———	
Screech owl			————	————	————	————
Barred owl			————	————	————	————
Great gray owl			———			
Long-eared owl			————	————	————	————
Whip-poor-will			————	————	————	————
Chimney swift			————	————	————	————
Ruby-throated humming bird			————	————	————	————
Redheaded woodpecker			————	————	————	————
Eastern king bird			————	————	————	————
Western king bird			———			
Great crested flycatcher			————	————	————	————
Eastern wood pewee			————	————	————	————
Rough-winged swallow			————	————	————	————
Purple martin			————	————	————	————
Blue jay			————	————	————	————
White-breasted nuthatch			————	————	————	————
House wren			————	————	————	————
Long-billed marsh wren			———		———	
Short-billed marsh wren			———		———	
Catbird			————	————	————	————
Brown thrasher			————	————	————	————

	Eskimoan	Hudsonian	Canadian	Illinoian	Carolinian	Austro-riparian
Wood thrush			———	———	———	———
Veery			———		—	
Eastern bluebird			———	———	———	———
Bohemian waxwing			———			
Yellow-throated vireo			———	———	———	———
Warbling vireo			———		———	———
Black and white warbler			———	———	———	———
Gold-winged warbler			———		—	
Nashville warbler			———			
Parula warbler			———	———	———	———
Black-throated blue warbler			———		———	———
Chestnut-sided warbler			———		———	———
Pine warbler			———	———	———	———
Bobolink			———		—	
Eastern meadowlark			———	———	———	———
Western meadowlark			———			
Baltimore oriole			———	———	———	
Brewer's blackbird			———			
Scarlet tanager			———		———	———
Cardinal			———	———	———	———
Rose-breasted grosbeak			———		—	
Indigo bunting			———	———	———	———
Evening grosbeak			———		———	———
American goldfinch			———	———	———	———

	Eskimoan	Hudsonian	Canadian	Illinoian	Carolinian	Austro-riparian
Rufous sided towhee			X	X	X	X
Grasshopper sparrow			X	X	X	X
Leconte's sparrow			X	X		X
Henslow's sparrow			X	X	X	X
Vesper sparrow			X	X	X	X
Lark sparrow			X	X	X	
Tree sparrow			X	X	X	
Field sparrow			X	X	X	X
Snapping turtle			X	X	X	X
Wood turtle			X	X	X	
Blanding's turtle			X			
Map turtle			X			
Painted turtle			X		X	
Five-lined skink			X	X	X	X
Kintland's water snake			X			
Common water snake			X	X	X	X
Brown snake			X	X	X	X
Redbellied snake			X	X	X	X
Butler's garter snake			X			
Shortheaded garter snake			X			
Ribbon snake			X	X	X	X
Eastern hognose snake			X	X	X	X
Eastern ringneck snake			X	X	X	X
Fox snake			X			
Racer			X	X	X	X

	Eskimoan	Hudsonian	Canadian	Illinoian	Carolinian	Austro-riparian
Smooth green snake			X			
Rat snake			X	X	X	X
Milk snake			X	X	X	X
Massasauga			X	X		
Mudpuppy			X		X	
Jefferson salamander			X		X	
Tiger salamander			X	X	X	X
Newt			X	X	X	X
Redbacked salamander			X	X	X	
Fourtoed salamander			X			
Spring salamander			X			
Cricket frog			X	X	X	X
Spring peeper			X	X	X	X
Gray treefrog			X	X	X	X
Bull frog			X	X	X	X
Green frog			X	X	X	X
Pickerel frog			X	X	X	
Opossum				X	X	X
Least shrew				X	X	X
Eastern mole				X	X	X
Eastern pipistrelle				X	X	X
Evening bat				X	X	X
Cottontail rabbit				X	X	X
Black tailed prairie dog				X		
Thirteen-lined ground squirrel				X	X	

	Eskimoan	Hudsonian	Canadian	Illinoian	Carolinian	Austro-riparian
Plains pocket gopher				—		
Hispid pocket mouse				—		—
Plains harvest mouse				—		
Western harvest mouse				—		
Southern plains woodrat				—		
Prairie vole				—		
Red wolf				—		
Bison				—	—	—
Eastern spotted skunk				—	—	—
Least tern				—	—	—
Black vulture				—	—	—
Mississippi kite				—	—	—
Snowy egret				—	—	—
Yellow-crowned night heron				—	—	—
Little blue heron				—	—	—
Common egret				—	—	—
Turkey			—	—	—	—
Barn owl				—	—	—
Chuck-will's-widow				—	—	—
Redbellied woodpecker					—	—
Acadian flycatcher					—	—
Carolina chicadee					—	—
Tufted titmouse					—	—
Carolina wren					—	—
Mocking bird					—	—

	Eskimoan	Hudsonian	Canadian	Illinoian	Carolinian	Austro-riparian
Blue gray gnatcatcher				———	———	———
Loggerhead shrike				———	———	———
White-eyed vireo				———	———	———
Prothonotary warbler				———	———	———
Wormeating warbler				—	———	———
Swainson's warbler				———		—
Yellow-throated warbler				———		———
Prairie warbler				———	———	———
Louisiana water thrush				———	———	———
Kentucky warbler				———	———	———
Yellow-breasted chat				———	———	———
Hooded warbler				———	———	———
Orchard oriole				———	———	———
Summer tanager				———	———	———
Tree sparrow				———		
Blue grosbeak				———		———
Painted bunting				———		———
Bachman's sparrow				———		———
White-crowned sparrow				———		———
Alligator snapping turtle				———		———
Mud turtle				———		———
Stinkpot				———	———	———
Box pot				———	———	———
Diamond-back terrapin				———	———	———
False map turtle				———		

	Eskimoan	Hudsonian	Canadian	Illinoian	Carolinian	Austro-riparian
Cooter				—		—
Pond slider				—		—
Spiny softshell turtle				—	—	—
Smooth softshell turtle				—		
Eastern fence lizard				—	—	
Slender glass lizard				—	—	—
Six-lined race runner				—	—	—
Ground skink				—	—	—
Southeastern five-lined skink				—	—	—
Glossy water snake				—		—
Green water snake				—		—
Plain-bellied water snake				—		—
Diamond-backed water snake				—		
Rough earth snake				—	—	—
Smooth earth snake				—	—	—
Worm snake				—	—	
Mud snake				—	—	—
Eastern coachwhip				—	—	—
Rough green snake				—	—	—
Corn snake				—	—	—
Prairie king snake				—	—	—
Common king snake				—	—	—
Scarlet snake				—	—	—
Flatheaded snake				—		

	Eskimoan	Hudsonian	Canadian	Illinoian	Carolinian	Austro-riparian
Plains blackheaded snake				—		
Eastern coral snake				—		—
Copperhead				—	—	—
Cotton mouth				—		—
Pigmy rattlesnake				—		—
Timber rattlesnake				—	—	—
Diamond back rattlesnake				—		
Lesser siren				—		—
Spotted salamander				—	—	—
Marbled salamander				—	—	—
Smallmouth salamander				—		
Amphiuma				—		—
Dusky salamander				—	—	—
Slimy salamander				—	—	—
Eastern spadefoot				—	—	—
Woodhouse's toad				—	—	—
Green tree frog				—		—
Bird-voiced tree frog				—		
Spotted chorus frog				—		
Strecker's chorus frog				—		
Narrowmouthed toad				—		—
Gray myotis					—	—
Indiana myotis					—	
Small-footed myotis					—	
Alleghany wood rat					—	

	Eskimoan	Hudsonian	Canadian	Illinoian	Carolinian	Austro-riparian
Fish crow					—	—
Bluewinged warbler					—	
Boattailed grackle					—	—
Spotted turtle				—	—	
Bog turtle				—	—	
Redbellied turtle				—	—	
Coal skink					—	
Queen snake				—	—	
Hellbender					—	
Mountain salamander					—	
Seal salamander					—	
Blackbellied salamander					—	
Pygmy salamander					—	
Zigzag salamander					—	
Jordan's Salamander					—	
Ravine salamander					—	
Wehrle's salamander					—	
Shenandoah salamander					—	
Yonaalossee salamander					—	
Many-lined salamander					—	
Pine Barren's tree frog					—	
Mountain chorus frog					—	
Brimley's chorus frog					—	
Southeastern shrew						—
Marsh rabbit						—

	Eskimoan	Hudsonian	Canadian	Illinoian	Carolinian	Austro-riparian
Rabinesque's big-eared bat						———
Marsh rice rat					—	———
Eastern harvest mouse					—	———
Eastern wood rat					—	———
Golden mouse					—	———
Black rat						———
Louisiana heron						———
Black rail						———
Purple gallinule						———
Ruddy turnstone						———
Western sandpiper						———
Marbled godwit						———
Blacknecked stilt						———
Foster's tern						———
Redcokaded woodpecker						———
Brown headed nuthatch						———
Palm warbler						———
Eastern glasslizard						———
Brown water snake						———
Rainbow snake						———
Pine snake						———
Crowned snake						———
Greater siren						———
Mole salamander					—	———

	Eskimoan	Hudsonian	Canadian	Illinoian	Carolinian	Austro-riparian
Mud salamander					—	———
Pinewoods tree frog					—	———
Barking tree frog					—	———
Little grass frog						———
Squirrel tree frog					—	———

APPENDIX H

HABITAT PREFERENCES OF SOME OF THE ANIMAL
SPECIES OF THE EASTERN UNITED STATES

Deciduous Forest.--Bear, Raccoon, Bobcat, Woodchuck, Striped skunk, Gray squirrel, Southern flying squirrel, Gray wolf, Gray fox, Long-eared owls, Broad-winged hawk, Scarlet tanager, Summer tanager, Hermit thrush, Whitebreasted nuthatch, Redbreasted nuthatch, Whip-poor-will, Chuck-will's-widow, Pileated woodpecker, Great horned owel, Ruffed grouse, Turkey, Redheaded woodpecker, Hairy wood-pecker, Downy woodpecker.

Deciduous Forest Edge.--Deer, Elk, Bear, Raccoon, Bobcat, Wood-chuck, Chipmunk, Striped skunk, Opossum, Least weasel, Fox squirrel, Gray squirrel, Coyote, Gray wolf, Harvest mice, Gray fox, Eastern spotted skunk, Cardinal, Blue jay, Sparrows, Yellow-billed cuckoo, Black-billed cuckoo, Bobwhite, Common night hawk, Yellow-shafted flicker, Common crow, Loggerhead shrike, Red-winged blackbird, Screech owl, Barn owl, Red-tailed hawk, Turkey, Redheaded woodpecker, Robin, Common grackle, Eastern Box turtle.

Grasslands.--Elk, Deer mouse, Badger, Jackrabbit, Coyote, Gray wolf, Black-tailed prairie dog, Spotted ground squirrel, Plains pocket gopher, Eastern spotted skunk, Ferruginous hawks, Golden eagle, Prairie chickens, Short-eared owls, Longbilled curlew, Sandhill crane, Upland curlew, Red-tailed hawk, Red-shouldered hawk, Downy woodpecker, Common raven, Western box turtle.

Conifer Forest.--Gray wolf, Moose, Bear, Wolverine, Snowshoe hare, Lynx, Porcupine, Northern flying squirrel, Longtail shrew, Marten, Red fox, Red squirrel, Fisher, Goshawk, Spruce grouse, Great gray owl, Boreal owl, Blackheaded three-toed woodpecker, Pileated woodpecker, Great horned owl, Sharptail grouse, Common raven, Slatecolored junco, Bohemian waxwing, Northern shrike, Gray jay.

Aquatic.--Raccoon, Beaver, Muskrat, Mink, Otter, Water shrew, Osprey, Ducks, Geese, Swans, Loons, Herons, Grebes, Cranes, Plovers, Rails, Gallinules, American coot, American bittern,

Bald eagle, Snapping turtle, Alligator snapping turtle, Stinkpot, Mud turtle, Spotted turtle, Bog turtle, Wood turtle, Blanding's turtle, Diamondback terrapin, Map turtle, False map turtle, Painted turtle, Cooter, Pond slider, Redbellied turtle, Spiny softshell, Smooth softshell.

APPENDIX I

ARCHAEOLOGICAL OCCURRENCE OF VARIOUS VERTEBRATE
SPECIES OF THE EASTERN UNITED STATES

Number on Map	Approximate Date of Sites	Identification
1	4000 B.C.-1000 B.C.	A Bog
2		Accokeek
3	A.D. 1400-	Albert Ibaugh Site
4	A.D. 1000-1400	Anderson
5		Southeast Manitoba
	4000 B.C.-1000 B.C.	Whiteshell Focus
	1000 B.C.-300 B.C.	Larter Focus
	300 B.C.-A.D. 500	Anderson Focus
	A.D. 500-A.D. 1000	Nutimik Focus
	A.D. 1000-A.D. 1400	Selkirk Focus
	A.D. 1400-	Manitoba Focus
6	A.D. 1400-	Anker Site
7	A.D. 1400-	Arkansas City Country Club
8		Ash Grove (Cave ?)
9	A.D. 1000-A.D. 1400	Aztalan
10	A.D. 1000-A.D. 1400	Baum
11	A.D. 800-A.D. 1300	Juntunen
12	A.D. 800-A.D. 1300	Bluff Cave
13		Boone Rockshelter and Campsite
14	1000 B.C.-300 B.C.	Buchanan Rock Shelter
15	A.D. 1000-A.D. 1400	Cahokia
16	A.D. 1400-	Campbell Island (Ohio)
17	A.D. 1000-A.D. 1400	Campbell Site (Missouri)
18		Canter Caves
19	A.D. 100-A.D. 1400	Chucalissa
20	?	Campsite
21	?	Clear Lake Site
22	A.D. 1000-A.D. 1400	Cramer Village
23	300 B.C.-A.D. 500	Dickison Mounds
24	A.D. 1400-	Dietz

Number on Map	Approximate Date of Sites	Identification
25	A.D. 1400-	Doniphan
26		Durtz Shelter
	4000 B.C.-1000 B.C.	Middle Archaic Zone V
	1000 B.C.-	Late Archaic Zone V
27	A.D. 1400-	Elliott
28	A.D. 1400-	Eschelman
29	A.D. 1000-A.D. 1400	Etowah
30	5200 B.C.±500 B.C.	Eva
	4000 B.C.-1000 B.C.	
31	A.D. 1400-	Fanning
32	A.D. 1400-	Fatherland
33	2000 B.C.	Feeheley Site
34	A.D. 1400-	Feurt
35	A.D. 1400-	Fisher
36	A.D. 1400	Fox Farm
37	4000 B.C.-1000 B.C.	Frontenac Site
38	A.D. 1400-	Fullerton
39	A.D. 1400-	Furton
40	A.D. 1000-A.D. 1400	Gartner Site
41		Gaston
42	300 B.C.-A.D. 500	Havana Mound Group
43	4000 B.C.	Hillsite
44	A.D. 732±150	Heins Creek
45	A.D. 1400-	Isle Royale
46	4000 B.C.-1000 B.C.	Indian Knoll
47	A.D. 500-A.D. 1000	Irving
48	A.D. 1400-	Johnston
49	A.D. 1400-	Kaw Village
50	A.D. 1000-A.D. 1400	Kenner
51		Kettle Hill Cave
52	A.D. 1000-A.D. 1400	Kingston Village
53	A.D. 1400-	Madisonville
54	300 B.C.-A.D. 500	Donaldson
55	A.D. 1400-	Malone
56	A.D. 500-A.D. 1000	Burley
57		Inverhuron
	1000 B.C.-300 B.C.,	Late Archaic
	300 B.C.-A.D. 500	
	A.D. 1400-	Late Woodland
58	A.D. 1400-	Middleport
59	4000 B.C.-1000 B.C.	Modoc
60	A.D. 500-A.D. 1000	Lagoon Pond

Number on Map	Approximate Dates of Sites	Identification
61	4000 B.C.-1000 B.C.	Lamoka Lake
62	A.D. 1400-	Larcom-Haggard
63	A.D. 1400-	Law Site
64	4000 B.C.-1000 B.C.	Little Bear Creek
65	4000 B.C.-1000 B.C.	Oberlander
66		New England Coast
67	A.D. 1400-	Oak Forest
68	1000 B.C.-300 B.C.	Picton
69	300 B.C.-A.D. 500	Pool
70	A.D. 500-A.D. 1400	Pottorff
71	A.D. 1400-	Proctorville Site
72	4000 B.C.-300 B.C.	Raddatz
73	A.D. 1400-	Reed Fort
74	300 B.C.-A.D. 500	Renner
75	A.D. 1400-	Roebuck Village Site
76	A.D. 1400-	Scott County State Park
77	300 B.C.-A.D. 500	Steuben Site
78	A.D. 1400-	Thompson Site
79	A.D. 1400-	Tobias Site
80		Twinsburgh Rockshelter
81	A.D. 500-A.D. 1000	Walter
82	A.D. 1400-	Wolf
83	A.D. 1000-A.D. 1400	Younge
84	A.D. 1000-A.D. 1400	Zimmerman
	A.D. 1400	Kaskaska
85		Various Sites in York County, Ontario
86		Clearville
	A.D. 1000-A.D. 1400	Occupation Number 1
	A.D. 1400-	Occupation Number 2
87	A.D. 1000-A.D. 1400	Crawford
88	A.D. 1000-A.D. 1400	Angel Site
90	A.D. 500-A.D. 1000	Carpenter Brook
91	A.D. 1400-	Flanagan
92		Lander Shelter
93	A.D. 1400-	Lawson Site
94	A.D. 1400-	Parker Earth works
95	4000 B.C.-1000 B.C.	Riverside Cemetery
96	A.D. 1000-A.D. 1400	Robinson Reserve
97	A.D. 1400-	Uren
98	A.D. 1400-	Scarem Site
99	1000 B.C.-300 B.C.	Stony Brook Site

Number on Map	Approximate Date of Sites	Identification
100	A.D. 1000-A.D. 1400	Goessens
101	A.D. 1400-	Sidey-Mackay
102	A.D. 1000-A.D. 1400	Varner Site
103	A.D. 1000-A.D. 1400	Matthews Site
104		Westfield Site
105	300 B.C.-A.D. 500	Snyders
106	3000 B.C.-1000 B.C.	Dixon Rock Shelter
107	A.D. 1000-A.D. 1400	Mill Creek
108	A.D. 300-A.D. 1000	Serpent Mound, Ontario
109		Prescott
110	4000 B.C.-	Stanfield-Worley
111	A.D. 1400-	St. Louis Site
112	A.D. 500-A.D. 1000	Krieger Site
113	4000 B.C.-	Scarborough
114	A.D. 1156±200	Snell
115	300 B.C.-A.D. 500	Indian Point
116	A.D. 1000-A.D. 1400	Moccasin Bluff
117	A.D. 1400-	Fort Michilimackinac
118	A.D. 1000-A.D. 1400	Lawhorn
119	A.D. 1400-	Bell Site
120	A.D. 1400-	Wilson Sand Hill
121	4000 B.C.-	Lime Creek (level 1)
122	300 B.C.-A.D. 500	Steuben Village
123		Quaker State Rockshelter
124	300 B.C.-A.D. 500	Kamp Mound Group
125		Kipp Island
126	A.D. 500-A.D. 1000	Kamp Mound (Jersey Bluff)
127	300 B.C.-A.D. 500	JA-63 Jim Woodruff Reservoir.
128	4000 B.C.-	J-5 Jim Woodruff Reservoir
129	4000 B.C.-	Itasca Bison Site
130		Washington Island
131	A.D. 300	Weaver Site
132	A.D. 1000-A.D. 1400	Fair Port Harbor
133	A.D. 1000-A.D. 1400	Tuttle Hill
134	A.D. 1000-A.D. 1400	South Park
135	A.D. 1000-A.D. 1400	Lee Mill Cave
136	A.D. 1400-	Grott
137	A.D. 1400-	Buyer Site
138	A.D. 1400-	Nichols Pond

Number on Map	Approximate Date of Sites	Identification
139	A.D. 1000-A.D. 1400	Hicks Site
140	A.D. 1400-	Wayland Smith (Cameron)
141	A.D. 1400-	Pen Site
142		Keyser Farm
143		Mt. Carbon Site
144	A.D. 1400-	Crawford Farm
145	500 B.C.-A.D. 500	Schuitz
146	A.D. 1170	Lasley's Point
147	A.D. 1400-	Oakfield Site
148	3000 B.C.-1500 B.C.	Four preceramic sites in Florida
149	A.D. 1000-	Bintz
150	A.D. 1200	The Mankaway Site
151	A.D. 500-A.D. 1000	Tick Creek Site
152	A.D. 1000-A.D. 1400-	Kingston Lake Site
153	400 B.C.-A.D. 400	Norton Mound Site
154	A.D. 1000-A.D. 1400	Silver Lake Site
155	400 B.C.-A.D. 400	The Bar Site, Spoonville
156	400 B.C.-A.D. 400	The McGraw Site
157	A.D. 1000-A.D. 1400	The Morrison Site
158	A.D. 800	Chesser Cave
159	A.D. 1000-A.D. 1400	Graham Village
160	A.D. 960±80	Spring Creek Site.

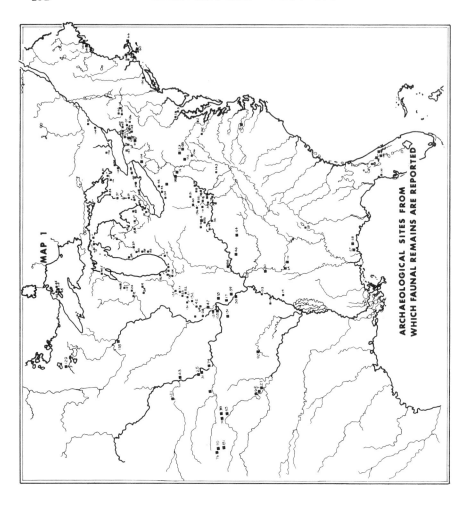

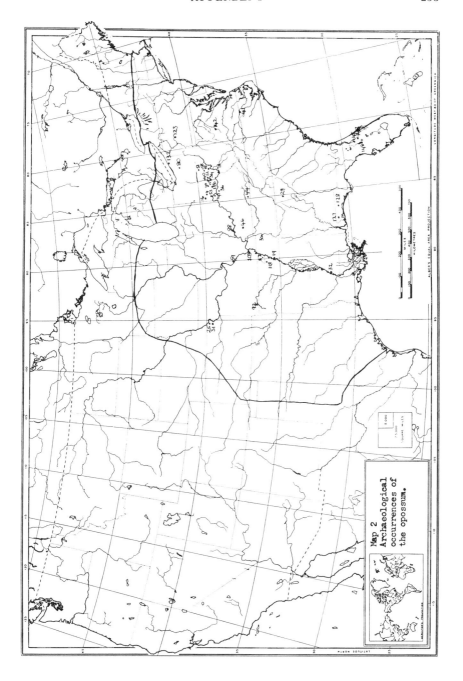

Map 2
Archaeological
occurrences of
the opossum.

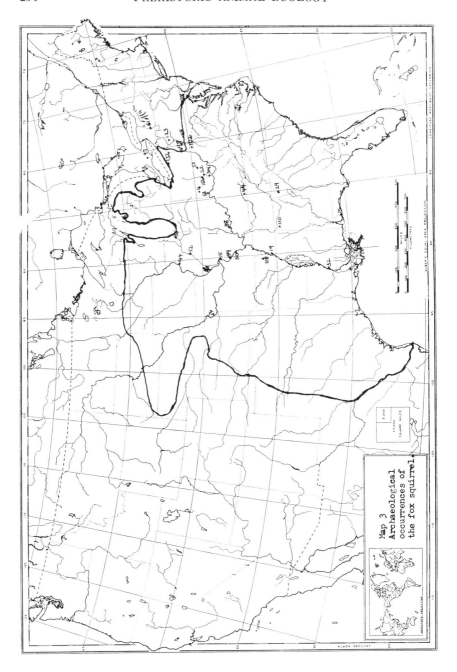

Map 3
Archaeological
occurrences of
the fox squirrel.

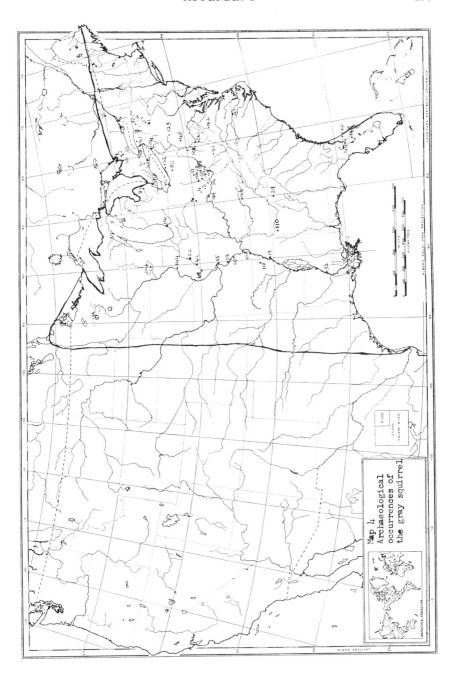

Map 4
Archaeological
occurrences of
the gray squirrel

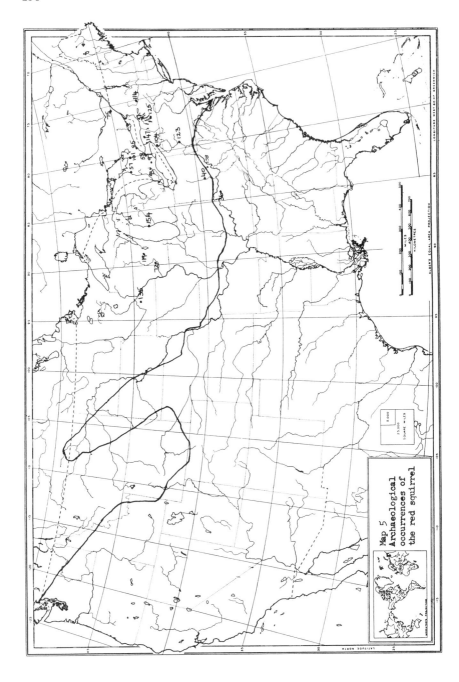

Map 5
Archaeological
occurrences of
the red squirrel

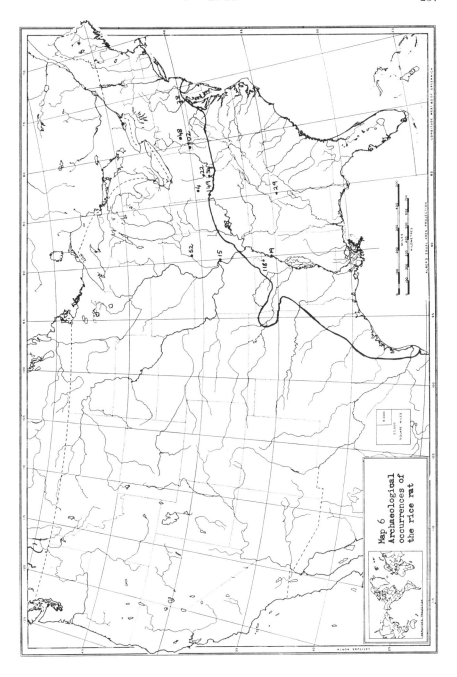

Map 6
Archaeological
occurrences of
the rice rat

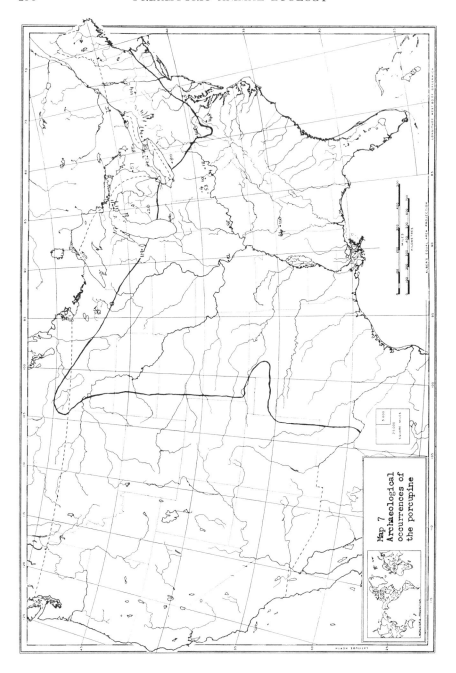

Map 7
Archaeological
occurrences of
the porcupine

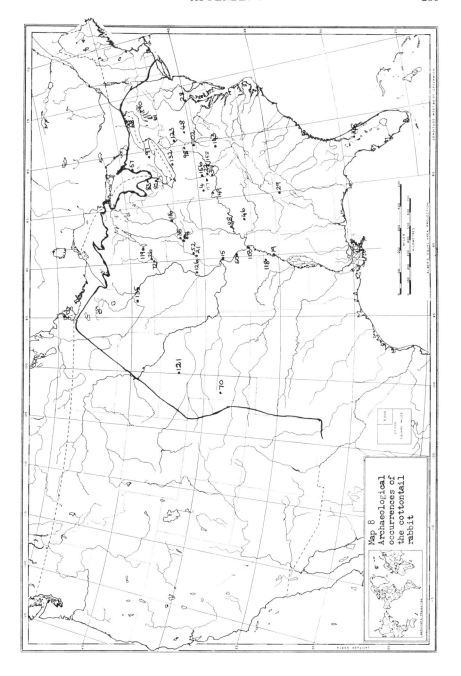

Map 8
Archaeological
occurrences of
the cottontail
rabbit

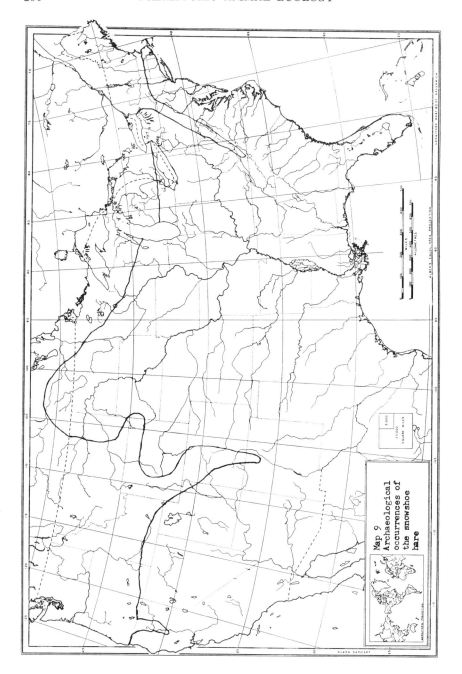

Map 9
Archaeological
occurrences of
the snowshoe
hare

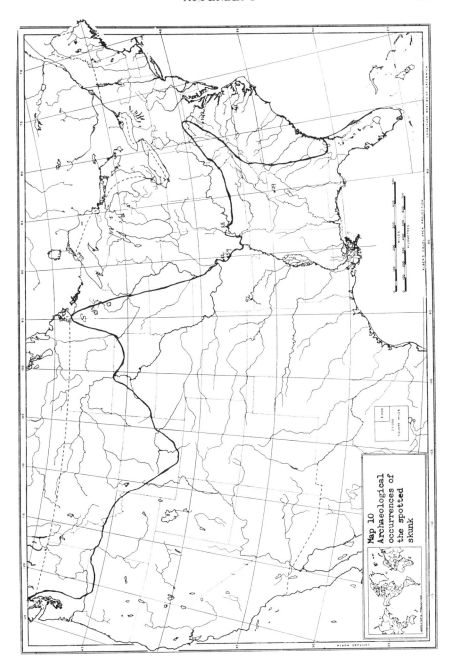

Map 10
Archaeological
occurrences of
the spotted
skunk

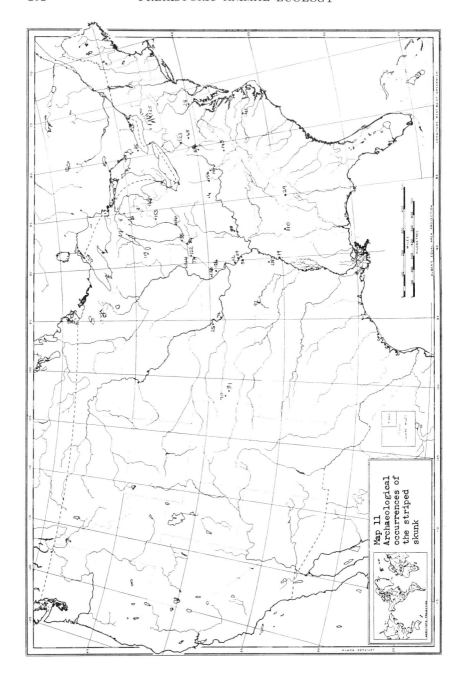

Map 11
Archaeological
occurrences of
the striped
skunk

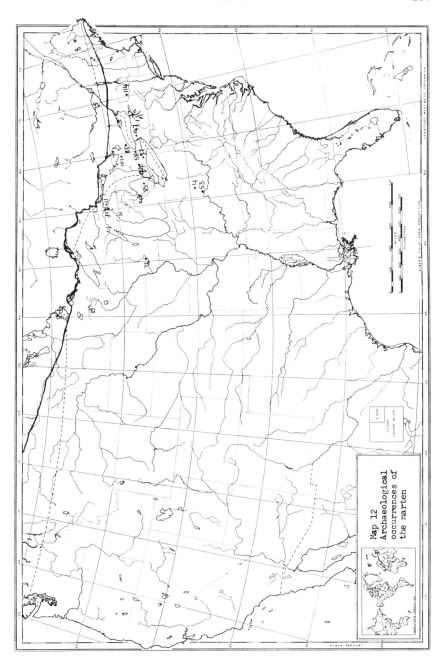

Map 12
Archaeological
occurrences of
the marten

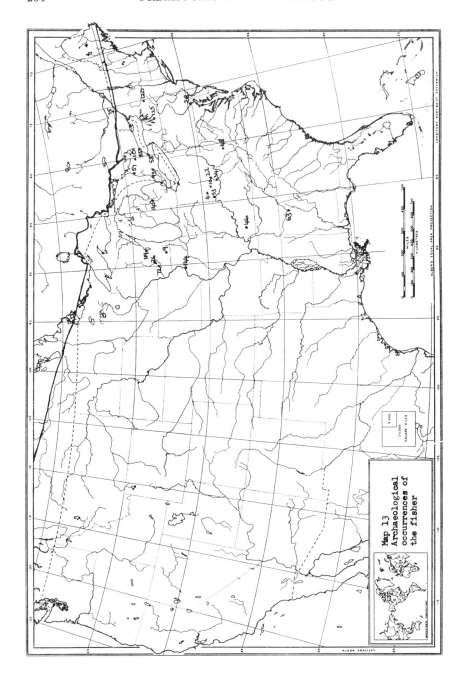

Map 13
Archaeological
occurrences of
the fisher

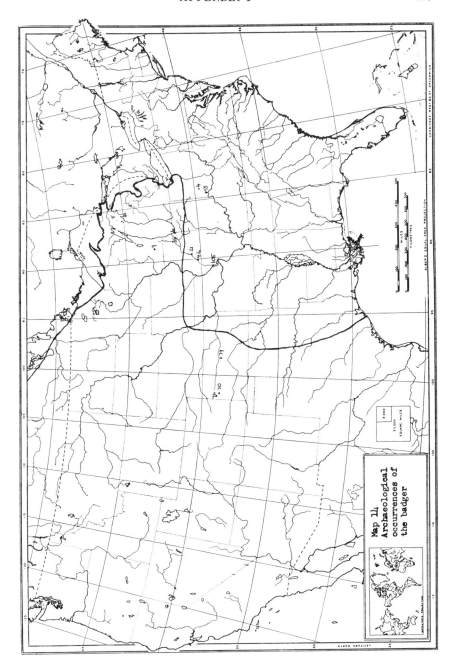

Map 14
Archaeological
occurrences of
the badger

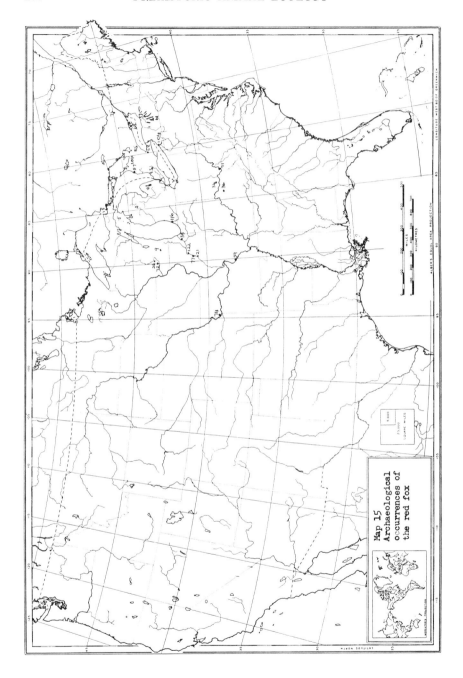

Map 15
Archaeological
occurrences of
the red fox

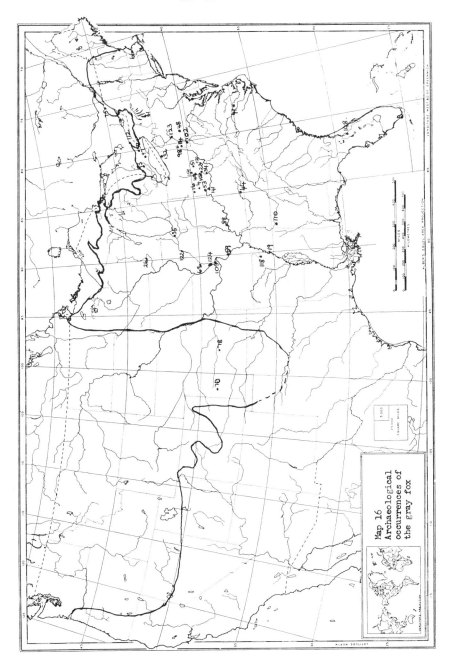

Map 16
Archaeological
occurrences of
the gray fox

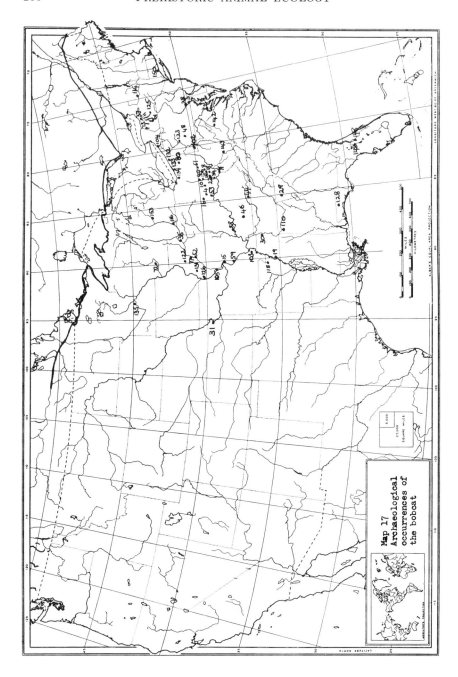

Map 17
Archaeological
occurrences of
the bobcat

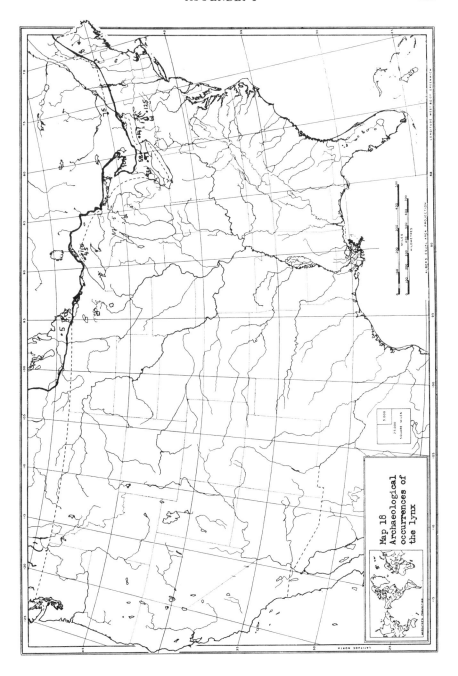

Map 18
Archaeological
occurrences of
the lynx

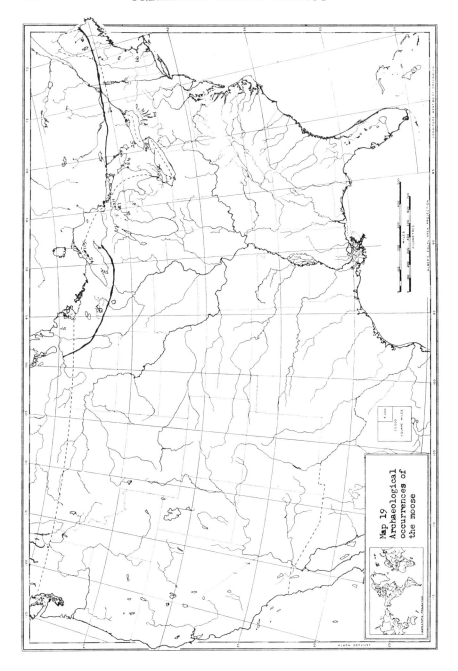

Map 19
Archaeological
occurrences of
the moose

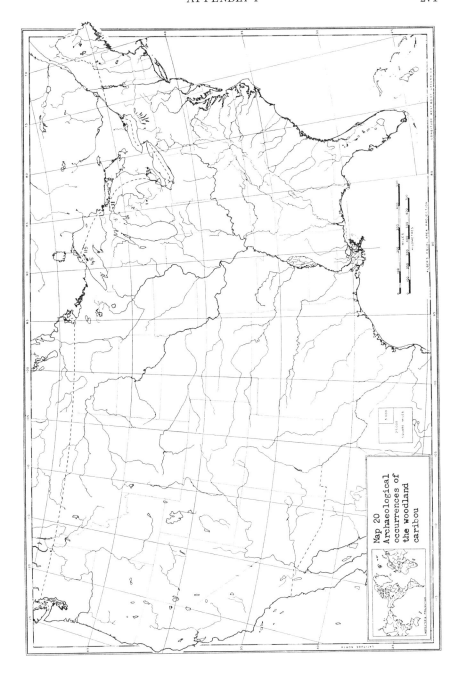

Map 20
Archaeological
occurrences of
the woodland
caribou

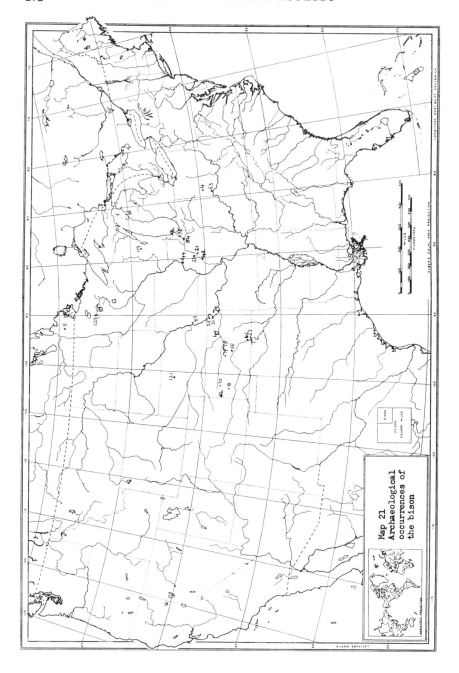

Map 21
Archaeological
occurrences of
the bison

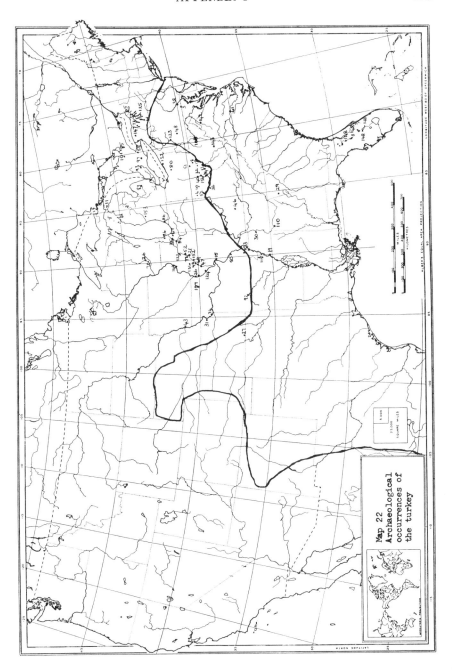

Map 22
Archaeological
occurrences of
the turkey

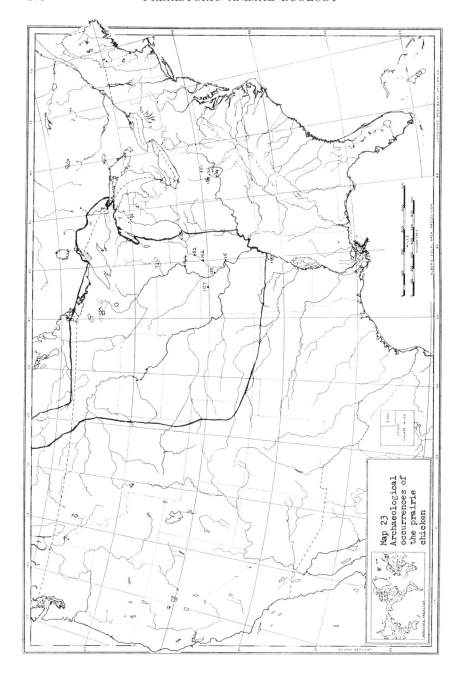

Map 23
Archaeological
occurrences of
the prairie
chicken

LITERATURE CITED

Adams, William R.
(n.d.) Archaeozoological Studies at Cahokia. Unpublished manuscript on file at the Museum of Anthropology, The University of Michigan. Ann Arbor.

Agogino, G. A. and Frankforter, W. D.
1960 A Paleo-Indian Bison Kill in Northwestern Iowa. American Antiquity, Volume 25, Number 3, pp. 414-415. Salt Lake City.

Allen, Glover M.
1920 Dogs of the American Aborigines. Bulletin of the Museum of Comparative Zoology, Harvard College, Volume LXIII, Number 9, pp. 429-517. Cambridge, Massachusetts.

Andersen, S. T.
1954 A Late-Glacial Pollen Diagram from Southern Michigan, U.S.A. Danmarks Geologiske Undersøgelse, Series 2, Number 80, pp. 140-155. Copenhagen.

Atwater, W. O. and Bryant
1899 The Chemical Composition of American Food Materials. U.S. Department of Agriculture Bulletin 28. Washington, D.C.

Ayers, Anderson, Chandler and Lauff
1956 Currents and Water Masses of Lake Huron. Great Lakes Research Institute (Michigan), Technical Paper Number 1 and Ontario Department of Lands and Forests Research Report, Number 35. Ann Arbor

Baerreis, David A.
(n.d.) Climatic Interpretations and the Mississippian Cultures in Wisconsin. Mimeographed paper presented before the American Association for the Advancement of Science, 1963.

Barreis, David and Bryson, Reid
1965 Climatic Episodes and the Dating of Mississippian Cultures. Wisconsin Archeologist, Volume 46, Number 4, pp. 203-220. Lake Mills, Wisconsin.

Benninghoff, W. S. and Hibbard, Claude W.
  1961   Fossil Pollen Associated with a Late-Glacial Musk
          Ox in Michigan. Papers of the Michigan Academy of
          Science, Arts and Letters, Volume XLVI (1960), Part
          I, pp. 155-159. Ann Arbor.

Binford, Lewis R.
  1963a   The Hodges Site - A Late Archaic Burial Station. In
          Miscellaneous Studies in Typology and Classification.
          Anthropological Papers, Museum of Anthropology,
          University of Michigan, Number 19, pp. 124-148.
          Ann Arbor.

  1963b   The Pomranky Site - A Late Archaic Burial Station.
          Ibid., pp. 149-192. Ann Arbor.

Blair, Emma Helen
  1911   The Indian Tribes of the Upper Mississippi Valley and
          Region of the Great Lakes, 2 Volumes. Cleveland:
          Arthur H. Clark

Bourne, Edward G. (Editor)
  1922   The Voyages and Explorations of Samuel de Champlain
          1604-1616, 2 Volumes. New York: Allerton Brook
          Company.

Broecker, W. and Farrand, W. R.
  1963   Radiocarbon Age of the Two Creeks Forest Bed, Wis-
          consin. Geological Society of America, Bulletin 74,
          pp. 795-802. Washington, D.C.

Brose, David
  (n.d.) Molluscan Fauna from the Schultz Site, Saginaw County,
          Michigan. Unpublished manuscript on file at the Museum
          of Anthropology, The University of Michigan. Ann Arbor.

Brown, James A.
  1964   The Identification of a Prehistoric Bone Tool from the
          Midwest: The Deer-Jaw Sickle. American Antiquity,
          Volume 29, Number 3, pp. 381-386. Salt Lake City.

Burt, W. H.
  1954   The Mammals of Michigan. Ann Arbor: University of
          Michigan Press.

Byers, Douglas S.
  1942   Fluted Points from Wisconsin. American Antiquity,
          Volume 7, Number 4, page 400. Salt Lake City.

1959   The Eastern Archaic: Some Problems and Hypotheses. American Antiquity, Volume 24, Number 3, pp. 233-256. Salt Lake City.

Cain, Stanley A. and Slater, J. V.
1948   Palynological Studies at Sodon Lake, Michigan, Part III, The Sequence of Pollen Spectra Profile 1. Ecology, Volume 29, Number 4, pp. 492-500. Brooklyn, New York.

Caldwell, Joseph R.
1958   Trend and Tradition in the Prehistory of the Eastern United States. American Anthropological Association, Memoir Number 88. Menasha.

Carver, J.
1818   Three Years Travels Through the Interiors of North America. Philadelphia: Hindman Company.

Catlin, George
1926   North American Indians - 1832-1839. Edinburgh: Oliver and Boyd.

Cleland, Charles E.
1965a Faunal Remains from Bluff Shelters in Northwest Arkansas. The Arkansas Archeologist, Volume 6, Number 2-3, pp. 39-63. Fayetteville.

1965b Barren Ground Caribou _Rangifer_ _arcticus_ from an Early Man Site in Southwestern Michigan. American Antiquity, Volume 30, Number 3, pp. 350-351. Salt Lake City.

(n.d.) A Comparison of Food Remains from the French and British Occupations of Fort Michilimackinac, Emmet County, Michigan. Unpublished manuscript on file at the Museum, Michigan State University. East Lansing.

Conant, Roger
1958   A Field Guide to Reptiles and Amphibians. Boston: Houghton Mifflin Company.

Cooper, L. R.
1933   Red Cedar Variant of the Wisconsin Hopewell. Bulletin of the Public Museum of the City of Milwaukee, Volume 16, Number 2. Milwaukee.

Crane, H. R.
1956   University of Michigan Radiocarbon Dates I. Science, Volume 124, Number 3224, pp. 664-672. Washington D.C.

Crane, H. R. and Griffin, J. B.
  1958a University of Michigan Radiocarbon Dates II. Science,
          Volume 127, Number 3306, pp. 1098-1105. Washington
          D.C.

  1958b University of Michigan Radiocarbon Dates III. Ibid.,
          Volume 128, Number 3332, pp. 1117-1123. Washington,
          D.C.

  1959   University of Michigan Radiocarbon Dates IV. American
          Journal of Science, Radiocarbon Supplement 1, pp. 173-
          198. New Haven.

  1960   University of Michigan Radiocarbon Dates V. American
          Journal of Science, Radiocarbon Supplement 2, pp. 31-
          48. New Haven.

  1961   University of Michigan Radiocarbon Dates VI. Radio-
          carbon, Volume 3, pp. 105-125. New Haven.

  1962   University of Michigan Radiocarbon Dates VII. Ibid.,
          Volume 4, pp. 183-203. New Haven.

  1963   University of Michigan Radiocarbon Date VIII. Ibid.,
          Volume 5, pp. 228-253. New Haven.

  1964   University of Michigan Radiocarbon Dates IX. Ibid.,
          Volume 6, pp. 1-24. New Haven.

  1965   University of Michigan Radiocarbon Dates X. Ibid.,
          Volume 7, 11. 123-152. New Haven.

Cunningham, Wilbur M.
  1948   A Study of the Glacial Kame Culture in Michigan, Ohio
          and Indiana. Occasional Contributions from the Museum
          of Anthropology of the University of Michigan, Number
          12. Ann Arbor.

de Vos, Antoon
  1964   Range Changes of Mammals in the Great Lakes Region.
          The American Midland Naturalist, Volume 71, Number
          1, pp. 210-231. Notre Dame, Indiana.

Dice, Lee R.
  1932   A preliminary Classification of the Major Terrestrial
          Ecologic Communities of Michigan, Exclusive of Isle
          Royale. Papers of the Michigan Academy of Science,
          Arts and letters, Volume XVI (1931), pp. 217-239.
          Ann Arbor.

1938   The Canadian Biotic Province with Special Reference
        to Mammals. Ecology, Volume 19, Number 4, pp.
        503-514. Brooklyn, New York.

1943   The Biotic Provinces of North America. Ann Arbor:
        University of Michigan Press.

Driver, Harold E. and Massey, William C.
1957   Comparative Studies of North American Indians.
        Transactions of the American Philosophical Society
        (n.s.), Volume 47, Number 2, pp. 163-456. Lancaster,
        Pennsylvania.

Fitting, James E.
1963   The Hi-Lo Site: A Late Paleo-Indian Site in Western
        Michigan. Wisconsin Archeologist, Volume 44, Number
        2, pp. 87-96. Lake Mills, Wisconsin.

1964a   Some Characteristics of Projectile Point Bases from
        the Holcombe Site, Macomb County, Michigan. Papers
        of the Michigan Academy of Science, Arts and Letters,
        Volume XLIX (1963), Part II, pp. 231-238. Ann Arbor.

1964b   Ceramic Relationships of Four Late Woodland Sites
        in Northern Ohio. Wisconsin Archeologist, Volume
        45, Number 4, pp. 160-175. Lake Mills, Wisconsin.

1965a   A Quantitative Examination of Paleo-Indian Projectile
        Points in the Eastern United States. Papers of the
        Michigan Academy of Science, Arts and Letters, Volume
        L (1964), Part II, pp. 365-371. Ann Arbor.

1965b   Observations on Paleo-Indian Adaptive and Settlement
        Patterns. The Michigan Archaeologist, Volume 11,
        Numbers 3-4, pp. 103-109. Ann Arbor.

1965c   Late Woodland Cultures of Southeastern Michigan.
        Anthropological Papers, Museum of Anthropology,
        University of Michigan, Number 24. Ann Arbor.

(n.d..) Middle Woodland Manifestations in Eastern Michigan.
        Paper presented at the 30th Annual Meeting of the
        Society for American Archaeology.

Flanders, Richard E.
1963   Marion Thick Pottery in Michigan. The Coffinberry
        News Bulletin, Volume 10, Number 5. Michigan
        Archaeological Society, Grand Rapids.

1965   A Comparison of Some Middle Woodland Materials from Michigan and Illinois. Ph.d dissertation, University Microfilms, Ann Arbor.

Flanders, Richard E. and Cleland, Charles E.
1964   The Use of Animal Remains in Hopewell Burial Mounds, Kent County, Michigan. Jack Pine Warbler, Volume 42, Number 4, pp. 302-309. Michigan Audubon Society, Kalamazoo.

Fogel, I. L.
1963   The Dispersal of Copper Artifacts in The Late Archaic Period of Prehistoric North America. Wisconsin Archeologist, Volume 44, Number 3, pp. 129-180. Lake Mills, Wisconsin.

Goodrich, Calvin
1932   Mollusca of Michigan. Michigan Handbook Series Number 5. Ann Arbor: University of Michigan Press.

1945   Goniobasis lirescens of Michigan. Miscellaneous Publications, Museum of Zoology, University of Michigan, Number 65. Ann Arbor.

Greenman, E. F.
1943   An Early Industry on a Raised Beach Near Killarney, Ontario. American Antiquity, Volume 8, Number 3, pp. 260-265. Salt Lake City.

1945   The Hopewellian in the Detroit-Windsor Area. Papers of the Michigan Academy of Science, Arts and Letters, Volume XXX (1944), pp. 457-464. Ann Arbor.

1957   Wintering in the Lower Peninsula, 1675-1676. Michigan Archaeologist, Volume 3, Number 3, pp. 62-69. Ann Arbor.

Greenman, E. F. and Stanley, G. M.
1940   A Geologically Dated Camp Site, Georgian Bay, Ontario. American Antiquity, Volume 5, Number 3, pp. 194-199. Salt Lake City.

Griffin, James B.
1960a   Climatic Change: A Contributory Cause of the Growth and Decline of Northern Hopewellian Culture. Wisconsin Archeologist, Volume 41, Number 1, pp. 21-33. Lake Mills, Wisconsin.

1960b A Hypothesis for the Prehistory of the Winnebago. In Culture and History, S. Diamond Editor, pp. 809-868. New York: Columbia University Press.

1961a Post Glacial Ecology and Culture Change in the Great Lakes Area of North America. Publication Number 7, Great Lakes Research Division, Institute of Science and Technology, The University of Michigan. Ann Arbor.

1961b Some Correlations of Climatic and Cultural Change in Eastern North American Prehistory. Annals of the New York Academy of Sciences, Volume 95, Article 1, pp. 710-717. New York.

1961c Lake Superior Copper and the Indians: Miscellaneous Studies of Great Lakes Prehistory. University of Michigan, Museum of Anthropology, Anthropological paper Number 17. Ann Arbor.

1961c Lake Superior Copper and the Indians: Miscellaneous Studies of Great Lakes Prehistory. University of Michigan, Museum of Anthropology, Anthropological Paper Number 17. Ann Arbor.

1965 Late Quaternary Prehistory in the Northeastern Woodlands. In The Quaternary of the United States, H. E. Wright, Jr. and David G. Frey, Editors, pp. 655-667. Princeton: Princeton University Press.

Guilday, John E.
1958 The Prehistoric Distribution of the Opossum. Journal of Mammalogy, Volume 39, Number 1, pp. 39-43. Baltimore.

Guilday, John E., Martin, P. S. and McCrady, A. D.
1964 New Paris Number 4: A Late Pleistocene Cave Deposit in Bedford County, Pennsylvania. Bulletin of the National Speleological Society, Volume 26, Number 4, pp. 121-194. Arlington, Virginia.

Guta, Margaret (Translator)
1957 Journal of the Last Winter Mission of Father Henry Nouvel, Superior of the Missions of the Ottawa. Michigan Archaeologist, Volume 3, Number 3, pp. 71-80. Ann Arbor.

Haag, William
    1948   An Osteometric Analysis of some Aboriginal Dogs.
            University of Kentucky, Reports in Anthropology, Volume
            VII, Number 3. Lexington.

Hall, Robert L.
    1962   The Archaeology of Carcajou Point: With an Interpreta-
            tion of the Development of Oneota Culture in Wisconsin,
            2 Volumes. Madison: University of Wisconsin Press.

Handley, Charles O., Jr.
    1953   Marine Mammals in Michigan Pleistocene Beaches.
            Jouranl of Mammalogy, Volume 34, Number 2, pp.
            252-253. Baltimore.

Hibbard Claude W.
    1951   Animal Life in Michigan during the Ice Age. Michigan
            Alumni Quarterly Review, Volume 57, Number 18, pp.
            200-208. Ann Arbor.

Hickerson, H.
    1962   The Southwestern Chippewa: An Ethnohistorical Study.
            American Anthropological Association, Volume 64,
            Number 3, Part 2, Memoir Number 92. Menasha.

Hinsdale, W. B.
    1932   Distribution of the Aboriginal Population of Michigan.
            Occasional Contributions from the Museum of Anthro-
            pology of the University of Michigan, Number 2. Ann
            Arbor.

Hough, Jack L.
    1963   The Prehistoric Great Lakes of North America. Amer-
            ican Scientist, Volume 51, Number 1, pp. 84-109.
            Easton, Pennsylvania.

Howard, Lynn
    1948   The Birdsell Pottery Collection from Moccasin Bluff.
            Unpublished manuscript on file at the University of
            Michigan, Museum of Anthropology. Ann Arbor.

Hubbs, Carl L.
    1940   The Cranium of a Fresh-water Sheepshead from
            Postglacial Marl in Cheboygan County, Michigan.
            Papers of the Michigan Academy of Science, Arts
            and Letters, Volume XXV (1939), pp. 293-296. Ann
            Arbor.

Hudgins, Bert
  1961   Michigan: Geographic Backgrounds in the Development
          of the Commonwealth. Ann Arbor: Edwards Brothers
          Inc.

Jelgersma, Saskia
  1962   A Late-Glacial Pollen Diagram from Madelia, South-
          central Minnesota. American Journal of Science,
          Volume 260, pp. 522-529. New Haven.

Jenness, D.
  1935   The Ojibwa Indians of Parry Island, Their Social and
          Religious Life. National Museum of Canada, Bulletin
          Number 78, Anthropological Series Number 17. Ottawa.

Jenks, A. E.
  1900   Wild Rice Gatherers of the Upper Lakes. Bureau of
          American Ethnology, Annual Report 19, pp. 1011-1161.
          Washington, D.C.

J. R.   The Jesuit Relations and Allied Documents. See
          Thwaites, Reuben Gold, Editor.

Jury, Wilfred and Jury, Elsie
  1952   The Burley Site. University of Western Ontario,
          Museum of Indian Archaeology and Pioneer Life,
          Bulletin Number 9, pp. 57-71. London, Ontario.

Kapp, R. O. and Kneller, W. A.
  1962   A Buried Biotic Assemblage from an Old Saline River
          Terrace at Milan, Michigan. Papers of the Michigan
          Academy of Science, arts and Letters, Volume XLVII
          (1961), Part I, pp. 135-145. Ann Arbor.

Kellogg, C. E.
  1941   Climate and Soil. In Climate and Man. Yearbook of
          Agriculture, United States Department of Agriculture,
          pp. 265-291. Washington D. C.

Kellogg, Louise P. (Editor)
  1923   Charlevoix's Journal of a Voyage to Northern America,
          2 Volumes. Chicago: Caxton Club.

Kenyon, Walter
  1959   The Inverhuron Site. The Royal Ontario Museum, Art
          and Archaeology Division--Occasional Papper Number
          1. Toronto: University of Toronto Press.

Kincer, J. B.
    1941   Climate and Weather Data for the United States. In
            Climate and Man. Year book of Agriculture, United
            States Department of Agriculture, pp. 685-699. Wash-
            ington, D.C.

Kinietz, W. Vernon
    1940   The Indians of the Western Great Lakes, 1615-1760.
            Ann Arbor: University of Michigan Press.

Kroeber, Alfred L.
    1939   Cultural and Natural Areas of Native North America.
            University of California Publications in American
            Archaeology and Ethnology, Volume 38, pp. xii + 1-242.
            Berkeley.

La Potherie, Claude Charles Leroy, Bacqueville de
    1911   History of the Savage Peoples Who are Allies of New
            France. In The Indian Tribes of the Upper Mississippi
            Valley and Region of the Great Lakes, Emma Blair,
            Editor. Cleveland: Arthur H. Clark.

Leacock, Eleanor
    1954   The Montaignais "Hunting Territory" and the Fur Trade.
            American Anthropologist, Volume 56, Number 5, Part
            2, Memoir Number 78. Menasha.

Lee Thomas E.
    1952   A preliminary Report on an Archaeological Survey of
            Southwestern Ontario for 1950. National Museum of
            Canada Bulletin Number 126, pp. 64-75. Ottawa.

    1954   The First Sheguiandah Expedition, Manitoulin Island,
            Ontario. American Antiquity, Volume 20, Number 2,
            pp. 101-111. Salt Lake City.

    1955   The Second Sheguiandah Expedition, Manitoulin Island,
            Ontario. Ibid., Volume 21, Number 1, pp. 63-71.
            Salt Lake City.

    1960   The Lucas Site, Inverhuron, Ontario. National Museum
            of Canada, Bulletin Number 167, Contributions to
            Anthropology, 1958. Ottawa.

MacNeish, Richard S.
    1952   A Possible Early Site in the Thunder Bay District,
            Ontario. National Museum of Canada Annual Report
            1950-1951, Bulletin Number 126, pp. 23-47. Ottawa.

1958   An Introduction to the Archaeology of Southeast Manitoba. National Museum of Canada Bulletin Number 157. Ottawa.

MacWhite, Eóin
1956   On the Interpretation of Archaeological Evidence in Historical and Sociological Terms. American Anthropologist, Volume 58, Number 1, pp. 3-25. Menasha.

Mason, O. T.
1896   Influence of Environment upon Human Industries or Arts. Smithsonian Institution Annual Report to July, 1895, pp. 639-665. Washington, D.C.

Mason, Ronald J.
1958   Late Pleistocene Geochronology and the Paleo-Indian Penetration into the Lower Michigan Peninsula. University of Michigan, Museum of Anthropology, Anthropological Papers, Number 11, pp. 1-48. Ann Arbor.

1963   Two Late Paleo-Indian Complexes in Wisconsin. Wisconsin Archeologist, Volume 44, Number 4, pp. 199-211. Lake Mills, Wisconsin.

1966   Two Stratified Sites on the Door Peninsula. University of Michigan, Museum of Anthropology, Anthropological Papers, No. 26. Ann Arbor.

Mason, R. and Irwin, C.
1961   An Eden-Scottsbluff Burial in Northeast Wisconsin. American Antiquity, Volume 26, Number 1, pp. 43-57. Salt Lake City.

McCallum, K. J. and Dyck, W.
1960   University of Saskatchewan Radiocarbon Dates II. American Journal of Science, Radiocarbon Supplement, Volume 2, pp. 73-81. New Haven.

McCallum, K. J. and Wittenberg, J.
1962   University of Saskatchewan Radiocarbon Dates III. Radiocarbon, Volume 4, pp. 71-80. New Haven.

1965   University of Saskatchewan Radiocarbon Dates IV. Ibid., Volume 7, pp. 229-235. New Haven.

McGregor, John C.
1952   The Havana Site. In Hopewellian Communities of Illinois, Thorne Deuell, Editor. Illinois State Museum, Scientific Papers Volume V, pp. 43-94. Springfield.

McKern, W. C.
   1931   A Wisconsin Variant of the Hopewell Culture. Bulletin
          of the Public Museum of the City of Milwaukee, Volume
          10, Number 2. Milwaukee.

   1945   Preliminary Report on the Upper Mississippi Phase
          in Wisconsin. Ibid., Volume 16, Number 3. Milwaukee.

McPherron, Alan L.
   1963   Late Woodland Ceramics in the Straits of Mackinac.
          Papers of the Michigan Academy of Science, Arts and
          Letters, Volume XLVIII (1962), Part II, pp. 567-576.
          Ann Arbor.

   1965   Pottery Style Clustering, Marital Residence and Cul-
          tural Adaptations at an Algonkian/Iroquoian Interface.
          A paper presented before The Iroquois Conference,
          Glen Falls, New York, 1965.

Mershon, W. B.
   1907   The Passenger Pigeon. New York: Outing Publishing
          Company.

M. P. H. C.
   1881   Edward Foote - A Historical Sketch of the Early Days
          of Eaton County. In Michigan Pioneer and Historical
          Collections, Volume 3 (1879-80), pp. 379-407. Lansing.

   1886   Ephraim S. Williams - Personal Reminiscences. Ibid.,
          Volume 8 (1885), pp. 233-259. Lansing.

   1891   George Willard - The Making of Michigan. Ibid.,
          Volume 17 (1890), pp. 295-310. Lansing.

   1892   Letter from Captain D. Campbell to Colonel H. Beuguet.
          Ibid., Volume 19 (1891), p. 121. Lansing.

   1906   Dwight Goss - The Indians of the Grand River Valley.
          Ibid., Volume 30 (1905), pp. 172-190. Lansing.

Muckenhirn, R. J. and Berger, K. C.
   1957   The Northern Lake States. In Soil. Yearbook of
          Agriculture, United States Department of Agriculture,
          pp. 547-552. Washington, D. C.

Nelson, T.
   1956   The History of Ornithology at the University of Michi-
          gan Biological Station. Minneapolis: Burgess Pub-
          lishing Company.

Odum, Eugene P.
    1953   Fundamentals of Ecology. Philadelphia: W. B. Saunders
            Company.

Ogden, J. G. and Hay, Ruth
    1965   Ohio Wesleyan University Natural Radiocarbon Measure-
            ments II. Radiocarbon, Volume 7, pp. 166-173. New
            Haven.

Oltz, Donald F. and Kapp, Ronald O.
    1963   Plant Remains Associated with Mastodon and Mammoth
            Remains in Central Michigan. The American Midland
            Naturalist, Volume 70, Number 2, pp. 339-346. South
            Bend, Indiana.

Parker, Arthur C.
    1910   Iroquois Uses of Maize and Other Plant Foods. New
            York State Museum Bulletin 144. Albany.

Parmalee, Paul W.
    1959   Animal Remains from Raddatz Rockshelter, Sk5, Wis-
            consin. Wisconsin Archeologist, Volume 40, Number
            2, pp. 83-90. Lake Mills, Wisconsin.

    1960a   Animal Remains from the Aztalan Site, Jefferson
            County, Wisconsin. Ibid., Volume 41, Number 1, pp.
            1-10. Lake Mills, Wisconsin.

    1960b   Animal Remains from the Durst Rockshelter, Sauk
            County, Wisconsin. Ibid., Volume 41, Number 1, pp.
            11-17. Lake Mills, Wisconsin.

    1963   Vertebrate Remains from the Bell Site, Winnebago
            County, Wisconsin. Ibid., Volume 44, Number 1, pp.
            58-69. Lake Mills, Wisconsin.

    1965   The Vertebrate Fauna of the McGraw Site. In The
            McGraw Site, A Study in Hopewellian Dynamics, Olaf
            H. Prufer, Editor. Cleveland Museum of Natural
            History, Scientific Papers, Volume 3, Number 1, pp.
            115-118. Cleveland.

Peske, G. Richard
    1963   Argillite of Michigan: A Preliminary Point Classifica-
            tion and Temporal Placement from Surface Materials.
            Papers of the Michigan Academy of Science, Arts and
            Letters, Volume XLVIII (1962), Part II, pp. 557-566.
            Ann Arbor.

Potzger, J. E.
1946   Phytosociology of the Primeval Forest in Central-Northern Wisconsin and Upper Michigan and a Brief Post-Glacial History of the Lake Forest Formation. Ecological Monographs, Volume 16, pp. 211-250. Durham: Duke University Press.

Pruitt, W. O.
1954   Additional Animal Remains from Under Sleeping Bear Dune, Leelanau County, Michigan. Papers of the Michigan Academy of Science, Arts and Letters, Volume XXXIX (1953), pp. 253-256. Ann Arbor.

Quimby, George I.
1941a   The Goodall Focus, An Analysis of Ten Hopewellian Components in Michigan and Indiana. Indiana Historical Society, Prehistory Research Series, Number 2, pp. 61-161. Indianapolis.

1941b   Hopewellian Pottery Types in Michigan. Papers of the Michigan Academy of Science, Arts and Letters, Volume XXVI (1940), pp. 489-494. Ann Arbor.

1943   The Ceramic Sequence within the Goodall Focus. Ibid., Volume XXVIII (1942), pp. 543-548. Ann Arbor.

1944   Some New Data on the Goodall Focus. Ibid., Volume XXIX (1943), pp. 419-423. Ann Arbor.

1952   The Archeology of the Upper Great Lakes Area. In Archeology of the Eastern United States, J. B. Griffin, Editor. Chicago: University of Chicago Press.

1959   Lanceolate Points and Fossil Beaches in the Upper Great Lakes Region. American Antiquity, Volume 24, Number 4, pp. 424-426. Salt Lake City.

1960   Indian Life in the Upper Great Lakes, 11,000 B.C. to A.D. 1800. Chicago: University of Chicago Press.

1962   A Year with a Chippewa Family 1763-1764. Ethnohistory, Volume 9, Number 3, pp. 217-239. Bloomington, Indiana.

1963   A New Look at Geochronology in the Upper Great Lakes Region. American Antiquity, Volume 28, Number 4, pp. 558-559. Salt Lake City.

Ridley, Frank
1952   The Huron and Lalonde Occupations of Ontario.
       American Antiquity, Volume 17, Number 3, pp. 197-210.
       Salt Lake City.

Ritchie, William A.
1945   An Early Site in Cayuga County, New York. Researches
       and Transactions of the New York State Archaeological
       Association, Volume X, Number 1. Rochester.

1965   The Archaeology of New York State. Garden City,
       New York: The Natural History Press.

Ritzenthaler, Robert E. and Quimby, George I.
1962   The Red Ocher Culture of the Upper Great Lakes and
       Adjacent Areas. Chicago Natural History Museum,
       Fieldiana: Anthropology, Volume 36, Number 11, pp.
       243-275. Chicago.

Roosa, William B.
1963   Some Michigan Fluted Point Types and Sites. Michi-
       gan Archaeologist, Volume 9, Number 3, pp. 44-48.
       Ann Arbor.

1965   Some Great Lakes Fluted Point Types. Ibid., Volume
       11, Numbers 3 and 4, pp. 89-101. Ann Arbor.

Rostlund, Erhard
1952   Freshwater Fish and Fishing in Native North America.
       Berkeley and Los Angeles: University of California
       Press.

Ruthven, Alexander G.
1911   A Biological Survey of the Sand Dune Region on the
       South Shore of Saginaw Bay, Michigan. Michigan
       Geological and Biological Survey, Publication 4,
       Biological Series 2. Lansing.

Sahlins, Marshall D. and Service, Elman R. (Editors)
1960   Evolution and Culture. Ann Arbor: University of
       Michigan Press.

Sauer, Carl O.
1950   Grassland Climax, Fire and Man. Journal of Range
       Management, Volume 3, pp. 16-22. Baltimore.

Schoolcraft, Henry R.
1820   Narrative Journal of Travels in 1820, Williams, Editor.
       East Lansing: Michigan State University Press.

Schultz, C. B. and Frankforter, W. D.
1948	Preliminary Report on the Lime Creek Sites: New Evidence of Early Man in Southwestern Nebraska. Bulletin of the University of Nebraska State Museum, Volume 3, Number 4, Part 2, pp. 43-62. Lincoln.

Scott, W. B.
1954	Freshwater Fishes of Eastern Canada. Toronto: University of Toronto Press.

Semken, H. A., Miller, B. B., and Stevens, J. B.
1964	Late Wisconsin Woodland Muskoxen in Association with Pollen and Invertebrates from Michigan. Journal of Paleontology, Volume 38, Number 5, pp. 823-835. Menasha, Wisconsin.

Senninger, Earl J., Jr.
1964	Atlas of Michigan. Flint: Flint Geographical Press.

Service, Elman R.
1962	Primitive Social Organization: An Evolutionary Perspective. New York: Random House.

Shay, Creighton T.
1963	A Preliminary Report on the Itasca Bison Site. The Minnesota Academy of Science, Volume 31, Number 1, pp. 24-27. Minneapolis.

Shelford, V. E.
1913	Animal Communities in Temperate America. Geographical Society of Chicago, Bulletin Number 5. Chicago.

Skeels, M. A.
1962	The Mastodons and Mammoths of Michigan. Papers of the Michigan Academy of Science, Arts and Letters, Volume XLVII (1961) Part I, pp. 101-133. Ann Arbor.

Smith, Philip W.
1957	An Analysis of Post-Wisconsin Biogeography of the Prairie Peninsula Region Based on Distributional Phenomena Among Terrestrial Vertebrate Populations. Ecology, Volume 38, Number 2, pp. 205-218. Durham, North Carolina.

Smith, H. M. and Snell, M. M.
1891	Fisheries of the Great Lakes in 1885. United States Commission of the Fish and Fisheries Part XV, Report of the Commissioner for 1887. Washington, D. C.

Speck, Frank G. and Eiseley, Loren C.
1942   The Significance of the Hunting Territory Systems of the Algonkian in Social Theory. American Anthropologist, Volume 44, pp. 269-280. Menasha.

Steward, Julian H.
1938   Basin-Plateau Aboriginal Socio-political Groups. Bureau of American Ethnology, Bulletin 20. Washington, D. C.

Stewart, O. C.
1956   Fire as the First Great Force Employed by Man. In Man's Role in Changing the Face of the Earth, Thomas, Sauer, Bates and Mumford, Editors. Chicago: University of Chicago Press.

Stoutamire, W. P. and Benninghoff, W. S.
1964   Biotic Assemblage Associated with a Mastodon Skull from Oakland County, Michigan. Papers of the Michigan Academy of Science, Arts and Letters, Volume XLIX (1963), Part I, pp. 47-59. Ann Arbor.

Struever, Stuart
1964   The Hopewell Interaction Sphere in Riverine-Western Great Lakes Culture History. In Hopewellian Studies, J. R. Caldwell and R. L. Hall, Editors. Illinois State Museum Scientific Papers, Volume 12, pp. 85-106. Springfield.

Taggart, David
(n.d.) Field Summary of University of Michigan Museum of Anthropology Excavations at Green Point (Schultz Site, 20SA2), Saginaw County, Michigan, during the Summer of 1963. Unpublished paper on file at the Museum of Anthropology, University of Michigan. Ann Arbor.

Taylor, Walter P.
1956   The Deer of North America. The Stackpole Company, Harrisburg, Pennsylvania and the Wildlife Management Institute, Washington, D. C.

Terasmae, J.
1961   Notes on Late Quaternary Climatic Changes in Canada. Annals of the New York Academy of Science, Volume 95, Number 1, pp. 658-675. New York.

Thwaites, Reuben Gold (Editor)
1896-1901   The Jesuit Relations and Allied Documents, 73 Volumes. Cleveland: Burrows Brothers.

Tooker, Elisabeth
1964   An Ethnography of the Huron Indians, 1615-1649.
Bureau of American Ethnology, Bulletin 190. Washington, D. C.

Trautman, Milton B.
1957   The Fishes of Ohio. Columbus: Ohio State University Press.

Trigger, Bruce G.
1962   The Historic Location of the Hurons. Ontario History, Volume 54, Number 2, pp. 137-148. Toronto.

Veatch, J. O.
1928   The Dry Prairies of Michigan. Papers of the Michigan Academy of Science, Arts and Letters, Volume VIII (1927), pp. 269-278. Ann Arbor.

1959   Presettlement Forest in Michigan. Department of Resource Development, Michigan State University. East Lansing.

Waugh, F. W.
1916   Iroquois Food and Food Preparation. Canada Department of Mines, Geological Survey, Memoir 86, Number 12, Anthropological Series. Ottawa.

White, Leslie A.
1949   The Science of Culture. New York: Farrar Strauss.

White, Theodore
1953   A Method of Calculating the Dietary Percentage of Various Food Animals Utilized by Aboriginal Peoples. American Antiquity, Volume 18, Number 4, pp. 396-398. Salt Lake City.

Whitford, Philip B.
1958   A Study of Prairie Remnants in Southeastern Wisconsin. Ecology, Volume 39, Number 4, pp. 727-733. Brooklyn, New York.

Wilford, Lloyd A.
1943   A Tentative Classification of the Prehistoric Cultures of Minnesota. The Minnesota Archaeologist, Volume IX, Number 4, Minneapolis.

1955   A Revised Classification of the Prehistoric Cultures of Minnesota. American Antiquity, Volume 21, Number 2, pp. 130-142. Salt Lake City.

Williams, Ephraim
  1885   Personal Reminiscences. See M. P. H. C.

Wintemberg, W. J.
  1948   The Middleport Village Site. National Museum of
          Canada, Bulletin 109, Anthropological Series 27. Ottawa.

Winter, T. C.
  1962   Pollen Sequence at Kirchner Marsh, Minnesota.
          Science, Volume 138, Number 3539, pp. 526-528.
          Washington, D. C.

Winters, Howard D.
  1963   An Archaeological Survey of the Wabash Valley in
          Illinois. Illinois State Museum Report of Investiga-
          tions, Number 10. Springfield.

Wissler, Clark
  1917   The American Indian. New York: Douglas C. McMurtrie.

Wittry, Warren
  1957   A Preliminary Study of the Old Copper Complex.
          Wisconsin Archeologist, Volume 38, Number 4, pp.
          204-221. Lake Mills, Wisconsin.

  1959a   The Raddatz Rockshelter, SK5, Wisconsin. Ibid.,
          Volume 40, Number 2, pp. 33-69. Lake Mills, Wis-
          consin.

  1959b   Archeological Studies of Four Wisconsin Rockshelters.
          Ibid., Volume 40, Number 4, pp. 137-267. Lake Mills,
          Wisconsin.

  1965   The Institute Digs a Mastodon. Cranbrook Institute of
          Science Newsletter, Volume 35, Number 2, pp. 14-19.
          Bloomfield Hills, Michigan.

Wood, N. A.
  1949   The Birds of Michigan. University of Michigan,
          Museum of Zoology, Miscellaneous Publications, Num-
          ber 75. Ann Arbor.

Wright, Henry T.
  1964   A Transitional Archaic Campsite at Green Point
          (20SA 1). The Michigan Archaeologist, Volume 10,
          Number 1, pp. 17-22. Ann Arbor.

(n.d.) The Geological Sequence of the Schultz Site, Saginaw County, Michigan. Unpublished manuscript on file at the Museum of Anthropology, University of Michigan, Ann Arbor.

(n.d.) The Geology of the Juntunen Site, Mackinac County, Michigan. Unpublished manuscript on file at the Museum of Anthropology, University of Michigan, Ann Arbor.

Wright, Henry T. and Morlan, Richard E.
1964 The Hart Site. The Michigan Archaeologist, Volume 10, Number 3. Ann Arbor.

Wright, J. V. and Anderson, J. E.
1963 The Donaldson Site. National Museum of Canada Bulletin Number 184, Anthropological Series, Number 58. Ottawa.

Yarnell, Richard A.
1964 Aboriginal Relationships between Culture and Plant Life in the Upper Great Lakes Region. University of Michigan, Museum of Anthropology, Anthropological papers, Number 23. Ann Arbor.

Zumberge, James H. and Potzger, John E.
1956 Late Wisconsin Chronology of the Lake Michigan Basin Correlated with Pollen Studies. Geological Society of America, Bulletin Number 67, pp. 271-288. Baltimore.

13-300